Palgrave Studies in American Economic History

Series Editor
Barbara Alexander
Department of Economics
Babson College
Babson Park, MA, USA

Since the social upheavals of the 1960s and 1970s and the free-market resurgence of the 1980s, American society has been enmeshed in a continuing process of profound change. Economic change has been oriented around the regulation of business, the information and telecommunication revolutions, and widening roles played by women and minority groups. Authors in the innovation area will assess how America arrived at its current position of technological dominance that is nonetheless under pressure from institutions that arguably are not well-configured for the future. Regulatory and legal historians will evaluate the reasons for concurrent regulatory breakdown and overreach in industries ranging from finance and health care to energy and land use. Finally, researchers working at the intersection of society and economic history will explore continuing struggles around issues of gender, ethnicity, and family structure, and the distribution of income, wealth, and political power. The series will address topics of interest to scholars, undergraduate and graduate students, and general readers drawn to the interplay of economics and cultural issues. Series contributors will be economics and business historians, or economists working with historians.

More information about this series at
http://www.palgrave.com/gp/series/14650

John H. Wood

Who Governs?

Legislatures, Bureaucracies, or Markets?

palgrave
macmillan

John H. Wood
Department of Economics
Wake Forest University
Winston-Salem, NC, USA

ISSN 2662-3900 ISSN 2662-3919 (electronic)
Palgrave Studies in American Economic History
ISBN 978-3-030-33082-8 ISBN 978-3-030-33083-5 (eBook)
https://doi.org/10.1007/978-3-030-33083-5

This Palgrave Macmillan imprint is published by the registered company Springer Nature Switzerland AG.
The registered company address is: Gewerbestrasse 11, 6330 Cham, Switzerland

Contents

List of Figures

List of Tables

CHAPTER 1

Introduction

Who Governs?

Market problems such as monopoly, fraud, speculation, and/or manipulation are perceived, the legislature passes a law to correct them, a bureaucracy is assigned to interpret and enforce the law, buyers and sellers comply, and the problems are solved or at least lessened. Markets are remedied along the lines of officials' understanding of the public's welfare. Or are they? Are the promises of politicians, the powers of regulators, and the stories of textbooks believable?

This is a lot to ask because we have learned from hard experience that mistaken legislators' perceptions and/or the inability or unwillingness of bureaucracies to enforce the law or the public to comply are also possible. All are subject to complex and changeable influences. In addition, the market interests believed to have been a source of the problems may persist along with incentives to obstruct the law or bend it to their own advantages. To the extent that markets continue to have their often inscrutable and unpredictable ways, legislatures and bureaucracies are undermined and government is by private interests.

This approach resembles the "iron triangle" theory of government consisting of congressional committees, the bureaucracy, and interest groups, except that, more generally, it begins with the making of the law and also considers markets of which private interests are parts (Adams 1981). There is no simple general pattern of these interactions because the laws have different origins and the distributions of power between the

J. H. Wood, *Who Governs?*, Palgrave Studies in American Economic History, https://doi.org/10.1007/978-3-030-33083-5_1

groups are variable and changing. For example, the massive securities losses of the Great Depression of 1929–33 led to the securities acts of the New Deal that were intended to correct the secrecy and greed of financial firms by means of enforced transparency and limits on such suspect practices as short selling and margin trading.

An alternative explanation is that typical securities issues of the 1920s were honest and transparent, with good prospects, but lost their values after 1929 with the disappearing profits of issuers, a cause which should be laid at the door of monetary policy rather than corporate greed. A more logical official response to such a crisis would have been reform of the monetary authority in the interest of price stability.

A similar story applies to the creation of the Federal Reserve in 1913. The country had experienced several financial crises, and the Panic of 1907, with the help of the Progressive movement and the presidency of Woodrow Wilson, sparked the establishment of a powerful public bank to deliver an elastic currency and profitable banks. Unfortunately, during the next twenty years, American finance experienced the greatest fluctuations in its history because it was used by the government to finance a major war followed by its unthinking submission to gold-reserve restraints which inhibited it from moderating the ensuing deflation.

In fact, the chief cause of the fragility of the American banking system had been overregulation, particularly state prohibitions of branching that resulted in a plethora (30,000 in 1920 and 13,000 after the failures of the 1920s and the Great Depression) of mainly small undiversified banks, as well as rigid reserve requirements that discouraged crisis lending by the money-center banks. Most failures were of small agricultural banks unable to survive the post-World War I falls in the prices of agricultural products.

Added to the sometimes misdirection of laws has been their hasty emotional constructions by temporary political majorities on the heels of crises. Should we necessarily conclude that the plethora of laws enacted during President Franklin Roosevelt's famous first 100 days were evidences of legislative achievement when we realize that crises, reactions to them, and the distribution of political powers are transient? A law and its enforcement might endure because of persistent economic and political conditions, aided by inertia, or they might not. The Securities and Exchange Commission, created in 1934, still exists along with its reporting requirements. On the other hand, several of the provisions of the Securities Exchange Act of 1934 directed at risks and monopolies have yet to be applied, and the SEC was moribund from the time the supporting administration's attention turned elsewhere in the mid-1930s until the 1960s, and its efforts continue to be uneven.

Bureaucracies' responsibilities have expanded with lawmakers' ambitions relative to their knowledge. So-called laws often in fact mostly consist of general directions to make and enforce rules (which are the effective laws) such as those pertaining to bank risk, required capital, leverage, and liquidity in the 2010 Dodd-Frank Wall Street Reform and Consumer Protection Act. Nor is this approach to lawmaking an innovation. The originators of the 1934 *Securities Exchange Act* wanted substantial changes to what they deemed too risky and too monopolistic exchange trading practices, but to get the Act passed, had to settle for Securities and Exchange Commission studies which decades later have still been unable to move the interests involved.

The other agency that we consider, the Federal Reserve System, soon deviated from the purposes specified by its founding 1913 Act—among which were currency stabilization and maintenance of the gold standard—as it monetized the government's World War I deficits and failed to deal with the subsequent deflations.

The question remains: Who or what governs the financial markets in our more-or-less competitive economy? Do the legislature's rules as implemented matter? Even pertinent laws and competent bureaucracies are faced with formidable tasks in their attempts to modify the behavior of often recalcitrant market participants. There are general influences on regulation—including private interests, Congress, and bureaucratic preferences—but no simple general result. Bureaucracies are less systematic and predictable than is sometimes supposed (Niskanen 1971; Moe 1997). They desire large budgets, of course, but their behavior is also affected by changing ideologies, political pressures, and private interests.

On the other hand, there seem to be some regularities in financial institutions' defensive responses to legislation. Effective prudential legislation is exceedingly difficult. The future is uncertain and wide open. Prohibitions or requirements regarding specific activities, which is the approach typically taken in financial legislation and regulation, can have little effect on the risk exposures of institutions with an infinity of choices among activities and portfolios. Such laws and their bureaucracies may enjoy long and busy lives, and even good reputations, with little inconvenience to market participants.

Regulations seek predictable behavior which is typically unobtainable (and perhaps undesirable) in developing environments in which discretion and adaptation are fundamental. This is nowhere truer than with respect to the disclosure requirements of the 1930s securities acts, which presume that reputations and expected results are less dependent on past performances than on standardized promises.

The Federal Reserve has also sometimes conformed more closely to traditional practices than to modern legislation. The ancient principal (though often denied) practice of central banks has been more to monetize government deficits, although sometimes restrained by the public's aversion to inflation, than to pursue their advertised goal of monetary stability. How they actually behave during any particular time period depends on executive, congressional, and private pressures as well as the ideologies existing within the agency—leading in the 1960s to a contest between the needy executive and a cautious agency. Guess who won.

This book looks at the outcomes of two experiences of government stimulated by the securities acts of the 1930s and the post-World War II monetary-policy responsibilities of the Federal Reserve. Similarities in our stories are furthered by the involvement of William McChesney Martin, Jr., in both, as president of the New York Stock Exchange, that is, a representative of the financial industry, in the 1930s, and as chairman of the Federal Reserve Board, a government agency, from 1951 to 1970. It is interesting that Martin's conservative, free-market, ideology influenced events in both situations even though it came from a private interest group in one case and a government agency in the other.

Born in 1906 into a St. Louis family with a history of finance and public service—his father was president of the Federal Reserve Bank of St. Louis—Martin was educated before the coming of Keynesian economics and the New Deal, although the Progressive (government interventionist) movement was already part of American politics. Martin's experiences revealed not only the interplay of Congress, bureaucracy, and market interests but also the Old School's mixture of resistance and accommodations to regulation. As president of the NYSE (1938–40), he was caught between the reforming pressures of government and the resistance of members of the Exchange struggling for profits and even survival, and second, as chairman of the Federal Reserve (1951–70), between the Fed's official mandate of financial stability and political and intellectual pressures for easy money. He showed similar economic views in the two cases as well as substantial bureaucratic skills. In the first case, he held off the reformers, with mixed success, until his goodwill had been exhausted. His record as chairman of the Fed is well-known: low inflation for a dozen years followed by as much resistance as he could manage consistent with the Fed's survival to presidents' easy-money pressures during the remainder.

Legislation's probable influences are often complex and uncertain when adopted, and might or might not become more straightforward with time. We might expect a law to diminish in effectiveness over time as technology and political conditions change. On the other hand, market adaptations could as easily, in principle, strengthen as weaken the effectiveness of laws. We will look at the practical development of the securities and Federal Reserve acts and compare them with subsequent related legislation, such as Dodd-Frank, which was inspired by the 2008 financial crisis, and is the most recent substantial effort to improve the financial system by legislation.

This book builds on the many excellent studies of the Securities Acts of the 1930s and the Federal Reserve Act of 1913, by examining their changing effectiveness over time as they respond to developing political, bureaucratic, and market pressures. Histories of the Acts are alive with personalities and their interactions with the private and political conditions of their times. New to the financial center, the young Martin, for example, was thrust into a prominent position with conflicting obligations to the bureaucracy and the stock market. The directions of his efforts were affected by the political climate, first emphasizing the reforms of the Exchange envisioned by the Securities Exchange Act of 1934, but also subject to traditional profit-seeking practices under pressure from the Exchange as administration pressures turned elsewhere.

Similarly, although as Chairman of the Fed, Martin's stable-price preference had not changed, his efforts were affected by political pressures. Observations of Martin at the New York Stock Exchange and the Federal Reserve allow us to study the interactions and relative importance of private interests, laws, bureaucracies, and ideologies. General theories of legislatures or government bureaucracies are difficult, but examinations of them in the contexts of particular conditions and personnel may improve our understanding of them a little, even if only to find that their importance may sometimes be exaggerated.

A Background of Crises and Financial Regulation

Financial crises and government reactions have been with us for centuries, especially since the seventeenth century, by which time national and international financial *systems* had become important parts of economic development. A crucial part of our story stems from the failures of politicians and the press to appreciate that history as they seem always to have been surprised by these developments in the apparent belief that bankers and other financiers had until their latest transgressions occupied the heights of morality and public esteem. In his famous first inaugural address in 1933, President Franklin Roosevelt promised to "restore [the] temple [of finance] to the ancient truths [with] social values more noble than mere monetary profit." In 2008, in emphasizing the novelty and difficulties of dealing with the current crisis, Treasury Secretary Henry Paulson (formerly CEO of Goldman Sachs) declared that "There is no playbook for responding to turmoil [arising from unsuccessful loans, which have been the most common problem for banks] we have never faced" (*New York Times*, November 17, 2008).

We are interested in the causes and effects of government in the marketplace, particularly financial markets consisting of suppliers and demanders of funds in roughly competitive circumstances. These markets have been essential to the development of modern economies. The Industrial Revolution that was driven by growing national and international manufacturing, transportation, and other corporations is unthinkable without the Financial Revolution which enabled the transfers of resources from savers/investors to producers. Walter Bagehot (1873) and J.R. Hicks (1969) argued that the financial system played a critical role in industrialization by facilitating the mobilization of capital for "immense works." Joseph Schumpeter (1912) argued that banks spur "innovation by identifying and funding those entrepreneurs with the best chances of successfully implementing innovative products and production processes" (Levine 1997). "Creative destruction" was enabled by finance (Schumpeter 1942).

Figure 1.1 indicates the growing though uneven importance of finance in the American economy. The financial industry grew from about 1.5 percent of GDP in the mid-nineteenth century to 8 percent today. The pattern of growth is consistent with the 1890s and 1920s being times of rapid entry by firms with large financial needs and government supplanting private finance during the two World Wars. A structural shift happened after World War II, when large established firms with high cash flows

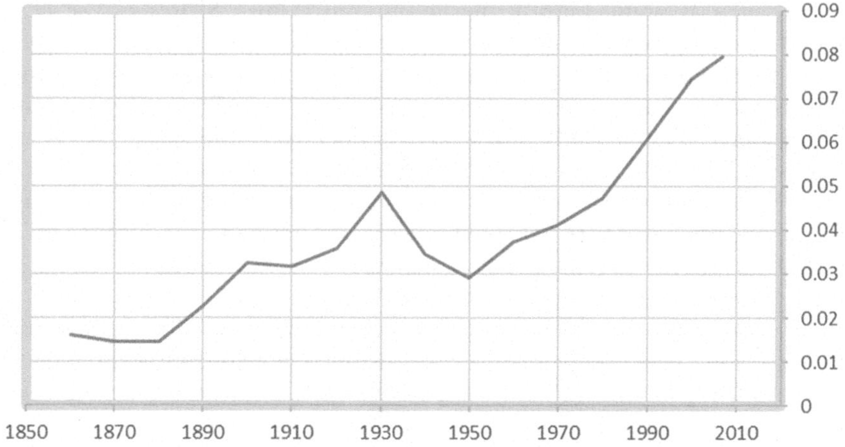

Fig. 1.1 GDP share of U.S. financial services. (Source: Based on data from Philippon 2008)

appear to have had the best investment projects. As a result, the demand for financial intermediation was small. Beginning in the 1970s, investment opportunities shifted toward young, especially information technology, firms with low current cash flows, and the demand for intermediation increased (Philippon 2008).

Although useful, perhaps necessary, to high incomes and growth, financial markets have been subject to disruptions from their beginning. Bets on the future are bound to end in mistakes some of the time, and financial mistakes disrupt production and employment, resulting in severe distress. The history of finance has been one of speculations and panics, booms and busts, and the loosening and tightening of regulations. Charles Mackay's popular 1841 book on *Extraordinary Popular Delusions and the Madness of Crowds* compared financial bubbles to witch hunts, alchemy, and the crusades.

Going back only as far as the beginnings of large corporations and stock markets in the seventeenth century, financial crises have been followed by legislation intended to punish offenders and prevent recurrences. Amsterdam's bourse began trading company shares in 1602, along with goods such as grain, herring, whale-oil, and tulips.[1] Shares of the new Dutch East India Company were actively traded, and as early as 1608, their prices fell by a third "as a consequence of manipulations by a group of speculators," according to Joseph de la Vega in 1688 in *Confusion de Confusiones.* "These early stock-market operators sold large blocks of shares and, in addition, sought to depress the price both by selling 'short' and by spreading rumors … unfavorable to the Dutch Company. Consequently," in 1610, "the first edict was published prohibiting activities of this sort, especially the 'windhandel,' that is, the dealing in shares that were not in the possession of the seller."

In 1621, after the outbreak of war with Spain, more edicts against the "wind-trade" and other practices were issued. "[A]pparently the abuses could not be eliminated," but the crisis of 1672 led to still more decrees intended to protect shareholders of the East India Company.

In 1687, Amsterdam lawyer Nicholas van Holy published a pamphlet on the evils of speculation. He pointed to "professional dealers in stocks who were anxious to worm out the secrets of the State and of the Companies in order to get the better of ordinary investors through the use of such 'inside' information; and in an effort to reduce speculation, he proposed" with some success that stock trades be registered and taxed (de la Vega 1699, Introduction).

In 1711, the British Parliament chartered the South Sea Company which took on much of the government war debt. Debt holders were persuaded to exchange their claims for shares in the Company. The government undertook to pay the company 6 percent interest plus expenses annually, distributed as a dividend to shareholders. The Company was also given a theoretical monopoly of trade with South America, which, controlled by Spain, never became profitable for the Company.

In 1720, rising expectations of earnings from trade and government debt produced an increase in the Company's shares which developed into a speculative frenzy, sending the share price from £128 in January to £1050 in June—before collapsing in August and falling below £200 by year's end. The overall market shared the fate of South Sea stock, thousands of investors gained and/or lost large amounts, and the public and government were enraged.

[1] The name *bourse* was derived from Roger Van der Burse's inn in Bruges, Belgium, where merchants gathered to trade.

The euphoria associated with the boom had encouraged a multitude of schemes, including those

- for supplying the town of Deal with fresh water.
- for trading in hair.
- for assuring of seamen's wages.
- for insuring of horses.
- for the transmutation of quicksilver into a malleable fine metal.
- for insuring and increasing children's fortunes.
- for a wheel for perpetual motion.
- for importing walnut-trees from Virginia.
- for paying pensions to widows and others, at a small discount.

and most famous of all,

- for carrying on an undertaking of great advantage; but nobody to know what it is (Mackay 1841, pp. 55–62).

A parliamentary committee reported in January 1721 that the South Sea Company's books contained fictitious entries, optimistic advertisements had been without foundation, and government favors had been obtained through bribes. Chancellor of the Exchequer John Aislabie was found guilty of the "most notorious, dangerous, and infamous corruption," expelled from Parliament, and confined in the Tower. He was named in the legislation which confiscated the estates of those deemed responsible for the bubble in order to compensate losers, although he was allowed to keep the property he had possessed on October 20, 1718. Other Company directors were treated similarly and several government ministers were impeached.

> Parliament made repeated attempts between the 1690s and 1770s to check the growth of Exchange Alley [a narrow alley of shops, coffee houses, and goldsmiths, where there was "lively trading in stocks and commodities," including by stock jobbers who had been expelled from the Royal Exchange for their rude manners]. Most of these attempts, however, were ineffectual, owing to their time-honoured but futile identification of economic pressures with human wickedness or folly. (Dickson 1967, p. 516)

After the crisis of 1697, when "the badly muddled" recoinage led to a shortage of money because the mint was slow to replace surrendered worn and clipped coins, Parliament decided that blame rested with the financial community, and pursued correction through regulation. Stockbrokers were licensed and limited in number, required to record their orders, and brokerage was limited to ½ percent. "Since the Lord Treasurer Earl Godolphin was aware that keeping government securities at par and preventing heavy falls in prices could not be accomplished by coercing the dealers, the measures had to be understood as a sop to public opinion rather than a serious attempt to regulate prices" (Feavearyear 1931, pp. 117–35; Dickson 1967, pp. 516–17). *Plus ça change, plus c'est la même chose.*

The Act was extended in 1708, and much of its detail and enforcement were delegated to a committee consisting of the Lord Mayor and others in the City, that is, to the financial community, who found its application beyond their capabilities or inclinations. Unlicensed brokers were complained of but unapprehended at least partly because of the difficulties of prosecution given the hostility of witnesses.

A bill "for the better Establishment of publick Credit by preventing … the infamous practice of Stock-Jobbing" passed the British House of Commons in 1720 but was rejected by the House of Lords. It finally passed both Houses in 1737 as Sir John Bernard's Act, after "the chief apostle of financial purity," probably inspired by a fall in security prices because of the prospects of war.[2] The Act also penalized options, dealings on margin, short sales, and broker-jobbing combinations, all without apparent effects on securities prices.

The definition of stockjobber in Samuel Johnson's *Dictionary*—"A low wretch who gets money by buying and selling shares in the funds"—may have reflected a public view, but finance was a powerful political interest, as must be the case with lenders to governments and businesses, and regulation had limited effects on practice. Stock trading's defenders were often diffident, relying on freedom of contract and its contributions to market liquidity and the government's ability to raise funds: "[T]hough stock-jobbing was an inconvenience, yet considering how much it contributed to the ready circulation of money, and to the supporting the credit of our funds, it was therefore to be tolerated," said a member of the House of Lords.

[2]Bernard was a City merchant, Member of Parliament for the City, and Lord Mayor (1737), known as a defender of the City's interests.

More than tolerance, however, the view that free trade should apply to finance as much as to other activities made considerable headway during the eighteenth century. Nevertheless, despite the ineffectiveness of restrictions on jobbers and time trades passed in 1697, 1708, and 1737, would-be regulators kept trying, and new bills aimed at stock-jobbing failed to pass Parliament in 1756 and 1771. It was said in Parliament in 1771 that "the trading of stock like every other thing ought to be free of interruption" (Dickson 1967, p. 520). The difficulties of effective regulation were being increasingly understood. "Whenever it shall be seriously intended to prevent or restrain this practice" [stock-jobbing], a London commentator wrote in 1725, "while they increase the difficulty of the most innocent and necessary transactions ..., will have little further effect on this practice than to force it into some other channel, and perhaps increase the profit and employment of the banker only, by making his credit or assistance further necessary" (Dickson 1967, p. 520).

A similar American ambivalence was revealed by the state of New York's 1812 ban on short selling, lifted in 1853, and resumed from time to time in the twentieth and twenty-first centuries, as we will see in Chap. 4 (Wyckoff 1972, p. 15). Stamp Brooksbank, merchant and director of the Bank of England, said in the House of Commons in 1733 that stock trading is "a sort of gaming, ... but of such a sort as cannot be entirely prevented, even by the bill now before us." Contracts were honored without legal sanction, under a moral code that was no less high-minded than others. To breach a contract was to ruin one's "honor" and "credit." "All the Affluence of Money, and the most immense Riches are of no Consequence if there be ground for the least suspicion of Disingenuity" (Harrison 1999). Adam Smith (1763, p. 252) argued similarly:

> There is no natural reason why £1000 in the stocks should not be delivered or the delivery of it enforced, as well as £1000 worth of goods. But after the South Sea Scheme this was thought upon as an expedient to prevent such practices, though it proved ineffectual. In the same manner all laws against gaming never hinder it, and though there is no redress for a sum above £5, yet all the great sums that are lost are punctually paid. Persons who game must keep their credit, else nobody will deal with them. It is quite the same in stockjobbing.

J.P. Morgan, Jr. and Kuhn, Loeb's Otto Kahn made the same point to a government investigative committee in 1933 (see Chap. 2). "An investment banker's credit is his most valuable possession; it is the result of years of fair and honorable dealing and, while it may be quickly lost, once lost cannot be restored for a long time, if ever."

The financial revolution supported the industrial revolution but crises persisted. The Federal Reserve Act brought an institution that was supposed to bring stability, but was followed by the greatest crash of them all in 1929. The U.S. government's reaction to this crash was also the greatest of them all. It reflected the increase in size, and potentially the influence, of government through its bureaucracy. German sociologist Max Weber wrote that bureaucracies are the effective government because they interpret and apply incomplete laws on a daily basis. Would the SEC be able to enforce regulations where earlier efforts had failed? And would the Federal Reserve improve the stability of money?

Plan of the Book

This book is about the effects of these laws and agencies on money and finance. We begin with markets and the institutions of which they are made. The legislature seeks improvements and passes a law or laws—such as the Securities Act of 1933 and the Securities Exchange Act of 1934—to be interpreted and applied by an agency—such as the SEC. What are the effects on the market? Are they significant? Are they those envisioned by the legislators?

These questions might seem frivolous to officialdom and the writers and readers of textbooks, but experience and logic suggest otherwise. First consider securities legislation. Think of markets consisting of people who have developed and grown used to procedures which advance their interests. Those interests might induce them to try to circumvent regulations. Much of economics is the study of market breakdowns caused by regulations such as price and wage controls, tariffs, and production limits.

Furthermore, at least in the United States, there is a good deal of democracy even in bureaucracy. Laws are passed and an agency is established by a particular Congress—there's a new one every two years—and often the terms of an act have to be worked out by the agency (whose membership is also changing) and the industry in concert—with Congress looking over their shoulders. The relevant subcommittees may pay close attention. A section of an act may have imposed a potentially severe restriction, details to be worked out, favored by a particular Congress and an ambitious agency. Good so far but this takes time. Less than half the 2010

Dodd-Frank Law was completed by 2015. Dodd-Frank was passed by the Democratic 111th Congress, but Republicans took the House the next and succeeding Congresses and the Senate shortly thereafter. Even when Democrats controlled Congress and the presidency from 1933 to 1947, their support of the securities acts was lukewarm.

Chapters 2, 3, and 4 treat these issues in the context of the Securities Act of 1933, the bureaucracy, and the effects of the Securities Act of 1934 and the Securities Exchange Commission on the New York Stock Exchange leading up to and during the 1938–40 presidency of Martin. We are interested in whether the government's responses to the Great Depression—its laws and agencies—affected the securities markets either temporarily or permanently.

Chapters 5 and 6 deal with American central banking before and during the early years of the Federal Reserve, followed by monetary policies during Martin's chairmanship as influenced by Congress, the Executive, and critical intellectual forces. Chapter 7 concludes with overviews of some of the experiences of market regulations, although it will "be far from a systematic treatment of" bureaucracies in markets, "and even farther from a rigorous testing of any theory of bureaucratization: Our knowledge of agency history and behavior is too sketchy to permit that," James Q. Wilson concluded (1976). Studies of bureaucracies in government tend to "assign little importance to the nature of the tasks an agency performs, the constitutional framework in which it is embedded, or the preferences and attitudes of citizens and legislators." Perhaps the best we can do is to identify the interests as well as the legislative and bureaucratic influences on markets in particular cases. We will see that the pair considered here suggests that official influences may have been exaggerated, especially in comparison with the permanent forces of finance.

References

Adams, Gordon. 1981. *The Iron Triangle. The Politics of Defense Contracting.* New York: Council on Economic Priorities.

Bagehot, Walter. 1873. *Lombard Street.* Henry King (Reprinted with Introduction by Harley Withers. New York: E.P. Dutton, 1920).

de la Vega, Joseph. 1688. *Confusion de Confusiones.* Trans. with Introduction by H. Kellenbenz, 1957. Cambridge: Harvard Graduate School of Business Administration.

Dickson, P.G.M. 1967. *The Financial Revolution in England. A Study in the Development of Public Credit, 1688–1756.* London: Macmillan.

Feavearyear, A.E. 1931. *The Pound Sterling: A History of English Money*. Oxford: Clarendon Press.

Harrison, Paul. 1999. The Causes and Consequences of Financial Market Regulation in 18th Century England, ms. Federal Reserve Board (from diss. *The More Things Change the More They Stay the Same. 300 Years of Stock Market Evolution*, Duke University).

Hicks, John R. 1969. *A Theory of Economic History*. Oxford: Clarendon Press.

Johnson, Samuel. 1755. *A Dictionary of the English Language*. London: J. and P. Knapton et al.

Levine, Ross. 1997. Financial Development and Economic Growth: Views and Agenda. *Journal of Economic Literature* XXXV: 688–726.

Mackay, Charles. 1841. *Extraordinary Popular Delusions and the Madness of Crowds*. London: Richard Bentley.

Moe, Terry M. 1997. The Positive Theory of Public Bureaucracy. In *Perspectives in Public Choice: A Handbook*, ed. D. Mueller. Cambridge: Cambridge University Press.

Niskanen, William. 1971. *Bureaucracy and Representative Government*. Chicago: Aldine-Atherton.

Philippon, Thomas. 2008. *The Evolution of the U.S. Financial Industry from 1860 to 2007*. Working paper, Stern School of Business.

Schumpeter, Joseph A. 1912. *The Theory of Economic Development* (German; published in English by Harvard University Press, 1934).

———. 1942. *Capitalism, Socialism, and Democracy*. New York: Harper & Brothers.

Smith, Adam. 1763. *Lectures on Justice, Police, Revenue, and Arms*, reported by a student, ed. E. Cannon. Oxford: Clarendon Press, 1896 (Reprinted New York: Kelley & Millman, 1956).

Wilson, James Q. 1976. The Rise of the Bureaucratic State. In *The American Commonwealth*, ed. Nathan Glazer and Irving Kristol. New York: Basic Books.

Wyckoff, Peter. 1972. *Wall Street and the Stock Markets: A Chronology, 1644–1971*. Philadelphia: Chilton.

CHAPTER 2

The Securities Act of 1933

I list an important place for that prize statement of principle in the platform here adopted calling for the letting in of the light of day on issues of securities, foreign and domestic, which are offered for sale to the investing public.
Franklin Roosevelt, presidential nomination acceptance speech, July 2, 1932.

The Crash

Politicians and the press reacted strongly to the collapse of security values during the Great Depression. The Democratic Party platform promised reforms although congressional enquiries had already begun. The Progressive Era's push for business and social reforms that had been relegated to a political back-seat during the 1920s was revived by the depression that began in 1929 and the election of Democrat/reformer Franklin Roosevelt in 1932.

The Report of the Senate Banking and Currency Committee following its hearings on *Stock Exchange Practices* began with the commissions and interest incomes of the members of 29 securities exchanges amounting to $2.4 billion, 92 percent at the New York Stock Exchange. What did the American public receive for this "staggering" cost "of maintaining the securities markets?" The committee's answer to its question was: "losses on an unprecedented scale" due to "speculation on the exchanges" that produced "the illusory boom which culminated in October 1929." The

J. H. Wood, *Who Governs?*, Palgrave Studies in American Economic History, https://doi.org/10.1007/978-3-030-33083-5_2

market value of stocks listed on the NYSE plummeted from $90 billion in September 1929 to $16 billion in July 1932, an 82 percent loss. The Dow Jones Industrial Average (of 30 blue chip stocks, including General Electric, General Motors, US Steel, and Sears, Roebuck) fell from 381 to 41. The crash of October 28–29, 1929, was the most dramatic event of the period, but that 2-day, 23-percent fall in the Dow Jones average from 300 to 230 was not the largest part of the four-year fall in security prices. "The annals of finance present no counterpart to this enormous decline in security prices," the Report accurately observed (U.S. Senate 1934a, pp. 6–7; Seligman 2003, pp. 1–2).

The House Committee on Interstate and Foreign Commerce reported that of $50 billion of securities floated in the United States during the postwar decade, "fully half ... have been proved to be worthless."

> These cold figures spell tragedy in the lives of thousands of individuals who invested their life savings, accumulated after years of effort, in these worthless securities. The flotation of such a mass of essentially fraudulent securities was made possible because of the complete abandonment by many underwriters and dealers in securities of those standards of fair, honest, and prudent dealing that should be basic to the encouragement of investment in any enterprise. Alluring promises of easy wealth were freely made with little or no attempt to bring to the investor's attention those facts essential to estimating the worth of any security. High-pressure salesmanship rather than careful counsel was the rule in this most dangerous of enterprises. (U.S. House of Representatives 1933b, p. 2; Seligman 2003, p. 5)

President Herbert Hoover and the 71st Congress, beneficiaries of the Republican landslide of 1928, had refrained from direct political action. The president "deplored the idea of extending Federal power over organizations which had the power to remedy their own evils. The Stock Exchange properly conducted is a vital part of the free-enterprise system. In any event, the primary responsibility for initiation of official action lay on Governor Franklin Roosevelt of New York" (Wilber and Hyde 1937, p. 347; Hoover 1952, p. 126). He remained "convinced we have passed the worst and with continued effort we shall rapidly recover" (Hoover 1952, p. 58).

The November 1930 elections gave Democrats control of the House of Representatives and one vote shy of Senate control. The first three days of the new Congress saw the introduction of ten bills to regulate securities markets, most directed at short sales.

New York Stock Exchange President Richard Whitney changed few minds when he argued in a national broadcast on October 16, 1931, that short selling was "essential to an open market for securities.... Every man who has sold short is ... a potential buyer of securities, and this is a great source of stability to a market, because experience shows that when prices suddenly decline the short sellers purchase stock in order to discharge their loans" (U.S. Senate 1934b, pp. 187–93). Nevertheless, one congressional proposal would have imposed a 25 percent tax on short-selling profits, another declared that "short sales ... exert a vicious influence and produce abnormal and disturbing declines of prices that are not responsive to actual supply and demand," and one would have sent short sellers to prison (Seligman 2003, p. 9).

Losses on foreign investments struck a special chord, and in December 1931, the Progressive Republican Senator Hiram Johnson secured approval of a Finance Committee investigation of the sale of foreign bonds to Americans and the profits of the bankers who had placed them. William Randolph Hearst's *New York American* had waged a campaign against the bankers who between 1923 and 1930 sold $6.3 billion of foreign securities, a tenth of the securities sold in the United States, 90 percent of which were depreciated (*New York American*, Nov. 8, 9, 10, 12, 15, 16, 19, 1931; *Historical Statistics of the U.S.*, v. 2, p. 1006. Fiorello LaGuardia called these articles to the attention of the House, *Congressional Record*, December 11, 1931). Many were in default. The market value of the debt of Latin American countries was about 20 percent of their face value, 7 percent for Peru (U.S. Senate 1932, pp. 324–27; *CR*, March 15, 1932, pp. 6057–58). European bonds were worth about half their face values.

American investment banks had competed vigorously for the high commissions paid to place these securities, sometimes engaging in questionable practices. They used political connections to secure placements and advertised rosy prospects for countries with suspect finances. Instead of waiting for bonds in accordance with conservative investment banking tradition, newer and more aggressive banks had sent agents abroad to encourage and compete for issues (Seligman 2003, p. 10; U.S. Senate 1932, *CR*, March 15, 1932).

Not as well publicized was the fact that most of these bonds had paid interest regularly and maintained their values throughout the 1920s, and most resumed payments after the depression (Mintz 1951, p. 29; Wynne 1951). Price falls and defaults began during the spring of 1931, "under the combined influence of the fall in business activity and in prices, the imposition of the tariff of 1930, and the cessation of new foreign investment" (Mintz 1951, p. 3). The price of copper, a major Peruvian export, fell more than two-thirds between 1929 and 1932, and the value of the country's exports fell 50 percent. Payments from the United States to foreign countries fell from $7400 million in 1929 to $2400 million in 1932, while the reverse debt-service obligations continued.

> Under such circumstances it was inevitable that many of these obligations should be defaulted. By comparison with the magnitude of these strains, all other explanations of the relatively unsatisfactory outcome of the past foreign lending experience of the United States must be of distinctly secondary importance. (Ilse Mintz, *Deterioration in the Quality of Foreign Bonds Issued in the U.S.*, p. 3)

The severity of the Great Depression was unanticipated, but the interest premiums on the bonds of developing countries suggest that investors had understood at least some of their risks (Mintz 1951, p. 61; Young 1930, p. 62; Madden et al. 1937, p. 14; and periodic reports on "Stock Exchange Bonds" in the *Wall Street Journal*, e.g., January 10, 1925, p. 15, and December 14, 1929, p. 8). Furthermore, the size and prestige of investment bankers and the performance of their bonds were positively correlated. As expected, newer and smaller firms placed the less attractive issues. Nevertheless, perhaps because of the political risk of subjecting small firms to cross examination, the Finance Committee limited its examinations to the big bankers.

> Senator Johnson (to Otto Kahn of Kuhn, Loeb & Co.): I will say to you that I am not bringing any small bankers here, because I do not want them to have to be submitted to any sort of irritation on the part of any of those with whom they have to deal. (*Foreign Bond Hearings*, p. 394)

Johnson had heard of small banks complaining of being coerced by the large banks to take the riskier issues. Kahn disagreed, saying that small firms had been seekers of risk. "These little bankers" were eager "for bonds, especially those yielding high rates of interest."

> Such practices as what you might term "strong-arm methods" of selling, making raids on rather unwilling buyers, exercising undue persuasiveness, tempting buyers by undue facilities, inducements or expectations; in short, high-powered methods of salesmanship, are against the dignity and the

> ethics of banking. They are not within the permissible functions of a bank or banker and, least of all, within the permissible functions of a bank of deposit.

The Committee was not impressed by witnesses' protests that they had not intentionally taken a gullible American public for a ride.

> Senator William King (Utah Democrat): Mr. Kahn, … isn't one of the reasons for the decline in American … corporate [as well as foreign government] bonds, [the fact that] corporations have unloaded upon investors not only stock but bonds at higher prices by far than the conditions of the corporations warranted? In other words, taking advantage of the inflated condition brought about by brokers and speculators and by banks that contributed to it, corporations unloaded upon the investing public millions and hundreds of millions of dollars of bonds and … stock at prices far beyond their intrinsic value.
>
> Mr. Kahn: As a general proposition, I very respectfully beg to differ, Senator, though I admit that errors have been made and that in some respects ground for criticism does exist. The price at which a bond is sold is determined not by the banker, as no banker has the power to do that, and no combination of bankers or of corporations, has the power to do that, but is determined by supply and demand. If the people want to buy bonds or are in a mood to buy bonds, if the market conditions and the monetary conditions of the time are such that bonds are in great demand, the bankers' job, among other things, is to form an estimate as to what the market price at which a bond that they believe to be good, intrinsically, according to their investigations, can be sold, according to their best judgment. (U.S. Senate 1932, pp. 341, 394; Collins 2003, pp. 269–95)

Kuhn, Loeb & Co. was founded in New York in 1867 and took a leading part in financing railroads and other growing companies, such as Western Union and Westinghouse. It was John D. Rockefeller's principal investment bank and the chief rival of J.P. Morgan & Co. Its connections were far-reaching. Paul Warburg, partner in the Hamburg family firm of M.M. Warburg & Co., and future advocate of the Federal Reserve and member of its Board of Governors (1914–18), married Nina Loeb in 1895, settled in the United States, and became a partner in Kuhn Loeb in 1902. The firm declined after World War II, when, it was said, it failed to keep up with an increasingly aggressive investment banking industry in which Kuhn, Loeb's genteel relational ways no longer fitted. In 1977, it merged with Lehman Brothers, creating

Lehman Brothers, Kuhn, Loeb Inc., which was acquired in 1984 by American Express to form Shearson Lehman/American Express (Geisst 2001, pp. 70–78).

Ferdinand Pecora wrote of Kahn, smooth in manner and a well-known patron of the arts, that "No suaver, more fluent, and more diplomatic advocate could be conceived" (Pecora 1939, p. 293). If anyone could succeed in presenting the customs and functions of the private bankers in a favorable and prepossessing light, it was he. Kahn may have been the model for the Monopoly game logo. Nevertheless, the senators resisted Kahn's as much as Morgan's and other investment bankers' claims of their values, although after fifteen days of hearings in January 1932, the Committee made no report. This is not surprising, for notwithstanding exclamations of the unprecedented nature of the recent bond defaults, they in fact were an old and much investigated problem. One is reminded of Treasury Secretary Henry Paulson's defense that nothing like the crisis of 2008, which was a consequence of rapid increases in inadequately collateralized bank loans that were effectively speculations on house prices, had ever happened. In fact, rapid expansions of loans on commodities or houses whose prices eventually stop rising have been the most common causes of bank failures. Pretending otherwise opens the door to new regulations on allegedly new problems. Regulatory failure and government shocks are also dismissed, such as the government's promotion of home mortgages before 2008, including pressures on banks to take on risk, and the Federal Reserve's volatile monetary policies which brought the Great Depression.[1]

An earlier crisis examined by an 1875 British parliamentary committee concluded that the only remedy with any chance of success had to be the self-education and caution of investors (Great Britain 1875, p. 1). "[D]ownward swings of the business cycle" had typically "caused the failure of governments and other foreign borrowers to meet their external obligations," although the recurrence of these periods of default did not fail to arouse "considerable public resentment and brought foreign securities into general disfavor from time to time." In 1875, outrage over

[1] For the government's support of the housing bubble by its pressures on banks to extend subprime mortgages, the promise of bailouts, and the Fed's easy money, see Hetzel (2012), and Wood (2015, ch. 6). For gold, prices, and causes of the Great Depression, see Eichengreen (1992) and Mazumder and Wood (2013).

defaults on the bonds of Honduras, Costa Rica, Paraguay, and Santo Domingo sold on the London market led to a parliamentary inquiry "into the circumstances attending the making of … loans with certain Foreign States, and also the causes which have led to the non-payment of [their] principal moneys and interest" (Madden et al. 1937, p. 107; *New York Times*, April 12, 1875).

The Johnson committee's hearings might have been taken from the 1875 committee's. Although the loans differed in several respects, there were "incidents for the most part common to all. [T]hose who introduced them to the public seem to have been regardless of the financial resources of the borrowing state; … In no case … with one unimportant exception, has the borrowing Government repaid any portion of its indebtedness incurred in respect of these loans, except from the proceeds of the loans themselves; by means of exaggerated statements in the prospectus the public have been induced to believe that the material wealth of the contracting state formed a sufficient security for the repayment of the money borrowed"; very little of the loans was applied to their ostensible purposes, which were to improve the industrial capacities of the countries; and "the buying and selling of the stock on behalf of the contractor created a fictitious market" (Great Britain 1875, pp. xliv–xlv).

The only policy recommended by the committee was to advise banks to require a more complete prospectus for foreign loans, including the authority from the borrowing state, its public debt, and the source of revenue securing the loan (Great Britain 1875, xlix). There was little evidence, however, that future behavior benefitted from either the experience or the advice. The Baring crisis of 1890 followed the failure of Argentine debt because the Bank of England had taken a substantial position in the country's securities for which it was the primary issuer (Weidenmier 2009). Defaults before the 1930s on issues in the United States included Mexico's government and railways after 1913, and Russian and Chinese government issues of 1916 and 1919, respectively (Madden 1937, p.108). Government defaulters were also found domestically. The U.S. government repudiated the gold clause protection of its debt in 1933, and state and local governments have a long history of default. Eight states and the territory of Florida defaulted in 1841–42. In the 1930s, 4770 governmental units defaulted, including 417 counties, 1532 municipalities, and 1241 school districts. Of the defaulting issues of incorporated municipalities, nearly half were rated Aaa in 1929, and 78 percent were rated Aa and better.[2]

Nevertheless, each crisis was treated by politicians and the press as an unprecedented consequence of modern greed calling for additional government control. President Hoover believed falling security prices were due to manipulation, and pressed for reforms, especially at the NYSE. Although the Exchange's directors "repeatedly promised they would … amend their rules so as to stop manipulation," Hoover recalled in his *Memoirs*, they "made only minor changes" (1952, p. 126). At a press conference on February 19, 1932, he demanded that "the managers of the Exchange … take adequate measures to protect investors from artificial depression of the price of securities for individual profit" (Wilber and Hyde 1937, p. 344). When no response was forthcoming, Hoover summoned Republicans Frederick Walcott and Peter Norbeck of the Senate Banking Committee to a highly publicized meeting at the White House, during which he threatened an investigation of stock exchange practices (Hoover 1952, p. 127; Wilber and Hyde 1937, pp. 345–46; *New York Times*, Feb. 27, 1932).

Reactions

It is not clear whether the president wanted hearings that would lead to federal control, or more likely, to put pressure on the exchanges to take action on their own (Seligman 2003, p. 12). The Committee chose the more ambitious path and obtained the Senate's approval for "a thorough and complete investigation" of stock exchange practices, leading to the submission of "recommendations for the necessary remedial legislation … as soon as practicable" (*New York Times*, March 4, 1932). "Ultimately," it has been said, "the Senate Banking Committee's stock exchange hearings

[2]After the Bryan silver scare of the 1890s, it was standard practice for private and government bond payments to be defined in terms of gold. For example, a $20 coupon was expressed as a promise of an ounce of gold (approximately, that is, because gold was valued at $20.67), which became $35 when the gold value of the dollar was reduced in 1934. However, Congress, upheld by the courts, repudiated the promise, and the $20 coupon remained unchanged despite the increase in the price of gold.

The 1841–42 defaults have been attributed by some to bad luck caused by the depression that began with the panic of 1837, but Dewey (1922, pp. 243–46) and Grinath et al. (2004) have pointed out that the aggressive underfunded investments in internal improvements came after 1837 (Hempel 1976, Exhibit 15, and 1971, pp. 108–109).

would transform American capitalism." This was an exaggeration, as will be seen, but Professor Joel Seligman was right when he wrote that "They would be directly responsible for the Securities and Banking Acts of 1933, the Securities Exchange Act of 1934, and the creation of the Securities and Exchange Commission" (Seligman 2003, p. 15).

The hearings' beginning was unimpressive. The first witness, Exchange spokesman Richard Whitney, dominated the hearings for two days, extolling the existing system and denying both the existence and the potential harm of bear raids. He would later call the NYSE "a perfect institution" (Alsop and Kintner 1938, p. 9). The unprepared senators and their counsels could only respond with hearsay. The hearings sputtered along for two months, but unsupported accusations of scandalous behavior were not enough to assure their continuation. When the hearings adjourned on June 24, no one knew whether they would be resumed, but the question was decided in the affirmative by Roosevelt's election in November.

Although his presidential nomination acceptance speech is best remembered for its "pledge ... to a new deal for the American people," it was devoted largely to the "dry subject of finance," partly reproduced in the opening quotation of this chapter. While the Republican platform and candidate virtually ignored financial regulation, Roosevelt made it a centerpiece of his campaign. His program of securities law reform included "truth telling" by securities issuers, federal regulation of securities exchanges, more rigid federal supervision of banks, separation of commercial and investment banking, and the prevention of Federal Reserve funds from being used for speculative enterprises (Columbus speech, August 20, 1932; Roosevelt, i, pp. 669–84).

Nine days after FDR's election, Senate Finance Committee Chairman Norbeck announced plans to resume the stock exchange hearings, and recruited New York City Assistant District Attorney Ferdinand Pecora as committee counsel. Reputed to be "the most brilliant cross-examiner in New York," Pecora was "a compact, swarthy man with curling black and gray hair" who "punctuated his [questioning] with the vigorous jabbing of a stubby finger." His manner was alternately genial, courtly, mocking, and belligerent. It was always relentless and he treated prestigious witnesses unused to such treatment as if they had something to hide. J.P. Morgan, Jr., complained that Pecora pursued him as if he were "a horse thief" (Seligman 2003, p. 21; *Time*, June 12, 1933; *Newsweek*, June 10, 1933).

The importance of the Stock Exchange Practices hearings owed much to their counsel.

> Intermittently throughout the year 1933 the Senate Committee on Banking and Currency, with the aid of its inexorable counsel, Ferdinand Pecora, had been putting on one of the most extraordinary shows ever produced in a Washington committee room: a sort of protracted coroner's inquest upon American finance. (Frederick Lewis Allen, *Since Yesterday*, pp. 135–36)

> Coldly Pecora made his witnesses recollect the gilded past—the stupendous bonuses they had received and the taxes they had avoided, the stock market pools they had rigged, the holding companies they had launched, the bad investments they had palmed off on a trusting nation. From their reluctant testimony emerged the portrait of a world of insiders where for years businessmen had greedily stuffed their own pockets at the expense of the innocent and dumb American citizen. (Arthur M. Schlesinger, Jr. *The Coming of the New Deal*, p. 437)

The committee produced little evidence to support legislation, but it fed the hostile attitude toward finance which cried out for action of some kind. Pecora's interrogations started slowly, but he soon found what worked with a press more interested in the personal foibles of high-paid executives than the technicalities of finance (Perino 2010, pp. 122–43).

This was demonstrated by its coverage of Pecora's attack on Charles Mitchell, who had led the National City Bank of New York from a modest size when he joined it in 1916 to the largest financial organization in the country. The method was in large part the expansion of investment bank activities forbidden to commercial banks, which were legally confined to making loans and taking deposits. National City got around this restriction through a company that was legally separate but practically the same as the bank. The company, financed by the bank, engaged in extra-commercial bank activities, selling securities by innovative and aggressive tactics, such as selling door-to-door, making it a formidable competitor of the large and prestigious investment banking houses. In 1928, journalist Edmund Wilson called Mitchell "Sunshine Charlie … the banker of bankers, the salesman of salesmen, the genius of the New Economic Era."

Pecora began his attack with Mitchell's remuneration, including fees exceeding $1.3 million in 1928 and $1.1 million in 1929. These were astronomical figures when 50¢ was a good hourly wage. It was the committee's view, in the words of Senator James Couzens, that "these unreasonable salaries and these bonuses lead to unsound banking and unsound sales of securities." The committee pursued this line of questioning "not for the purpose of headlines or … delving into … people's personal affairs. I personally dislike this sort of thing, but I think the public should know what inspires some of these sales and some of these securities being foisted on the public" (U.S. Senate 1933, p. 1779).

Mitchell's admission that he had sold National City stock to his wife at fictitious prices to establish a capital loss "for tax purposes" led the U.S. attorney for New York City to announce an investigation of possible tax fraud. Mitchell resigned from his National City positions. Other revelations concerned security issues. Despite the state of Peru's finances, which National City knew were "distressing," it was accused of bribing the president's son for the business of selling the country's securities (Seligman 2003, pp. 26, 29; U.S. Senate 1932, pp. 214–15; *New York Times*, February 25, 27, 28, 1933).[3]

On February 21, a confident Mitchell strode into the Banking Committee's hearing room surrounded by a bevy of bank executives and lawyers. Ten days later, Pecora looked down from a Senate Office Building window to see a solitary man, carrying his own suitcase, shuffling toward the train station. "'That's Mr. Mitchell,' Pecora pointed him out to Senator Norbeck" (Perino 2010, pp. 278–79; Pecora 1962, pp. 685–86, 851).

The National City hearings were conducted against the background of the wave of bank closures which culminated in the new president's declaration of a national "bank holiday" on March 6. After beginning his famous inaugural address two days earlier with "the only thing we have to fear is fear itself," Roosevelt had turned on the bankers. Distress had come "because the rulers of the exchange of mankind's goods have failed, through their own stubbornness and their own incompetence, have admitted their own failure, and abdicated. Practices of the unscrupulous money changers stand indicted in the court of public opinion, rejected by the hearts and minds of men.… The money changers have fled from their high seats in the temple of our civilization. We may now restore that temple to the ancient truths. The measure of the restoration lies in the extent to which we apply social values more noble than mere monetary profit."

[3] Mitchell was found not guilty of criminal charges but had to pay $1,000,000 to the government. Further testimony revealed that the president's son, unknown to the American bankers, had been a member of a group sharing in the loan placement (U.S. Senate 1932, pp. 1280–81).

Establishing himself as patron of the hearings, Roosevelt urged Duncan Fletcher, the new chairman of the Senate Banking Committee, to broaden the inquiry into "all the ramifications of bad banking so that the government will be able to guard against their continuance and prevent their return" ("President upholds banking inquiry," *New York Times*, March 14, 1933). FDR publicly asked the attorney general to prosecute violations of the law revealed by the Banking Committee, and in late March, Mitchell was indicted by a federal grand jury for income tax evasion (Seligman 2003, p. 30; *Newsweek*, April 1, 1933). The Committee acceded to Roosevelt's request to make the high-profile J.P. Morgan & Company the next target. Pecora told reporters he

> was reluctant to mention names of prospective witnesses before informal questioning in New York had established the existence of "evidence of such a character that would be of interest to the Senate committee," but he admitted the classification of private bankers to be questioned included J.P Morgan & Co., and others whom he defined as "private bankers who make their own rules and are not subject to examination at the hands of any public authority". (*New York Times*, March 16, 1933)

The Morgan hearings dominated the news for two weeks. Senior partner Thomas Lamont had testified for the company during the Foreign Bond Hearings, but he lacked the magic of the Morgan name. As with National City, Pecora began with the large earnings of the Morgan partners. The "milling, jostling, sweating crowd ... that fought to get into a stifling room" to see Morgan admit under oath that he paid no income taxes in 1931 or 1932, "loved it, loved the whole Big Show," *Time* magazine enthused (May 29, 1933). This particular revelation was explained by the fact that the company lost money those years, but that did not diminish the public's indignation. Nor was the use of capital losses to reduce income taxes "criminality. Mr. Pecora only makes it seem so," commented the *New York Evening Post* (Seligman 2003, p. 34).

Morgan's preferred lists which gave some customers early access to new issues (which is still a means of underwriting issues and compensating valuable customers) were condemned, as were the holding companies which Morgan organized in the 1920s, primarily, Pecora said, to generate promoters' profits. These revelations, if so they may be called, contained nothing illegal, or improper by ordinary standards, but because of their association with the most prestigious personality (although J. P. Morgan had been succeeded by his son) and financial firm in the country, "the modern embodiment of Croesus, Lorenzo the Magnificent, [and] Rothschild," according to the *Richmond Times Dispatch*, they helped set the stage for regulation (Seligman 2003, p. 31).

Morgan described itself as an ethical and public-spirited company: "we have never been satisfied with simply keeping the law." The reason for the firm's large sales without aggressive sales methods, J.P. Morgan, Jr. said in his opening statement to the committee, was "character" rather than "money or property." "I consider the private banker a national asset and not a national danger. As to the theory that he may become too powerful, it must be remembered that any power which he has comes, not from the possession of large means, but from the confidence of the people in his character and credit, and that that power, having no force to back it, would disappear at once if people thought that the character had changed."

The private banker has none of the privileges of commercial banks, Morgan said, "but as he does not have to conform to any special Government regulation, he has a somewhat greater freedom of action. The private banker is a member of a profession which has been practiced since the Middle Ages. In the process of time there has grown up a code of professional ethics and customs, on the observance of which depend his reputation, his fortune, and his usefulness to the community. [I]f in the exercise of his profession, the private banker disregards this code, which could never be expressed in legislation, but has a force far greater than any law, he will sacrifice his credit" which "is his most valuable possession; it is the result of years of fair and honorable dealing and, while it may be quickly lost, once lost cannot be restored for a long time, if ever" (U.S. Senate 1933, May 23, p. 5).

An account of one of Morgan's public contributions illustrates his enigmatic powers. In 1895, during a run on the dollar by Europeans fearful of its future, at the request of the government, he managed an American bond issue for the purchase of gold which ended the panic. He insisted on complete control. Skeptical Missouri Senator George Vest suggested during a Senate investigation that Morgan had wanted control because he wanted all the profits of the transaction.

> Vest: If the gold was abroad I take it for granted that anybody could get hold of it who had the means to do so. If you were actuated by the desire to prevent a panic, why were you not willing that other people should do it, if they wanted to.
>
> Morgan: They could not do it.

President Grover Cleveland later asked Morgan how he had known he could "command the cooperation of the great financial interests of Europe."

> Morgan: I simply told them that this was necessary for the maintenance of the public credit and the promotion of industrial peace, and they did it.

Of course there was more to his success than Morgan verbalized. He and his firm, along with many others, had stakes in a stable dollar and a government that did not default. Foreign investments in the United States, much of them represented by Morgan, depended on a stable gold value of the dollar. Jean Strouse (1999, pp. 349–52) wrote that Morgan's "power lay in his willingness to take on this kind of risk and responsibility, his knowledge of markets, [and a] record that had earned him the confidence of the world's leading financiers." Finally, there had to be confidence in the government's long-term commitment to the dollar (discussed near the end of Chap. 5). Efforts to bolster currencies in the presence of continuing inflations are bound to fail. Morgan's $68 million dollar estate was less than people had imagined, considerably less than his much-vaunted influence, leading billionaire John D. Rockefeller to comment: "And to think he wasn't even a rich man" (Strouse 1999, pp. 14–15).

I have quoted Morgan at length to compare the sources of their market powers as seen by investment bankers with those understood by the reformers/regulators. The stress on reputation anticipated academic research on the economics of information. Implied by this approach is the preference for dealing with people one knows.[4] FDR valued compulsory reports and controls over relationships and reputations.

Pecora and the press charged that Morgan's dealings had forfeited its claim to high character. Newspaper headlines repeated the former's "revelations" that "Morgan paid no income tax for the years 1931 and 1932,"

[4] See Lamoreaux (1994) for a discussion of insider lending.

and "Tax 'evasion' by Morgan in legal stock dealings is now hunted by Pecora" (*New York Times*, May 24 and June 2, 1933).

A *New York Times* editorial mourned the death of Morgan's character. "Here was a firm of bankers, perhaps the most famous and powerful in the world, which was certainly under no necessity of practicing the small arts of petty traders. Yet it failed under a test of its pride and prestige." Columnist Walter Lippman wrote that "the system of favoritism to insiders … can be explained but cannot be defended." He called on government to "reduce the sheer power of so much privately directed money" (*Literary Digest*, June 10, 1933, pp. 4–5). Though guilty of "no crude crime against the law," the House of Morgan, according to the *New York World-Telegram* (May 26, 1933, p. 21), was guilty of "the far deeper, more dangerous offence of what Lord Bryce well calls 'The submarine warfare which wealth can wage.' The country, the tone of its business, finance, and government, the whole capitalistic structure, will be better, safer, and more stable when this long-standing notion of wealth's high prerogatives and immunities has gone finally into the discard." "No banking is private," *Business Week* (June 7, 1933, p. 21) declared. The national comedian/spokesman Will Rogers summed up the feeling of many, John Brooks (1969, p. 203) wrote, when he said, "These old Wall Street boys are putting up an awful fight to keep the government from putting a cop on their corner."

Neglected in the popular furor was serious thought about the contribution of finance to history's most successful economy. The country's production and capital stock depended on the distributions of savings by financial institutions. Although not mentioned, the reformers' target was nonfinancial business as much as Wall Street, and prosecutors' revelations showed no more wrongdoing in the latter than society in general. Business failures were common in the volatile economy, symptoms of the willingness of entrepreneurs and investors to take risks. The failures of small security issues, sold door to door or not, were no more frequent than business failures generally. Discouraging them primarily threatened small businesses and growth, notwithstanding the avowals of hostility to bigness.

Much was made of Morgan's practice of dealing with the largest and most secure borrowers and lenders, lacking even a sign on its door at 23 Wall Street.

Peddling Money on the Street

Marcus Goldman, emigrated from Bavaria as a young man, became a dry-goods peddler and shopkeeper, father-in-law of Joseph Sachs, and entered New York finance in 1869. In the standard banker's uniform—tall silk hat and Prince Albert frock coat—he left his home uptown each morning to visit friends and acquaintances among the wholesale jewelers and hide and leather merchants downtown (where he was able to judge credit-worthiness first-hand). Marcus carried his business in his hat. He knew a merchant's chief need: cash. Since rates on loans from commercial banks were high, small merchants often sold their promissory notes (commercial paper) at a discount, often 8 to 9 percent to men like Marcus, who bought these notes in amounts ranging from $2500 to $5000, and tucked them inside the inner lining bank of his hat. As the morning and his walk progressed, his hat sat higher and higher on his forehead.

In the afternoon, he would head uptown to the commercial banks, where he would remove his hat and begin to dicker. From his earliest days of, "trading-on-the-street," Goldman handled as much as $5,000,000 of commercial paper a year, yielding a revenue for every 1% spread of $50,000 per annum (over one million in today's dollars). Who would say he was overcompensated?

(From Stephen Birmingham, *Our Crowd*, p. 88)

> Chairman (Democratic Senator Duncan Fletcher of Florida): I suppose if I went there, and had $10,000 I wanted to leave with the bank, you would take it in, wouldn't you?
>
> Mr. Morgan: No; we should not do it.... Not without an introduction.

Morgan mostly "did business with great corporations" that kept over half a billion dollars of deposits with the bank at the end of 1927. Pecora (1939) was aghast:

> This great reservoir of "other people's money" was wholly subject to the disposition of the partners of this one private banking establishment—in the last analysis, really, to the will of one man, Mr. Morgan—to manage as they pleased, uncontrolled in any manner by the slightest vestige of government regulation, examination, or supervision.

He questioned whether the large profits of investment bankers were justified by the risks they undertook. "No banker would underwrite a foreign issue unless he felt quite certain that he could sell it in his market?" Pecora intimated.

> Mr. Clarence Dillon (of Dillon, Read and Co.): I should not think that he would underwrite any issue unless he felt that, sir.

"Dillon emphasized particularly that it was precisely the leading bankers who took the least risks," Pecora recalled in his account of the hearings. "It was not the great houses [Dillon] pointed out, which, for example, financed the automobile industry in its infancy."

> Mr. Dillon: If you had relied on houses like ourselves you probably would not have had the automobile industry in this country. We would not have risked it....

"It was only after more venturesome persons had risked their money and developed the industry to the point where it was safe, that 'we, the smug, conservative bankers'," as Dillon described his fellows, "stepped in and 'now are very pleased to handle automobile securities'." What risk there was seems to have been passed on "to the shoulders of the little fellows, the hundreds of retailers in the selling group," Pecora (1939, pp. 48–49) commented. "Mr. Dillon was good enough to say" that "We must not, in fairness, criticize the man who took the initial risks – although probably many went wrong.... I, for one, am not willing to put on a lower plane than ourselves that financier who does take those risks provided he states frankly and openly to the investor the nature of the investment" (U.S. Senate 1933, pp. 1629–30).

Morgan and Dillon gave much the same testimony as Kahn, in which their fragile powers depended on their reputations. Pecora also missed the point that the facilitation of risk-taking by bankers might assist growth. Of course they should be honest about those risks, but the hearings found little to suggest improper dealings. Their losses during the Great Depression were evidence not of wrongdoing but of the costs of risk-taking.

The Glass-Steagall bill to prohibit institutions from engaging in both investment and commercial banking—"to prevent the undue diversion of funds into speculative operations"—had made little progress since its introduction in 1930, but on the third day of the Morgan hearings it passed the Senate by voice vote, quickly followed by the House.[5] The bill's sudden success coincided with the ballyhoo surrounding the alleged risks that securities affiliates imposed on bank deposits (Kelly 1985).

In fact, banks with securities affiliates failed less frequently than others. The allegedly aggressive commercial banks had behaved about the same as the veteran investment banks (Benston 1990; White 1986). In a 1942 study of the corporate bond market, George Edwards (1942) concluded that the conflict-of-interest-laden commercial bank was myth rather than legend, for "legend at least has an element of historic truth." The adverse incentives attributed to the originate-and-distribute model (like securitization in the 2000s) may be overridden by the value of reputation. A fundamental reason for the bill's adoption was support from investment banks seeking to suppress competition (Shughart 1988; Flandreau et al. 2010; Mahoney 2001; Moore 1934).

Most of Glass-Steagall's legal separation of commercial and investment bank activities was repealed by the Gramm-Leach-Bliley Act in 1999, but it had not been effective. Depression had caused commercial banks to drop out of investment banking before 1933, although they returned in spite of the law when it became profitable to do so. Technological innovations and rising inflation and interest rates during the 1960s and 1970s induced commercial banks to find ways of paying interest on demand deposits (such as automatic transfers between time and demand deposits and interest on deposits in foreign branches). They also became active stock brokers while investment banks infringed on the supposed commercial bank monopoly of demand deposits by means of money market deposit accounts—all under the benign noses of the regulators.

Lawsuits arose as the firms sued each other to halt trespasses against what they had thought were protected practices. In April 1979, the U.S. Court of Appeals for the District of Columbia directed the regulators (including the SEC and the Federal Reserve) to enforce the law.

> It appears to the court that the development of [these practices] … in each instance represents the use of a device or technique … not authorized by the relevant statutes, although permitted by regulations of the respective institutions' regulatory activities.

[5] The Banking Act of 1933 touched on branch banking, deposit insurance, and deposit interest ceilings, as well as the separation of commercial and investment banking. The latter sections are referred to as Glass-Steagall, which is also used for 1932 legislation that permitted the Federal Reserve to use U.S. government securities as collateral for note issues. Both acts are in Krooss (1969).

The history of the development of these … techniques reveals each type of financial institution securing the permission of its appropriate regulatory agency to install these devices in order to gain a competitive advantage … without the benefit of Congressional consideration and statutory enactment (Wood and Wood 1985, pp. 58–63).

The judges were sympathetic. The new practices represented "enormous investments." However, that did not mean that regulators should rewrite the laws even though Congress appeared to be content with a state of affairs in which it had abandoned its legislative responsibilities to the regulators (or, should we say, the market?). Because of the disruptions likely to result from the withdrawal of these regulatory authorizations, upon which the financial community had "grown to rely," and to give Congress time to decide whether to override the Court by changing the law, about nine months, until January 1, 1980, were allowed to comply with the Court's ruling. Spurred into action, Congress held hearings in June 1979, passed legislation temporarily authorizing the practices found illegal by the Court and permanently in the Depository Institutions Deregulatory and Monetary Control Act of 1980.

The end of the separation of commercial- and investment-banking was effectively completed in 1998, when the commercial bank, Citicorp, merged with the Travelers Group insurance company to form the conglomerate Citigroup, which combined banking, securities, and insurance services, and the Federal Reserve gave Citigroup a temporary waiver for the merger before it was made legal by Gramm-Leach-Bliley the following year.

Returning to the New Deal, the administration preferred "fairness" to competition and growth. "As much as any single document can," David Kennedy (1999, p. 373) wrote, "Franklin Roosevelt's 1932 campaign address at San Francisco's Commonwealth Club … served as a charter for the New Deal's economic program:"

> As long as we had free land, as long as population was growing; by leaps and bounds; as long as our industrial plants were insufficient to supply our own needs, society chose to give the ambitious man free play and unlimited reward provided only that he produced the economic plant so much desired. During this period of expansion, there was equal opportunity for all and the business of government was not to interfere but to assist in the development of industry.

> [But now] our industrial plant is built; the problem just now is whether under existing conditions it is not overbuilt. Our last frontier has long since been reached, and there is practically no more free land.... We are now providing a drab living for our own people....
>
> Clearly, all this calls for a re-appraisal of values. A mere builder of more industrial plants, a creator of more railroad systems, an organizer of more corporations, is as likely to be a danger as a help. The day of the great promoter or the financial titan, to whom we granted everything, if only he would build, or develop, is over. Our task now is not discovery, or exploitation of natural resources, or necessarily producing more goods. It is the soberer, less dramatic business of administering resources and plants already in hand, of seeking to reestablish foreign markets for our surplus production, of meeting the problem of under-consumption, of adjusting production to consumption, of distributing wealth and products more equitably, of adapting existing economic organizations to the service of the people. The day of enlightened administration has come.... As I see it, the task of government in its relation to business is to assist the development of ... an economic constitutional order.

Although this speech, written by FDR's liberal advisor Adolph Berle, was delivered to "a silent luncheon audience" consisting primarily of businessmen, it has been ranked in polls of academics among the 100 best American speeches and the second-best campaign speech of the twentieth century (Houck 2004). One thing it decidedly was not was innovative. Every generation for hundreds and even thousands of years has been treated to prophecies of doom resulting from new catastrophes, with the implication that government powers of salvation be expanded (Maurice and Smithson 1984).

> We cannot absolutely prove that those are in error who tell us that society has reached a turning point, that we have seen our best days. But so said all before us, and with just as much apparent reason ... On what principle is it that, when we see nothing but improvement behind us, we are to expect nothing but deterioration before us. (Thomas Babington Macaulay, *Edinburgh Review*, 1830)

Roosevelt later remarked when laying the cornerstone of the new FTC building in 1935: "May this permanent home of the Federal Trade Commission stand for all time as a symbol of the purpose of the government to insist on a greater application of the golden rule to conduct the corporation and business enterprises in their relationship to the body politic."[6] These views cannot be reconciled with FDR's oft-stated goal of saving capitalism. Rather they suggest a conflict between the public Roosevelt as seen through the speeches of his liberal "brains-trust," on the one hand, and his frequently expressed optimism and conservative policy leanings on the other, making prospects and planning difficult for all.

Among the difficulties raised by the conflicts between FDR's policies and positions were the uncertainties facing the agencies charged with the enforcement of legislation. What did the president really want? The first chairman of the SEC, Joseph Kennedy (1934–35), was interested primarily in the health of finance, for which he was knowingly appointed by FDR. James Landis (1935–37), more conservative in applying than in writing the Securities Act, was similarly concerned for the industry. The liberal William O. Douglas (1937–39) and Jerome Frank (1939–41), on the other hand, had come to Washington to help FDR accomplish what they thought were going to be radical economic changes, but came up short because of the lack of support of the surprisingly conservative administration.

Precursors

FDR had started the ball rolling toward the *Securities Act of 1933* before assuming the presidency, and was eager to take advantage of the general sense of emergency, the administration's popularity, and the public's unhappiness with finance to enact his reforms quickly. He had been influenced by the progressive beliefs of Woodrow Wilson and his advisor Louis Brandeis that the immoral behavior of bankers could be corrected by public scrutiny. Roosevelt's speeches often drew on the first sentences of Chapter 5, "What Publicity Can Do," of Brandeis's 1914 book on *Other Peoples' Money*: "Publicity is justly commended as a remedy for social and industrial diseases. Sunlight is said to be the best of disinfectants, electric light the most efficient policeman."

[6] July 12, 1937, FDR *Public Papers*, vi, pp. 299–301. "Most of the great Federal Commissions were set up in the belief," he said, that "an ounce of prevention was worth a pound of cure. The Federal Trade Commission was no exception to that sound legislative intent. Prevention of unfair business practices is generally better than punishment administered after the fact of infringements, costly to the consuming public and to honest competitors."

Brandeis based his lessons on the corporate and banking "scandals" that were the subject of the 1912–13 congressional (Pujo, after Louisiana's Arsène Pujo) investigation of the "money trust." The Pujo enquiry was like Pecora's in uncovering little that was against the law or directly implying legislation, but in helping set the stage for whatever hostile financial legislation an administration might want (Carosso 1974). FDR, in particular, believed that replacement of the diverse and often lax state securities regulations by uniform and more rigorously enforced disclosure at the federal level would improve the credibility, contributions, and perhaps even the profits of finance. Virtue and profits might not be contradictory.

Financial regulation is as old as finance. Limits on interest, or usury, are thousands of years old, evidenced by the *Old Testament* and the Babylonian Code of Hammurabi (Homer and Sylla 2005, ch. 2, 6). Don Quixote noted the regulation of Spanish stock brokers at the beginning of the seventeenth century (Cervantes 1614, pt. 1, ch. 22). Regulation increased with the size and importance of financial markets, assisted by the public's hostility, ever present and whipped up as necessary. Jesus "overthrew the tables of the moneychangers," who had made the temple "a den of thieves" (Matthew 21:12–13). "[H]eavy losses suffered through the fraudulent manipulation of prices by brokers" led to a 1697 act of the English Parliament "to restrain the number and ill practice of brokers and stock jobbers" (de Bedts 1964, p. 2). The Bubble Act of 1720 condemned "dangerous and mischievous undertakings or projects under false pretences of publick good," and imposed stricter licensing requirements. Short selling was restricted in 1733, and mandatory disclosure was included in the English Companies Act of 1844. New York outlawed short sales in 1812 (repealed in 1858) (de Bedts 1964, pp. 2–3; McCormick 1948, pp. 3–8; Meeker 1930, p. 608; Loss 1983, pp. 1–3). Roosevelt's "ancient truths" of finance and the high public esteem of bankers were mythic.

Securities regulation in the United States was with few exceptions (such as common carriers regulated by the Interstate Commerce Commission) a state responsibility, and beginning with Kansas in 1911, frequently took the form of "blue sky" laws, so called because they were aimed at swindlers selling securities of "speculative schemes which have no more basis than so many feet of 'blue sky'," according to the 1917 U.S. Supreme Court decision in "the Blue Sky cases."[7] These laws went further than previous legislation in two ways. The first was the thoroughness of disclosure. Sale of a security to the public required a registration statement with full information not only of the company and the condition of its business but of its officers and directors and the purposes to which the funds were to be applied. False statements were punishable by fine and/or imprisonment (Carosso 1970, pp. 162–63; McCormick 1948, pp. 8–11).

In addition, no security covered by the act could be issued without a permit from the Bank Commissioner, whose grounds for denial were broad. Anything in the registration statement or accompanying documents that appeared "unfair, unjust, inequitable or oppressive to any class of contributors" was sufficient to deny sale of the security in the state. "If, after examining its affairs, the commissioner decided that a company was insolvent, did not 'intend to do a fair and honest business,' or that its securities did not 'promise a fair return,' he was authorized to prevent it from doing 'any further business'" in the state (Carosso 1970, pp. 163–64).

Nearly every state had a securities law in 1933, although with many exemptions, enforcement was often lax, and state regulations had been ruled unenforceable for interstate offerings through the mails, which was standard. The laws drew much of their support from "smaller commercial banks and savings institutions that saw blue sky legislation as a means for suppressing competition for depositors' funds." The investment banking community disliked the lack of uniformity of the state laws, but was unable to garner legislative support for a model blue sky law. They wanted enough government oversight to discourage aggressive and allegedly fraudulent challenges from new competitors without impeding their own activities (Carosso 1970, pp. 183–88; Macey and Miller 1991; Parrish 1970 pp. 5–14; McCormick 1948, pp. 11–12).

Ashwini Agrawal (2013) reported that state investor protection laws caused firms to pay greater dividends, issue more equity, and grow in size, as well as being associated with improvements in operating performance and market valuations. Reliance on them, however, was undermined by the security collapses of the Great Depression.

[7] *Hall* vs. *Geiger-Jones Co.*, 242 U.S. 539 (1917): "… the prevention of deception is within the competency of government and … the appreciation of the consequences of it is not open for our review." Also Kohr (1912) on the Kansas law and Parrish (1970, p. 5).

The first federal attempt at general securities regulation was by the Capital Issues Committee (CIC) created by Congress with the mandate "to utilize and direct economic resources" during World War I. The Committee consisted of representatives of the Federal Reserve Board and private finance (Willoughby 1934, p. 17). It announced "Plans for strangling hundreds of millions of dollars' worth of oil stocks and other speculative securities which the Government considers unnecessary in the war emergency, and [are] hindrances to [the] sale of liberty bonds" (*New York Times*, September 7, 1918).

Short of enforcement machinery, however, the committee was "unable to deal effectively with many enterprises whose promoters or managers remained deaf to every appeal to their patriotism." It was "astonished at the number of fraudulent, indifferent and actually bad propositions that come before us." It should be noted that the Federal Reserve's monetization of the government's deficit finance of the war made every project a speculation on inflation, which raises suspicions of the legitimacy of the CIC's complaint that in 1918, the task of "the purveyor of stock and bonds" is simply to persuade the public "to trade a Government bond bearing a low rate of interest for stocks and bonds baited with promise of high rate of return and prospect of sudden riches" (U.S. House 1918, pp. 1–3; Parrish 1970, pp. 15–16).

Of course the CIC "was not investor protection. Rather it rationed capital to give effect to the Government's policy of 'war business first'" (Loss 1983, p. 30). Nevertheless, supporters of the program recommended the establishment of a similar but stronger agency to continue its goal "to check the traffic in doubtful securities while imposing no undue restrictions upon the financing of legitimate industry." Federal supervision was necessary to fill "a crevice in our financial structure through which flows a constant torrent of funds in utter wastage." However, President Wilson's request to Congress to adopt a securities act "to prevent the fraudulent methods of promotion by which our people are annually fleeced of many millions of hard-earned money" got nowhere, nor did several other securities bills introduced between 1919 and 1927 (August 8, 1919, message to Congress, quoted in U.S. House 1933a, p. 91; Seligman 2003, pp. 49–50, 579; Loss 1983, pp. 116–17).

Many liberals in the 73rd (1933–34) Congress hoped to resume the expansion of government controls that had been interrupted by Republican majorities since 1919, but found that many of FDR's ideas were unattractively modest, better characterized as conservative than reformist. The more radical and ambitious elements of the New Deal (legislative and bureaucratic) often found themselves lacking the Executive's support.

Paths to the Act

One of its authors later noted the "scanty" legislative history of the Securities Act of 1933, following from the secrecy surrounding the act's progress as its promoters sought speedy passage untroubled by critics' delays and amendments (Landis 1959). Following his normal practice, the president assigned the drafting of a federal securities bill to competing groups, and chose the product of the team headed by former Federal Trade Commissioner Huston Thompson, western populist and Wilsonian anti-corporate reformer (Seligman 2003, pp. 50–53; Parrish 1970, pp. 17–18, 45–46). His proposal was based on the unsuccessful 1919 bill reflecting the views of the CIC (*CR* 1918, p. 16; U.S. House 1919, pp. 11–12, 19, 25; Thompson 1923, pp. 57–59; Parrish 1970, pp. 17–18). On March 29, Roosevelt submitted the bill to both houses of Congress with the following message:

> The Federal Government cannot and should not take any action which might be construed as approving or guaranteeing that newly issued securities are sound in the sense that their value will be maintained or that the properties which they represent will earn profit.
>
> There is, however, an obligation upon us to insist that every issue of new securities to be sold in interstate commerce shall be accompanied by full publicity and information, and that no essentially important element attending the issue shall be concealed from the buying public.
>
> This proposal adds to the ancient rule of caveat emptor the further doctrine: "Let the seller also beware." It puts the burden of telling the whole truth on the seller. It should give impetus to honest dealing in securities and thereby bring back public confidence. (U.S. CR, 73rd Cong., 1st sess. (March 29, 1933), pp. 937, 954)

The initial public, congressional, and even industry responses were favorable. "Such legislation, obviously, is in the interest of the commonweal," said *Financial Age*, "and will go a long way to prevent the plundering of the public. The sooner this legislation is on the books the better." The *Wall Street Journal* concluded that the "measure is in the main so right in its basic provisions … the country will insist upon its passage." The *New York Times* predicted that it "would be on the way to the statute books by the latter part of next week" (*Financial Age*, April 1, 1933; *Wall Street Journal*, March 31, 1933; *New York Times*, March 31, 1933).

In the House of Representatives, the bill was assigned to the Interstate and Foreign Commerce Committee chaired by the rural Texan Sam Rayburn, a legislative tactician experienced in securities legislation and later the longest-serving Speaker in the history of the House. Rayburn was not your standard southern conservative. He had decided upon entering Congress in 1913 that advancement depended on party loyalty and legislative expertise. He worked on government regulations of business, stimulated by suspicions of the latter. In his biography of Lyndon Johnson, Robert Caro wrote that Rayburn "hated the railroads, whose freight charges fleeced the farmer, and the banks, whose interest charges fleeced the farmer, and the utility companies, which refused to extend their power lines into the countryside, and thus condemned the farmer to darkness," as well as the trusts, interests, Yankees, Republicans, and the rich. His proposal to give the Interstate Commerce Commission supervision of railroad securities failed in 1914, but became part of the Transportation Act of 1920 (Seligman 2003, p. 55; U.S. House 1933b, p. 43; Caro 2003, p. 306; Mahoney 2001).

Rayburn shared the president's trust in the strategic advantage of moving swiftly in the new Democratic world of 1933, and he expected smooth sailing for the securities bill. Hearings began on March 31, with only two days of testimony scheduled. No opposition witnesses were invited. A law requiring transparency was being developed in secrecy. Rayburn soon discovered, however, that he had tried to move too fast. The Thompson bill referred to the inability of state laws to prevent the losses arising from the issue of "undesirable and worthless" securities, but ran into "a buzz saw of criticism, first from members of the Commerce Committee" as they became familiar with the bill, and then from opposition witnesses whom Rayburn reluctantly allowed to testify after he had begun to lose confidence in the bill (Seligman 2003, pp. 55–56).

The heart of the bill was registration. By requiring information about the firm and its securities before issue, the bill sought prevention rather than punishment of fraud after the fact. Registration statements to be signed by corporate executives and directors did not require more data than many states. The innovations in Thompson's bill were the elimination of exemptions and increased penalties for misinformation. Unlike existing state laws, registration on an exchange would not exempt securities from federal registration. Nor would histories of earnings and debt service.

Schedule A of the bill specified dozens of categories of information. A first look gives the impression of tedious but straightforward entries: such as the name and address of the issuer, date of organization, stock authorized and outstanding, and names of the underwriters. Soon encountered, however, were required estimates and decisions that might not be known at the time of issue: such as the specific purposes and amounts for which the funds are to be raised, expenses of the issue, options to be created in connection with the issue, with their prices and terms, and the names and addresses of the persons to be allotted more than 10 percent of such options (Lasser and Gerardi 1934, pp. 341–60). The flexibility, the last-minute decisions that are part of management, was assumed away.

The sharpest response was provoked by the punitive civil remedies for investors and the provisions for revocation of registration by the Federal Trade Commission which was charged with administering the law. *Section 9* provided that

> every person acquiring any securities specified in such [registration] statements … shall be presumed to rely upon the representations set forth in the said statement. In case any such statement shall be false in any material respect, any person acquiring any security to which such statement relates, either from the original issuer or from any other person, shall have the right to rescind the transaction and to obtain … any and all consideration given or paid for any such securities … either from any vendor knowing of such falsity or from the persons signing such statement…. Any persons acquiring any securities to which such statement relates shall also have the right to obtain damages … from any one or more of the signers of the statement in which such falsity occurs, or from any person who authorized the statement to be made.

Corporate executives and directors and initial and secondary securities dealers would be liable for an indefinite period. Investment Bankers Association counsel William Breed warned that the bill would be an indefinite opening to "litigation by crooked and unprincipled people" (Seligman 2003, p. 56). In the Senate Banking and Currency Committee, Tennessee Senator Thomas Gore thought the liability section would "paralyze business entirely." "You," Senator James Couzens of Michigan scolded Thompson, "as a director of General Motors could not investigate all their plants … you could not count all the automobiles, you could not value all their buildings … you could not check all their accounts receivable…. That is a thing that just cannot humanly be done." Upstate New York

Congressman James Parker said directors "cannot count every piece of steel and every machine. [I]f this law was in effect I would resign as director from some of the companies I happen to be in" (Parrish 1970, p. 52). Couzens and Parker were Republicans. Gore was a Democrat.

The bill's authors had little sympathy for big business, which they believed was a curse on the economy, anyway. There were too many directors, Thompson associate Ollie Butler told the Committee. He objected to exempting from civil liability a director who "in good faith makes a misstatement." "That would destroy the effect of the entire act" (Parrish 1970, p. 52; Moley 1966, pp. 311–12). Yale law professor and future chairman of the Securities and Exchange Commission and U.S. Supreme Court justice, William O. Douglas, thought *Section 9* "doubtless will drive many directors out," which "will be highly commendable" (*New York Times*, April 9, 1933, p. E8).

The bill empowered the FTC to investigate and prosecute fraudulent securities sales. For corporations above a certain size, no sale or offer to sell a security would be lawful until registered with the FTC. *Section 10* of the bill said that no action of the FTC could be represented as approval of a security, although *Section 6* invested the commission with the power to revoke the registration of any security whose issuer "has been or is about to engage in fraudulent transactions … is not conducting its business in accordance with law" or "is in any other way dishonest," or whose business is "in unsound condition or insolvent, … is not based upon sound principles, and … revocation is in the interest of the public welfare."

If any statement in a registration was false, the buyer had the right to recover the purchase price from the promoters, issuers, principal officers, and directors, who were required to sign the registration before a security could be offered for sale. That was too much even for Rayburn, who showed his dwindling enthusiasm for the bill on the second day of hearings, perhaps revealing more than he intended, when he asked a witness who had helped draft it: "Do you believe that an administrative officer of the Government ought to be given that much power … – to pass upon whether or not a man's business is based on sound principles? … If you were going to pass upon whether a man's business was based upon sound principles, you would want quite a corps of the ablest economists in the land to sit around you.… It is quite a hazard, is it not, realizing the personnel in the past of some of these Commissions" (U.S. House 1933a, p. 136)?

Presidential advisor Raymond Moley forwarded "a storm of protest from bankers and lawyers" to Rayburn, and before the scheduled end of the hearings Rayburn sent word to the White House that drastic alterations were needed. Roosevelt, who wanted a bill conservative enough to be rapidly enacted, agreed (Moley 1966, pp. 311–12; Parrish 1970, p. 57; Hardeman and Bacon 1987, p. 151).

He turned to his long-time advisor and administrative-law expert, Harvard Law School Professor Felix Frankfurter, who chose colleagues and former students to draft an acceptable bill. Frankfurter had emigrated from Austria with his family at age 12 to the lower East side of New York, and became a top student at the City College of New York and Harvard Law School, from which he graduated in 1906. He became assistant U.S. Attorney for the Southern District of New York under Henry Stimson, whom he followed when Stimson became William Howard Taft's Secretary of War. Frankfurter's work in Washington impressed the faculty at Harvard Law School, who used a gift from Jacob Schiff (head of Kuhn Loeb) to create a position for him. He taught administrative law, and with former student and fellow professor James Landis, advocated judicial restraint in dealing with government misdeeds, including greater freedom for administrative agencies from judicial oversight (Carrington 1999, p. 132). Frankfurter and Landis collaborated on the influential *Business of the Supreme Court: A Study in the Federal Judicial System* in 1928, and Landis's classic *Administrative Process* appeared in 1938 (Corwin 1928; Tushnet 2011).

Frankfurter had worked with Assistant Secretary of the Navy Roosevelt on the War Labor Policies Board, but they had little contact after 1918 until Roosevelt was elected governor of New York in 1928 (Baker 1969, pp. 77–83). Frankfurter was attracted by FDR's progressivism and offered his help to the receptive governor. He "was especially concerned with the recruitment of competent men for Roosevelt's administration, for he believed that an expert civil service was the key to successful government" (Dawson 1978). Frankfurter had maintained his Washington contacts during the 1920s and placed several of his students as law clerks for U.S. Supreme Court justices and in other positions. Former Frankfurter students in key positions in Washington during the early New Deal—"Felix's boys" or "the Happy Hot Dogs"—included Landis, Benjamin Cohen, and Thomas Corcoran—who in two days produced a draft of the *Securities Act* which they said was based on the English Companies Act, but had more in common with state blue sky laws. The Securities Act went beyond the Companies Act in possessing "a permanent supervisory body with broad powers to administer its provisions [and] in the respect that [its] disclosure requirements … go a good deal further than those under [English and] continental systems" (Kessler 1935; Barnett 1934).

Frankfurter shared Roosevelt's mix of liberalism and conservatism that wanted to see capitalism preserved but purified. He also believed in the "wickedness of Wall Street," and taking a page from Pecora, advised his boys that their legislative efforts would be helped by the "disclosure of financial self-interest" and emphasis on "commissions or profits. [W]e ought also to cover the mischief of peddling securities from door to door or over the telephone as was practiced so widely before 1929" (*Frankfurter Papers*, Reel 7; Seligman 2003, p. 57).

On April 10th, Frankfurter formally presented the draft to Rayburn at a meeting of the Commerce Committee, which gave the go ahead for further work on the bill. A revised draft was finished on April 21st. Gone were the FTC's power to judge the quality of securities, and several categories were exempted, including railroad and bank securities regulated under other legislation, commercial paper with maturities under nine months, so as not to interfere with short-term finance, and municipal securities because "the mayors of our various cities rose up en mass when we tried to bring [their issues] under the 1933 Act" (Seligman 2003, p. 65). The liabilities for untrue or omitted material statements on security registrations applied only if due diligence could not be proven.

Rayburn named a subcommittee to oversee the bill and dissuaded it from adopting further significant changes or discussing the bill's contents with others until a satisfactory draft was reported to the full committee. "Without even pausing for further committee hearings," wrote an admiring historian, "Rayburn whipped the new bill through the House with consummate skill and speed" (Seligman 2003, p. 66; Landis 1959; de Bedts 1964, p. 38).

Moley, who believed the bill interfered with recovery by "hampering … the process of issuing securities" later wrote that it "was the first appearance of the strategy that Cohen and Corcoran were to use so often … – ramming a too-severe bill through one House and using it for trading purposes in the other. Corcoran [said] 'When you want one loaf of bread, you've got to ask for two.' [T]his technique was to be one of the chief factors that undermined congressional confidence in Roosevelt. You can't cry 'Wolf!' indefinitely," Moley (1939, pp. 182–83; Lasser 2003, ch. 5–6) wrote. The reformers paid little heed to the possibility that the effectiveness of legislation founded on current sentiments might be transitory.

Cohen and Corcoran seemed effective in their short-term objectives, although their personal advancement was later hindered by their aggressive methods. After Corcoran left public employment, his success as a lobbyist led to charges of and even congressional investigations into influence peddling for private interests. There was no evidence that he did anything illegal, but "in the words of a friend," according to his December 12, 1981, *New York Times* obituary, his "trouble was that he worked as strenuously and in the same manner for private interests as he once had for the President: 'He has never been able to make a distinction between them, or to realize that what might be justified within the Government cannot be from outside it.'"

Rayburn presented the Landis-Cohen-Corcoran version of the Securities Bill to the Commerce Committee on May 3, which after another political concession—adding the issues of state banks to the list of exemptions—sent it to the House on May 4, which unanimously adopted it by voice vote on May 5.

Rayburn and Roosevelt were not finished. The Senate Banking Committee, moved by the Pecora hearings, still preferred the Thompson bill, albeit with some relaxations. The Banking Committee wanted more stringent regulations than the House. Chairman Duncan Fletcher, who had long had his sights on the "gambling sharks and rascals of Wall Street," told a corporate witness: "We do not want to spend our time hearing criticism of the bill, with people picking it to pieces here and there and getting nowhere" (U.S. House 1933a, p. 145; Seligman 2003, p. 67). Fletcher took umbrage at the Chamber of Commerce president's advice to investment bankers to oppose the bill: "It was not to be expected that a measure such as the Federal securities bill, ... designed to protect the public from the financial racketeering of certain classes of so-called investment bankers, could be enacted without arousing the most determined opposition on the part of that profession which has mulcted the people of some $50 billion during the past ten years" (Seligman 2003, p. 67; *CR*, May 20, 1933).

The Senate passed the Thompson bill three days after the House passed the Landis version. With prodding from Roosevelt, Rayburn was allowed to chair the conference committee, which agreed on what was essentially the Landis bill. Conference changes included the shortening of the House's waiting period from thirty to twenty days and surrender of the

Senate's severe liability and federal government power to enforce state blue sky laws when securities were sold across state lines. In spite of his secrecy and speed, Rayburn's bill was more attuned than the Senate's to the realities of what the industry and their congressmen would accept.

Would-be reformers of capitalism were disappointed. Adolph Berle (Columbia professor of corporate law, co-author of an influential book on corporate governance, and member of FDR's "brains-trust") wrote that the Act "leaves unsolved the major questions.... It must be conceded that the efforts to reduce finance to the place of an honest servant instead of discredited master have been fumbling in the extreme." Finance is power to distribute the national wealth. The next few years will probably determine whether [that] power ... remains in the hands of the financial group or whether they pass, measurably, into the hands of the community (Berle 1933).

Professor Douglas agreed. The Act was irrelevant. It "presupposes that the glaring light of publicity will give the investors needed protection. But those needing investment guidance will receive small comfort from the balance sheets, contracts, or compilation of data revealed in the registration statement. They either lack the training or intelligence to assimilate them and find them useful, or are so concerned with a speculative profit as to consider them irrelevant. And wise and conservative investors don't require mandatory reporting." He came close to saying that regulation was unnecessary because the judgment of experts will be reflected in the market price.

The Act was more appropriate to the simpler competitive conditions of the nineteenth century, which could not be regained, Douglas (1934) argued. It was "wholly secondary in any thoroughgoing and comprehensive program for social control in this field."

> [T]here is nothing in the Act which controls the power of the self-perpetuating management group which has risen to a position of dominance in our industrial organization. There is nothing in the Act which purports to deal with the protection of the rights of minorities. There is nothing which concerns the problem of capital structure, its soundness or unsoundness. There is nothing that deals with the problem of mobilizing the flow of capital to various productive channels. And finally, there is nothing which deals with the fundamental problem of the increment of power and profit inherent in our present forms of organization.

Douglas and other critics of capitalism were at odds with FDR, who mostly wanted the transparency advocated by his teacher, Louis Brandeis. The Pujo committee's 1913 report, upon which Brandeis's *Other Peoples' Money* was based and which shaped public attitudes for a generation and beyond, had, as Vincent Carosso (1973, 1985) argued, "a more profound influence on shaping the New Deal's banking and securities statutes than is generally acknowledged."

Robert Jackson (2003, pp. 74, 119), an ally in New York politics and poker buddy (with Douglas) of FDR, observed that the president did not think logically about issues or causes and effects, but in terms of right and wrong. "He had not engaged in business as my law practice compelled me to do, and he had no personal knowledge of its methods or its problems." He thought "of economic matters as personal rather than impersonal forces.... He was inclined to think that we were prosecuting a group of businessmen because they had done some moral wrong, and that if he talked to them and made them see that their course was morally wrong, they would do something about it." That their behavior was conditioned by circumstances did not occur to him.

Richard Posner (2003, p. 457) and others have observed that the legislation was rooted in the misconception that the securities losses of the Great Depression were due to fraud and other private abuses rather than to the collapse of corporate profits. On the other hand, it might be said that the Great Depression, reinforced by Pecora's sensationalism, created the atmosphere which enabled FDR to secure the reforms he and Brandeis had wanted for two decades.

The Act's Effectiveness

> It is doubtful whether any other type of public regulation of economic activity has been so widely admired as the regulation of the securities markets by the Securities and Exchange Commission. The purpose of this regulation is to increase the portion of truth in the world and to prevent or punish fraud, and who can defend ignorance or fraud? (George Stigler, *Journal of Business*, April 1964)

The economic costs and benefits of the New Deal securities acts received little explicit consideration during their writing and passage – although prospective costs must have been behind the financial industry's opposition. The market for information was not mentioned except in a moralistic manner. It did not seem fair that not everyone had the same information.

This attitude overlooks the fact that information is a scarce good which, like other goods, is supplied and demanded according to its cost and value. It is especially surprising when applied to the financial markets which are in the first instance a market for information. We look to our brokers and bankers for transactions, but before that for information.

"It is a curious fact," Friedrich Hayek wrote in his classic 1945 paper, "The use of knowledge in society," that knowledge of often temporary opportunities in a changing society is "generally regarded with a kind of contempt, and that anyone who by such knowledge gains an advantage over someone better equipped with theoretical or technical knowledge is thought to have acted almost disreputably…. The common idea now [certainly that of the Securities and Exchange Commission then and now] seems to be that all such knowledge should as a matter of course be readily at the command of everybody."

"The peculiar character of the problem of a rational economic order," however, "is determined precisely by the fact that the knowledge of the circumstances of which we must make use never exists in concentrated or integrated form, but solely as the dispersed bits of incomplete and frequently contradictory knowledge which all the separate individuals possess. The economic problem of society is thus not merely a problem of how to allocate 'given' resources," Hayek wrote. "It is rather a problem of how to secure the best use of resources known to any of the members of society for ends whose relative importance only these individuals know. Or to put it briefly, it is a problem of the utilization of knowledge which is not given to anyone in its totality." The solution to this problem is given by the price system, which is "a mechanism for communicating information."

This is nowhere truer than the financial markets, where the information advantage of professionals is small and temporary because prices quickly reflect information. Most of us are free-riders in these, as in other, markets. We have nearly free use of society's knowledge.

Lawyer and economist (once an unusual combination) and a founder of the field called *law and economics*, Henry Manne (1969, Introduction) observed that the "subject of securities regulation sprang full blown from lawyers' minds, and, from the beginning, policy was formulated and the law administered almost exclusively by lawyers." Not until the 1960s, he said, did the economics literature begin to address "even the most obvious economic problems of this field in any systematic way." The judiciary, on the other hand, had necessarily been deeply involved, and for a long time (to the dismay of Landis and Frankfurter) had been defenders of traditional markets. In *Lochner v. New York* (1904), for example, the U.S. Supreme Court ruled by a 5–4 vote that New York State's law setting the maximum hours of work for bakers violated the freedom of contract that was included in the "liberty" protected by the Fourteenth Amendment to the U.S. Constitution. Justice Oliver Wendell Holmes, Jr., wrote in his dissent:

> This case is decided upon an economic theory which a large part of the country does not entertain. If it were a question whether I agreed with that theory, I should desire to study it further and long before making up my mind. But I do not conceive that to be my duty, because I strongly believe that my agreement or disagreement has nothing to do with the right of a majority to embody their opinions in law.

"It is settled by various decisions of this court," Holmes continued, that state constitutions and laws may regulate life in many ways which we may personally think injudicious or worse, and which also interfere with the liberty to contract. "Sunday laws and usury laws are ancient examples.... The liberty of the citizen to do as he likes so long as he does not interfere with the liberty of others to do the same, which has been a shibboleth for some well-known writers, is interfered with by school laws, by the Post Office, by every state or municipal institution which takes his money for purposes thought desirable, whether he likes it or not.... Some of these laws embody convictions or prejudices which judges are likely to share. Some may not. But a constitution is not intended to embody a particular economic theory, whether of paternalism ... or of *laissez faire*. It is made for people of fundamentally differing views, and the accident of our finding certain opinions natural and familiar, or novel, and even shocking, ought not to conclude our judgment upon the question whether statutes embodying them conflict with the Constitution of the United States."

The Lochner decision held sway for several years. In 1923, in *Adkins v. Children's Hospital*, the Court held that minimum wage laws violated the due process clause, although Chief Justice William Howard Taft strongly dissented, arguing that Lochner itself should have been overturned. Eventually, though, Holmes' dissent became the majority view. In 1934, the Court ruled in *Nebbia v. New York* that no constitutional fundamental right to freedom of contract exists, and in 1937, upholding the state of Washington's minimum wage in *West Coast Hotel Co. v. Parrish*, repudiated the idea that freedom of contract should be unrestricted:

> The legislature has also recognized the fact, which the experience of legislators in many States has corroborated, that the proprietors of these establishments and their operatives do not stand upon an equality, and that their interests are, to a certain extent, conflicting. The former naturally desire to obtain as much labor as possible from their employees, while the latter are often induced by the fear of discharge to conform to regulations which their judgment, fairly exercised, would pronounce to be detrimental to their health or strength. In other words, the proprietors lay down the rules and the laborers are practically constrained to obey them. In such cases, self-interest is often an unsafe guide, and the legislature may properly interpose its authority.

Conservatives could no longer expect the judiciary's cooperation in resisting the government's expansion either on the grounds of freedom of contract or the Constitution's limit on federal regulation to "Commerce … among the several states" (Art. I, sec. 8). Cases for and against regulations would have to be made to legislatures and their agencies in the exercise of their *police powers* to regulate behavior and maintain order in the interests of health, safety, morals, and the general welfare, presumably in light of costs and benefits as understood by politicians, bureaucrats, and interests of the day. In 1955, in *Williamson v. Lee Optical of Oklahoma*, a unanimous Supreme Court ruled that "The day is gone when this Court uses the Due Process Clause of the Fourteenth Amendment to strike down state laws, regulatory of business and industrial conditions, because they may be unwise, improvident, or out of harmony with a particular school of thought."

Not until the 1960s, however, after a generation's experiences of substantial government interferences with markets, did economists seriously begin to evaluate them (although we know from Adam Smith that economists had been far from uncritical of government). A leader in this endeavor was University of Chicago Professor George Stigler, who compared the qualities of new issues before and after the *Securities Acts*, and found no significant differences in their returns relative to existing securities between the 1920s and 1950s, both boom decades.

Table 2.1 from Stigler compares the performances of new issues between 1923–28 and 1949–55 relative to the stock market. Neither period was particularly good for new issues (see the note at the bottom of

Table 2.1 New common stock prices relative to market averages (issue year = 100)

	Year after issue				
	1	*2*	*3*	*4*	*5*
Pre-SEC					
1923	93	85	78	62	67
1924	98	76	69	66	51
1925	85	67	55	42	33
1926	90	82	77	63	67
1927	85	69	60	73	103
1928	72	50	41	45	57
Average	82	65	56	53	58
Stan. Dev.	44	47	44	48	65
No. issues	84	87	88	85	84
Post-SEC					
1949	93	88	87	87	65
1950	84	76	53	58	47
1951	84	79	76	80	74
1952	88	74	71	70	70
1953	88	79	75	70	94
1954	53	49	56	48	42
1955	71	65	82	78	83
Average	82	73	73	72	70
Stan. Dev.	24	28	31	31	39
No. issues	47	47	47	47	47

Source: Stigler, "Public regulation of the securities markets"

For example, the 67 in the first row means that 1923 issues rose about 2/3 as much as (or fell a third more than) the market the next five years

the table), but they did about as well as the market before and after the establishment of the Securities and Exchange Commission.

Findings of less risk after the securities acts have been attributed by regulation's defenders to the reductions in uncertainty resulting from required disclosure (Friend and Herman 1964). An alternative explanation is that the regulations imposed relatively greater costs on newer, smaller, and riskier issues, and caused their withdrawal from the market. Regulatory discrimination against riskier ventures may be "inconsistent with social welfare maximization." Three pieces of evidence support this view. SEC rejections have been more frequent in risky industries such as precious metal mining and oil and gas exploration; "the wholesale substitution after 1934 from public offerings to private placements was more intense among" riskier bonds; and post-1934 saw a shift from stock to bond issues (Jarrell 1981).

Failure to find positive effects of regulation does not prove that none exists, but regulation's proponents have not felt a need to support their position by anything beyond scandalous anecdotes. Critics Irwin Friend and Edward Herman (1964) amazingly claimed "that a more convincing [than Stigler's] test of the SEC's accomplishments is provided in the Pecora hearings and ... *Report* with their documentation of the massive securities abuses of the earlier period and the much healthier post-SEC experience."

Stigler's was one of several studies finding little or no economic justification for additional regulation (Simon 1989). George Benston (1969, 1973), for example, could find no value to investors of the SEC's accounting disclosure requirements, which failed in several respects:

1. There was no systematic history of fraud in corporate accounting. Anecdotes of such behavior in the finance literature referred mainly to the nineteenth and early twentieth centuries, and the voluminous hearings and reports (including Pecora's) preceding the securities acts of 1933 and 1934 "turned up only one citation of fraudulently prepared financial statements.... Thus, the need for the disclosure requirements that are at the 'heart' of the Securities Act of 1933 appear to have had their genesis in the general folklore of turn-of-the-century finance rather than in the events of the 1920s" (Ripley 1927; Clews 1908).
2. There was a considerable amount of disclosure prior to the securities acts, as indicated in Table 2.2. Beginning in 1932, all corporations applying for a listing on the NYSE were required to have their annual statements audited by independent CPAs.
3. "The other stated goal of the securities acts (besides fraud prevention) is to assure that investors 'make a realistic appraisal of the merits of securities and thus exercise an informed judgment whether to purchase them'" (SEC 1967, p. 13). However, the information required is stale. Form 10K, the annual report, must be filed within 120 days after the close of the corporation's fiscal year. It would be useful to investors only if it added to their knowledge, which does not seem to have been the case. Benston found that data reported through the SEC had no significant effect on stock prices; they were not used by investors. Simon also found it "difficult to identify

Table 2.2 Financial accounting information disclosed by companies traded on the NYSE

	Year	*Percent reporting*
Balance sheet	1926	100
	1934	100
Current assets and liabilities	1926	100
	1934	100
Sales	1926	55
	1930	62
	1934	62
Cost of goods sold	1926	45
	1934	54
Depreciation	1926	71
	1934	93
New income	1926	100
	1934	99.6
Audited by CPA	1926	82
	1934	94

Source: *Moody's Manuals*, 1927–35. (From Benston, "Value of SEC's accounting disclosure requirements")

information required by the 1933 Act that had not been previously required by the NYSE."

A contemporary (1930) account noted that corporations with securities listed on the [NYSE] were required "to make public at suitable intervals their earnings and other essential and current statistics." If these regulations "should become excessive and inequitable, they would soon prove valueless since the corporations would refuse to list their securities there. The Exchange … does, however, employ moral suasion with the corporations …, and thus has been all along an important factor in the rising standards of corporation ethics which are apparent in this country" (Meeker 1930, p. 97).

Information was negotiable. In 1866, the Exchange's request for information drew a response that "The Delaware, Lackawanna & Western R.R, make no reports and publishes no statements – and has not done anything of the kind for the past five years" (Neumark 1960, p. 44). Yet listing requirements increased, presumably as determined by costs and benefits.

4. Some have argued that only sophisticated groups have the expertise and resources necessary to profit from the required information. However, even they apparently possess no such advantages because

the performances of mutual funds, for example, have not differed appreciably from unmanaged portfolios of similar securities. "Even very sophisticated users of the accounting reports required by the SEC are not able to profit from them," Benston concluded.

5. In some ways, the SEC has obstructed the disclosure of relevant information. It has reinforced traditional conservative accounting practices by forbidding market as opposed to original cost values, and thus in a period of inflation undervaluing corporations. The SEC has also forbidden corporate predictions of performances even when identified as such, even though these might be among the most useful information of all, inviting investors and their advisors to fill the gap.

In summary, there "was little evidence [as opposed to hearsay] of fraud related to financial statements" before the securities acts. "Nor was there a widespread lack of disclosure." The reporting required by the acts did not meet the standards of "information" in being either new or timely. In fact, the acts as administered by the SEC proved to be self-defeating in discouraging the development of genuinely useful information.

Going beyond disclosure, few of the abuses alleged by Pecora and others were supported by evidence (such as stock pools and fraud in securities sales; Mahoney 1999) and none were addressed seriously by the securities acts, including the effects of short sales, preferred lists, high salaries, commissions, bonuses, holding companies, and tax avoidance on which Pecora dwelled.

Finally, a case has been made for regulatory competition by means of the decentralization of securities regulation, like other parts of corporate law, to be handled by the States, in place of the growing federalization. Instead of encouraging a "race to the bottom," Roberta Romano (2003, p. 3) has argued, such an approach would enable competition for and by issuers, who might seek to enhance firm values by choosing the regulations most valued by investors.

So Who Governs?

We must wonder about the effectiveness of an act hurriedly adopted on the heels of a crisis, written and steered through the legislature by reformers with little knowledge of the industry—especially after the crisis has passed and been replaced on the political agenda by other issues, legislators have taken a conservative turn, prosperity returns, and the targeted industry regains its profitability and political influence. Also important, advances in communications technology have probably made information requirements less necessary than in 1933. We have to wonder why the Securities Act has endured and even thrived (Macey and Sommer 1995).

The Best Regulated Market in the World

Actions of all market participants are under continuous surveillance during the trading day. In addition, the NYSE reviews the success of assigned dealers in maintaining a fair and orderly market in the securities assigned to them....

The NYSE market is governed by a firm set of rules and regulations, approved by the SEC, to make the market fair and open for all investors....

The NYSE's efforts are part of a continuum of regulation that includes member firms, exchanges throughout the nation, and the SEC. Together these organizations share responsibility for enforcing federal statutes, rules and regulations ... and all are accountable to Congress.

[A]nyone who violates securities laws runs an extremely high risk of being caught and prosecuted. While no system is perfect, the NYSE provides the most meaningful market regulation in the world.

(*NYSE Fact Book* 1991, pp. 4–5)

Perhaps the principal justification for the act, FDR's beloved disclosure, was and is superfluous. It brings costs without benefits except possibly to large firms. Like the 2010 Dodd-Frank Act which supposedly targeted large banks, the substantial reporting and other costs of the 1930s Securities Acts bore heaviest on small firms lacking the resources to comply with them efficiently, forcing them to close or be absorbed by their larger competitors. The endurance of the written law despite variations in the political strengths of interests, parties, and institutions means a further shift in government from the floors of Congress to bureaucratic and judicial interpretations, and variable enforcements and industry desires. On the other hand, an industry's apparent regulation may give it a kind of seal of approval at a cost that is not excessive for large firms. It is even a source of commendation by the Exchange, as indicated in the box.

Table 2.3 Average real rates of return (%) on common stock and U.S. government bonds

Years	*Stocks*	*Long-term governments*	*Short-term governments*	*Consumer price inflation*
1802–1997	7.0	3.5	2.9	1.3
1802–1870	7.0	4.8	5.1	0.1
1871–1925	6.6	3.7	3.2	0.6
1946–1997	7.5	1.1	0.5	4.3

Source: Siegel, *Stocks for the long run*, pp. 10, 14

It is appropriate to bring this chapter to an end by noting two of the strongest arguments, from personal and public standpoints, against stock-market regulations designed "to protect investors." First, long-term stock investments have produced superior real returns, shown in Table 2.3, to the point of being called anomalous (Mehra and Prescott 1978). Second, informed stock choices in free markets are available to free-riders at small trading costs because market prices are generally determined by active and careful investors who take advantage of information that is better and more timely than required by law. Investors can readily insulate themselves against pools and other manipulated prices (false information) by random timing of transactions, resisting temptations to use runs and self-serving brokerage advice as guides.

In free markets, risk-takers have the ability to exercise their stock preferences. Official discouragement of those preferences still allows them freedom (or forces them) to turn elsewhere. It is not in the public interest that prospective traders in stock options (whose average return is zero less one or two percent trading costs) are forced to prove their qualifications to brokers while their purchases of state lottery tickets (sometimes with less than 50 percent payoffs) are unrestricted.

References

Agrawal, Ashwini. 2013. The Impact of Investor Protection Law on Corporate Policy and Performance: Evidence from the Blue Sky Laws. *Journal of Financial Economics* 107 (2): 417–435.

Allen, Frederick Lewis. 1940. *Since Yesterday – The Nineteen-Thirties in America, Sept. 3, 1929–Sept. 3, 1939.* New York: Harper & Row.

Alsop, Joseph., and Robert Kintner. 1938. The Battle of the Market Place. *Saturday Evening Post*, June 11.

Baker, Liva. 1969. *Felix Frankfurter*. New York: Coward-McCann.

Barnett, George E. 1934. The Securities Act of 1933 and the British Companies Act. *Harvard Business Review* 13 (1): 1–18.

Benston, George J. 1969. The Value of the SEC's Accounting Disclosure Requirements. *Accounting Review* XLIV: 515–532.

———. 1973. Required Disclosure and the Stock Market: An Evaluation of the Securities Exchange Act of 1934. *American Economic Review* 63: 132–155.

———. 1990. *The Separation of Commercial and Investment Banking: The Glass-Steagall Act Revisited and Reconsidered*. New York: Oxford University Press.

Berle, A.A. Jr. 1933. High Finance: Master or Servant. *Yale Review* 23: 42.

Birmingham, Stephen G. 1967. *Our Crowd*. New York: Harper & Row.

Brandeis, Louis. 1914. *Other People's Money, and How the Bankers Use It*. New York: Frederick A. Stokes Co.

Brooks, John. 1969. *Once in Golconda*. New York: Harper & Row.

Caro, Robert. 2003. *The Years of Lyndon Johnson. Master of the Senate*. New York: Knopf.

Carosso, Vincent P. 1970. *Investment Banking in America: A History*. Cambridge: Harvard University Press.

———. 1973. The Wall Street Money Trust from Pujo to Medina. *The Business History Review* 47: 421–437.

———. 1985. Comment. In Walter (1985).

Carrington, Paul. 1999. *Stewards of Democracy. Law as Public Profession*. New York: Basic Books.

Clews, Henry. 1908. *Fifty Years on Wall Street*. New York: Irving.

Collins, Theresa M. 2003. *Otto Kahn*. Chapel Hill: University of North Carolina Press.

Corwin, Edward S. 1928. Review of the Business of the Supreme Court. A Study in the Federal Judicial System. *Political Science Quarterly* 35: 255–271.

Dawson, Nelson L. 1978. Louis D. Brandeis, Felix Frankfurter, and Franklin D. Roosevelt: The Origins of a New Deal Relationship. *American Jewish History* 68: 36–41.

De Bedts, Ralph F. 1964. *The New Deal's SEC. The Formative Years*. New York: Columbia University Press.

de Cervantes, Miguel. 1614. *The Adventures of Don Quixote*. Trans. J.M. Cohen. Penguin Books, 1950.

Dewey, Davis R. 1922. *Financial History of the U.S.* 8th ed. London: Longmans, Green and Co.

Douglas, William O. 1934. Protecting the Investor. *Yale Review* 23: 521–533.

Edwards, George W. 1942. The Myth of the Security Affiliate. *Journal of the American Statistical Association* 37: 225–232.

Eichengreen, Barry. 1992. *Golden Fetters. The Gold Standard and the Great Depression*. New York: Oxford University Press.

Flandreau, Marc, Norbert Gaillard, and Ugo Panizza. 2010. *Conflicts of Interest, Reputation, and the Interwar Debt Crisis: Banksters or Bad Luck.* HEID Working Paper No. 02/2010.

Frankfurter, Felix. *Papers.* Harvard Law School.

Frankfurter, Felix, and James Landis. 1928. The Business of the Supreme Court. In *A Study in the Federal Judicial System.* New York: Macmillan.

Friend, Irwin, and Edward S. Herman. 1964. Through a Glass Darkly. *Journal of Business* (October).

Geisst, Charles R. 2001. *The Last Partnerships. Inside the Great Wall Street Dynasties.* New York: McGraw-Hill.

Great Britain. 1875. House of Commons. *Report from the Select Committee on Loans to Foreign States.*

Grinath, A., R. Sylla, and J. Wallis. 2004. *Sovereign Debt and Repudiation. The Emerging Market Crisis in the U.S., 1839–43.* NBER WP 10753.

Hardeman, D.B., and Donald C. Bacon. 1987. *Rayburn. A Biography.* Austin: Texas Monthly Press.

Hayek, F.A. 1945. The Use of Knowledge in Society. *American Economic Review* 35: 519–530.

Hempel, George H. 1971. *The Postwar Quality of State and Local Debt.* New York: Columbia University Press.

———. 1976. *Understanding the Market for State and Local Debt.* Washington, DC: Advisory Commission on Intergovernmental Relations.

Hetzel, Robert L. 2012. *The Great Recession. Market Failure or Policy Failure.* Cambridge: Cambridge University Press.

Homer, Sidney, and Richard Sylla. 2005. *A History of Interest Rates.* New York: Wiley.

Hoover, Herbert. 1952. *Memoirs: The Great Depression, 1929–41.* New York: Macmillan.

Houck, Davis W. 2004. FDR's Commonwealth Address: Redefining Individualism, Advocating Greatness. *Rhetoric and Public Affairs* (Fall).

House of Commons. 1875. Select Committee on Loans to Foreign States. *Report, Proceedings, and Minutes of Evidence.* In *British Parliamentary Papers*, Monetary Policy, General, 10. Shannon: Irish University Press, 1969.

Jackson, Robert H. 2003. *That Man.* New York: Oxford University Press.

Jarrell, Gregg A. 1981. The Economic Effects of Federal Regulation of the Market for New Security Issues. *Journal of Law and Economics* 24: 613–675.

Kelly, Edward J.I.I. 1985. Legislative History of the Glass-Steagall Act. In *Deregulating Wall Street: Commercial Bank*, ed. Ingo Walter. New York: Wiley.

Kennedy, David M. 1999. *Freedom from Fear: The American People in Depression and War, 1929–45.* New York: Oxford University Press.

Kessler, Friedrich. 1935. The American Securities Act and Its Foreign Counterparts. *Yale Law Journal* 44: 1133–1165.

Kohr, Harry F. 1912. The Blue Sky Law. *Technical World Magazine*. June 17.
Krooss, Herman E., ed. 1969. *Documentary History of Banking and Currency in the U.S.* New York: McGraw-Hill.
Lamoreaux, Naomi R. 1994. *Insider Lending. Banks, Personal Connections, and Economic Development in Industrial New England*. Cambridge: Cambridge University Press.
Landis, James M. 1959. The Legislative History of the Securities Act of 1933. *George Washington Law Review* 28: 176–193.
Lasser, William. 2003. *Benjamin V. Cohen. Architect of the New Deal*. New Haven: Yale University Press.
Lasser, J.K., and J.A. Gerardi. 1934. *Federal Securities Act Procedure*. New York: McGraw-Hill.
Loss, Louis. 1983. *Fundamentals of Securities Regulation*. Boston: Little, Brown and Co.
Macey, Jonathan R. and A.A. Sommer, Jr. 1995. Should the Securities and Exchange Commission Be Abolished? *ABA Journal* 81: 52–53.
Macey, Jonathan R., and Geoffrey Miller. 1991. Origin of the Blue Sky Laws. *Texas Law Review* 70: 348–397.
Madden, John T., Marcus Nadler, and Harry C. Sauvain. 1937. *America's Experience as a Creditor Nation*. New York: Prentice-Hall.
Mahoney, Paul G. 1999. The Stock Pools and the Securities Exchange Act. *Journal of Financial Economics* 51: 343–369.
———. 2001. The Political Economy of the Securities Act of 1933. *The Journal of Legal Studies* 30: 1–31.
Manne, Henry G. 1969. *Economic Policy and the Regulation of Corporate Securities*. Washington, DC: American Enterprise Institute.
Maurice, Charles, and Charles W. Smithson. 1984. *The Doomsday Myth*. Stanford: Hoover Institution Press.
Mazumder, Sandeep, and John H. Wood. 2013. The Great Deflation of 1929–33: It (Almost) Had to Happen. *Economic History Review* 66: 156–177.
McCormick, Edward T. 1948. *Understanding the Securities Act and the S.E.C.* New York: American Book Co.
Meeker, J. Edward. 1930. *The Work of the Stock Exchange*. New York: Ronald Press.
Mehra, Rajnish, and Edward C. Prescott. 1978. The Equity Premium: A Puzzle. *Journal of Monetary Economics* 22: 375–394.
Mintz, Ilse. 1951. *Deterioration in the Quality of Foreign Bonds Issued in the United States, 1920–30*. New York: National Bureau of Economic Research.
Moley, Raymond. 1939. *After Seven Years*. New York: Harper.
———. 1966. *The First New Deal*. New York: Harcourt, Brace & World.
Moore, Terris. 1934. Security Affiliate Vs. Private Investment Banker – A Study in Security Originations. *Harvard Business Review* 12: 478–484.

Neumark, John A., ed. 1960. *Wall Street, 20th Century*. New York: Investment Association of NY.

New York Stock Exchange. *Fact Book*, annual.

Parrish, Michael E. 1970. *Securities Regulation and the New Deal*. New Haven: Yale University Press.

Pecora, Ferdinand. 1939. *Wall Street Under Oath*. New York: Simon & Schuster.

———. 1962. *The Reminiscences of Ferdinand Pecora*. Oral History Collection of Columbia University.

Perino, Michael A. 2010. *The Hellhound of Wall Street. How Ferdinand Pecora's Investigation of the Great Crash Forever Changed American Finance*. New York: Penguin.

Posner, Richard A. 2003. *Economic Analysis of the Law*. 6th ed. New York: Aspen.

Ripley, William Z. 1927. *Main Street and Wall Street*. Boston: Little, Brown.

Romano, Roberta. 2003. *The Advantage of Competitive Federalism for Securities Regulation*. Washington, DC: American Enterprise Institute Press.

Roosevelt, Franklin D. 1938. 1941. 1950. In *Public Papers and Addresses*, ed. S.I. Rosenman. New York: Random House.

Schlesinger, Arthur M., Jr. 1945. *The Age of Jackson*. Boston: Little, Brown and Co.

———. 1958. *The Coming of the New Deal, 1933–35*. Boston: Houghton Mifflin.

———. 1965. *A Thousand Days*. Boston: Houghton-Mifflin.

Securities and Exchange Commission. 1935. *Annual Reports*.

———. 1967. *The Work of the Securities and Exchange Commission*. Washington, DC: United States Government Printing Office.

Seligman, Joel. 2003. *The Transformation of Wall Street. A History of the Securities and Exchange Commission and Modern Corporate Finance*. 3rd ed. New York: Wolters Kluwer.

Shughart, William F. 1988. A Public Choice Perspective of the Banking Act of 1933. *Cato Journal* 7: 595–613.

Siegel, Jeremy. 1998. *Stocks for the Long Run*. 2nd ed. New York: McGraw-Hill.

Simon, Carol J. 1989. The Effect of the 1933 Securities Act on Investor Information and the Performance of New Issues. *American Economic Review* 7: 295–318.

Stigler, George J. 1964. Public Regulation of the Securities Markets. *Journal of Business*, April, 117–142. Comment. Oct., pp. 414–422.

Strouse, Jean. 1999. *Morgan*. Boston: Random House.

Sylla, Richard, Robert E. Wright, and David J. Cowan. 2009. Alexander Hamilton, Central Banker: Crisis Management during the U.S. Financial Panic of 1792. *Economic History Review* 83: 61–86.

Thompson, Huston. 1923. Regulation of the Sale of Securities in Interstate Commerce. *American Bar Association Journal* 9: 157–159, 183.

Tomlins, Christopher L. 2005. *The United States Supreme Court*. Boston: Houghton Mifflin.

Tushnet, Mark. 2011. Administrative Law in the 1930s: The Supreme Court's Accommodation of Progressive Theory. *Duke Law Journal* 60: 1565–1638.

U.S. House of Representatives. 1918. *Report of Capital Issues Committee*, House Document 1485, 65th Cong., 3rd sess.

———. 1919. Final *Report of the Capital Issues Committee*, House Document 1836, 65th Cong., 3rd sess.

———. 1933a. *Federal Securities Act*, Hearings, Commerce Committee, 73rd Cong., 1st sess.

———. 1933b. *Federal Supervision of Traffic in Investment Securities in Interstate Commerce*, Report No. 85. 73rd Cong., 1st sess.

U.S. Senate. 1932. *Sales of Foreign Bonds or Securities in the U.S.*, Hearings Before the Finance Committee, 72nd Cong., 1st sess.

———. 1934a. *Stock Exchange Practices. Report No. 1455*, 73rd Cong., 2nd sess. June.

———. 1932–1934b. *Stock Exchange Practices*, Hearings. Committee on Banking and Currency.

Weidenmier, Marc. 2009. The Baring Crisis of 1890. In *The New Palgrave Dictionary of Economics; Online Edition*, ed. S.N. Durlauf and L.E. Blume. London: Palgrave Macmillan.

White, Eugene. 1986. Before the Glass-Steagall Act: An Analysis of the Investment Banking Activities of National Banks. *Explorations in Economic History* 23: 33–55.

Wilber, Ray L., and Arthur M. Hyde. 1937. *The Hoover Policies*. New York: C. Scribner's Sons.

Willoughby, Woodbury. 1934. *The Capital Issues Committee and War Finance Corporation*. Baltimore: Johns Hopkins Press.

Wilson, Edmund. 1928. Sunshine Charley. *New Republic*, June. Rep. Wilson, *The American Earthquake: A Documentary of the Twenties and Thirties*. London: W.H. Allen, 1958.

Wood, John H. 2015. *Central Banking in a Democracy*. New York: Routledge.

Wood, John H., and Norma L. Wood. 1985. *Financial Markets*. San Diego: Harcourt Brace Jovanovich.

Wynne, William H. 1951. *State Insolvency and Foreign Bondholders*. New Haven: Yale University Press.

Young, Ralph A. 1930. *Handbook on American Underwriting of Foreign Securities*. Washington, DC: U.S. Government Printing Office.

CHAPTER 3

Bureaucracies

In a modern state the actual ruler is necessarily and unavoidably the bureaucracy, since power is exercised neither through parliamentary speeches nor monarchical enunciations but through the routines of administrations.
—Max Weber, *Economy and Society* (1922, p. 1393).

The widening area of what in effect is law-making authority, exercised by officials whose actions are not subject to ordinary court review, constitutes perhaps the most striking contemporary tendency of the Anglo-American legal order.
—Felix Frankfurter, "The task of administrative law" (1927).

The Development of Bureaucracies

Was Weber correct about the importance of bureaucracy to government? Some Americans, such as Felix Frankfurter, Harvard professor of administrative law, thought he might be, although bureaucracies were less developed in the United States than in many other countries, such as Weber's Germany. This chapter looks at American bureaucracy in principle and practice, especially in reference to the 1930s securities acts.

The bureaucracy is identified here as the agencies established by Congress to enforce its legislation. Since in French a bureau is a desk, bureaucracy means government by people at desks. Supporters of bureaucracy (or the "administrative state") see it as an efficient and apolitical repository of analysis, oversight, and decisions by experts who enable

J. H. Wood, *Who Governs?*, Palgrave Studies in American Economic History, https://doi.org/10.1007/978-3-030-33083-5_3

government to keep pace with the complexities of society. Bureaucracy's critics, on the other hand, deplore its interferences with democracy and the rule of law and can point out that its growth has not eliminated or possibly even diminished the effects of politics and interests on government. Bureaucracies may not represent as much of a change as their advocates had hoped.

"The life of the law has not been logic," Oliver Wendell Holmes, Jr. (1881, p. 5), wrote, "it has been experience. The felt necessities of the time, the prevalent moral and political theories, intuitions of public policy, avowed or unconscious, even the prejudices which judges feel with their fellow-men" affect the understanding of the law. "The law embodies the story of a nation's development ..., and it cannot be dealt with as if it contained only the axioms and corollaries of a book of mathematics." There is no reason why this should not also apply to the bureaucracies charged with applying the law.

"The range of control conferred by Congress and the state legislatures upon subsidiary law-making bodies, variously denominated as ... departments, commissions, and boards," Frankfurter wrote in 1927, "penetrates ... the whole gamut of human affairs."

> Hardly a measure passes Congress the effective execution of which is not conditioned upon rules and regulations emanating from the enforcing authorities. These administrative complements are euphemistically called "filling in the details" of a policy set forth in statutes. But the "details" are of the essence; they give meaning and content to vague contours. The control of banking, insurance, public utilities, finance, industry, the professions, health and morals, in sum, the manifold response of government to the forces and needs of modern society, is building up a body of laws not written by legislatures, and of adjudications not made by courts and not subject to their revision.

All this had been made necessary by the growing demands of an increasingly complex society. "The real difficulty" of government, New York Senator Elihu Root (1912) said as he addressed the state bar association,

> appears to be that the new conditions incident to the extraordinary industrial development of the last half-century are ... demanding the readjustment of the relations between the great bodies of men and the establishment of new legal rights and obligations not contemplated when existing laws were passed or existing limitations upon the powers of government were prescribed in our Constitution.

"In place of the old individual independence of life in which every intelligent and healthy citizen was competent to take care of himself and his family," Root said, "we have come to a high degree of interdependence in which the greater part of our people have to rely for all the necessities of life upon the systemized cooperation of a vast number of other men working through complicated industrial and commercial machinery. Instead of the completeness of individual effort working out its own results in obtaining food and clothing and shelter we have specialization and division of labor which leaves each individual unable to apply his industry and intelligence except in cooperation with a great number of others whose activity conjoined to his is necessary to produce any useful result."

The "division of labor" reminds us of Adam Smith's (1776, pp. 1, 421, 423) study of markets that combine results from individual effort, "as if by an invisible hand," which benefit both the individual and society. For Root and many others, however, "the old reliance upon the free action of individual wills appears quite inadequate," so that "in many directions the intervention of that organized control which we call government seems necessary to produce the same result of justice and right conduct which obtained through … individuals before the new conditions arose."

Root, who also served as Secretary of War (1899–1904) and Secretary of State (1905–1909) and was awarded the Nobel Peace Prize for contributions to international law and arbitration, was called "the prototype of the 20th-century 'wise man,' who shuttled between Washington and legal practice in New York City" (Isaacson and Thomas 2012, ch. 6). The need for government to expand with society found its way into popular histories. The increased incomes brought by the expanding financial and industrial powerhouse had been accompanied by economic and social problems that cried for correction, Allan Nevins and Henry Steele Commager wrote in their *Short History of the United States* (p. 387):

> Science and machinery had outrun social science and political machinery. The practices and principles inherited from an eighteenth-century rural republic were no longer adequate to the exigencies of a twentieth-century urban state. This was true in the political realm, where the fear of government persisted into the period when only government could adequately control the forces that machinery had let loose on society…. The heroes of the day were all reformers, [who undertook to solve] the land question, the labor question, the woman question, the money question.

Solutions included the Elkins and Hepburn Acts (1903, 1906), which strengthened the Interstate Commerce Commission (1887), the Food and Drug Administration (1907), the Federal Reserve System (1913), and the Federal Trade Commission (1914).

The absence of free markets and other private arrangements from these discussions is remarkable. The "problems" which Frankfurter, Root, Nevins, and Commager wanted to correct were thought by some others to be more than compensated for by their benefits. An understanding of the costs and benefits of regulating laws and bureaucracies requires a comparison with the performances and possibilities of the alternative: free (unregulated) exchange in markets as well as hierarchies and organizations to mediate and economize the uncertainties and transaction costs of imperfect markets, which in less than a century had made a primitive agricultural society the richest and most advanced industrial country in the history of the world (Williamson 1973, 1975; Coase 1960, 1964).

Much of Smith's *Enquiry into the Nature and Causes of the Wealth of Nations* was given to examples of inefficiencies and even disasters arising from government interferences with private arrangements, such as tariffs, monopolies, and wage and price controls. There is more than a note of optimism, however, because

> The uniform, constant, and uninterrupted effort of every man to better his condition, the principal from which public and national as well as private opulence is originally derived, is frequently powerful enough to maintain the natural progress of things toward improvement, in spite both of the extravagance of government, and the greatest errors of administration. Like the unknown principle of animal life, it frequently restores health and vigour to the constitution, in spite, not only of the disease, but of the absurd prescriptions of the doctor. (p. 326)

The evaluation of regulations requires an understanding of markets, which, Friedrich Hayek (1945) wrote, are mechanisms "for communicating information." "There should be no dispute about whether planning is to be done or not"—in the small or the large, for the economy or for a particular price, quantity, or facility. The real dispute is whether "planning is to be done centrally, by one authority … or is to be divided among many individuals.… Which of these systems is likely to be more efficient depends mainly on the question under which of them we can expect that fuller use will be made of the existing knowledge." There is much to be said for many individuals, immersed, full time, and on the spot, with strong and specific goals, subject to rapid feedback, positive and negative, from right and wrong decisions, all of which make up the market, rather than remote part-timers with undefined objectives.

The belief in free exchange as an information mechanism is not universal. Many philosopher–reformers have thought otherwise. William Godwin's *Enquiry Concerning Political Justice* (1798) showed the confidence of the "age of reason," through which "the liberally educated and reflecting members" of society should, as in Plato, be "guides and instructors" to the people. Voltaire looked to absolute rulers—he compared the constitutionally limited governments of Western Europe unfavorably to Catherine the Great's Russia—for rational states. "It is most advantageous for the prince and the state when there are many philosophers. The philosophers having no particular interest to defend, can only speak up in favor of reason and the public interest" (Sowell 1987, pp. 43–46). John Stuart Mill wrote that much could be accomplished if "the most cultivated intellects" and "superior spirits would but join with each other," and the universities sent forth "a succession of minds, not the creatures of their age, but capable of being its improvers and regenerators" (Works xviii, pp. 86, 129; xv p. 632).

Godwin believed experience was overrated—"unreasonably magnified"—compared with "the general power of a cultivated mind. [W]e must bring everything to the standard of reason" (1798, ii, p. 172).

> Nothing must be sustained because it is ancient, because we have been accustomed to regard it as sacred, or because it has been unusual to bring its validity into question. (Godwin, *Enquiry Concerning Political Justice*, i, p. 185.)

The great conservatives for whom knowledge is social thought otherwise. Edmund Burke wrote:

> We are afraid to put men to live and trade each on his own private stock of reason; because we suspect that this stock in each man is small, and that the individuals would do better to avail themselves of the general bank and capital of nations and of ages. (Burke, *Reflections on the Revolution in France*, p. 182.)

Opposed to this was Frankfurter's (1936) confidence in the "disinterested enthusiasm" and freedom from imprisoning dogmatism and horizon-restricting "specialized experience" of the fresh young men called to public service in the 1930s. These are the people on whom we should rely to translate "the words on the statute books ... into life," besides which legislation is "child's play."

On the other hand, conservatism is not opposed to change because experience may be an effective as well as a dear teacher.

> The growth of knowledge and the growth of civilization are the same only if we interpret knowledge to include all human adaptations to environment in which past experience has been incorporated. Not all knowledge in this sense is part of our intellect, nor is our intellect the whole of our knowledge. Our habits and skills, our emotional attitudes, our tools, and our institutions – all are in this sense adaptations to past experience which have grown up by selective elimination of less suitable conduct. They are as much an indispensable foundation of successful action as is our conscious knowledge. (Friedrich Hayek, *The Constitution of Liberty*, p. 26.)

Man "is better served by custom than understanding," Hayek wrote, because he has "learnt to do the right thing without comprehending why it was the right thing." There is "more 'intelligence' incorporated in the system of rules of conduct than in man's thoughts about his surroundings" (Hayek 1979, p. 170). This does not mean that enlightened public policy is impossible, but we should be careful:

> Rage and phrenzy will pull down more in half an hour than prudence, deliberation, and foresight can build up in an hundred years. The errors and defects of old establishments are visible and palpable. It calls for little ability to point them out; and where absolute power is given, it requires but a word wholly to abolish the vice and establishment together.... To make every thing the reverse of what they have seen is ... easy.... No difficulties occur in what has never been tried. Criticism is almost baffled in discovering the defects of what has not existed. (Burke, *Reflections ...*, p. 274.)

Burke's lesson might have been learned from the disappointing performances of the agencies urged by Frankfurter, Landis, and others, including Congress, which seems always to be investigating the reasons for their unsatisfactory performances. Their growth has nevertheless continued, along with their surveillance and restrictions.

"At once to preserve and to reform is quite another thing," Burke continued:

> When the useful parts of an old establishment are kept, and what is superadded is to be fitted to what is retained, a vigorous mind, steady persevering attention, various powers of comparison and combination, and the resources of an understanding fruitful in expedients are to be exercised; they are to be exercised in a continued conflict with the combined force of opposite vices; with the obstinacy that rejects all improvement, and the levity that is fatigued and disgusted with every thing of which it is not in possession. But you may object – 'A process of this kind is slow. It is not fit for an assembly which glorifies in performing in a few months the work of ages. Such a mode of reforming possibly might take up many years'. Without question it might; and it ought. It is one of the excellencies of a method in which time is among the assistants, that its operation is slow and in some cases almost imperceptible. (Burke, *Reflections* ..., pp. 274–5.)

One of the questions raised in this book is whether Burke's way in fact wins out in the face of impatient reformers seeking to impose their changes on resistant interests.

Bureaucracies emerge beyond their necessities for several reasons. Root and Frankfurter admitted the sometimes too hasty political responses to crises, as well as dissatisfaction with existing agencies, illustrated by the SEC's replacement of the FTC's administration of securities. "A problem arises, a crisis occurs, a response is demanded," Charles Peters and Michael Nelson wrote in their *Culture of Bureaucracy*. "The President goes on television with a plan of action, Congress quickly approves it, perhaps with some alterations, and then political leaders and the public-at-large go back about their business."

American Bureaucrats

The classic study of public administration was developed in the early twentieth century by Weber, who grew up with Bismarck's welfare state administered by a professional bureaucracy. Weber wrote that "progress toward bureaucratic officialdom – characterized by formal employment, salary, pension, promotion, specialized training and functional division of labor, well-defined areas of jurisdiction, documentary procedures, hierarchical sub- and super-ordination – has been the ... yardstick for the modernization of the state, whether monarchic or democratic."

"Bureaucracy" may refer to the administrations of all large organizations, but is limited here to public institutions assigned by legislatures to administer their laws. Differences between ancient and modern bureaucracies, according to Weber, include the impersonality and permanence of the latter, staffed by agents of the state guided by rules, instead of, as in the past, personal servants of officials/rulers possessing considerable discretion. The modern bureaucrat exercising legal authority does so in his capacity as a member of a corporate group executing "the law." The complexity of the modern state and its laws call for highly educated, disinterested agents with permanent tenure and considerable prestige (1922, pp. 956–63, 1393; 1946; 1947, pp. 329–41).

"The advance of the bureaucratic structure rests upon 'technical' superiority," Weber wrote, which is why England, with its history of "administration by notables," was slow to bureaucratize. "Generally speaking, the trained permanent official is more likely to get his way in the long run than his nominal superior, the cabinet minister, who is not a specialist," Weber (1947, p. 338) claimed. In fact, the bureaucratic "expert" is often an invention that requires clear and technically precise laws rather than the often amorphous political compromises and evasions which characterize legislation. The avoidance of clarity and precision are often necessary to attract the votes necessary for passage, but their applications may be forced into dependence as much on the personal preferences and politics of bureaucrats as on their technical/scientific knowledge.

The United States had not seriously begun to bureaucratize in Weber's time. Steps had been taken toward job security for civil servants, but Andrew Jackson's spoils system still had many adherents. Government and its agencies have grown, but American civil servants have not achieved the numbers, professionalism, or status prevailing elsewhere.

The *grandes ècoles* supply the French civil service, and the British civil service exams are taken by the cream of Oxford and Cambridge, while their American counterparts aim for private professional or executive careers via the numerous law and business schools. Top students join law and consulting firms, investment banks, and corporations. Those having to go into government hope their situations are temporary, whether as bank examiners or assistant prosecutors, and strive for higher incomes and status by favorably impressing their private counterparties. Frankfurter saw and regretted this in the 1920s. "[T]he public as well as the utilities have suffered from too many mediocre lawyers appointed for political considerations, looking to the public service commissions not as means for solving difficult problems of government, but as opportunities for political advancement or more profitable future association with the utilities"—often through specialized knowledge of commission operations (Frankfurter 1930, p. 114; also Jenkins 1978).

Frankfurter deplored the "cult of mediocrity" in government espoused by such men as the president of the Chamber of Commerce, who said: "The best public servant is the worst one.... A thoroughly first-rate man in public service is corrosive. He eats holes in our liberties. The better he is and the longer he stays the greater is the danger." On the contrary, Frankfurter said,

> The American ideal of 'government of laws, not of men' ... is expressed in ... noble words.... But there can be no government of laws except through men. Administration of a statute, like the administration of a business, depends on the quality of its administrator. Sensible and humane government is impossible without well-trained, disciplined, imaginative, modest, energetic, and devoted administrators. Indeed, with its modern tasks, government will need even better talent than that which private enterprise enlists. For with us, not until individual initiative has proved its inability to manage enterprise does government take it over. (Frankfurter, "The young men go to Washington.")

Frankfurter looked forward to improvements in agency personnel. Neither "fear of brains" nor "typical bureaucrats interested in obeying the routine and holding their jobs as inconspicuously as possible for as long as possible will ... solve the intricate problems confronting the Social Securities Board in establishing a system of minimum security for the masses ...; nor be able to supervise wisely the chameleon-like financial transactions which the Securities and Exchange Commission has been instructed to protect, in the interests of both the investment market and the public" (Frankfurter 1936).

Key dates in the history of the American civil service include 1829, when Andrew Jackson became president, and 1885, when the Pendleton Act was passed. Public access to government employment was an important part of Jacksonian democracy, along with belief that the claims of the elite families descended from the founders, who apparently felt a moral property right in federal office, ought to be a thing of the past. Jackson was not unusually active in turning over the bureaucracy, nor did he originate the term, "to the victor belong the spoils," but it was roughly consistent with his beliefs (Johnson 1991, p. 941).

Jackson's announcement of his plans for reform of the public service in his first Annual Message to Congress included some of his views of the unfortunate tendencies of bureaucracy.

> There are, perhaps, few men who can for any length of time enjoy office and power without being more or less under the influence of feelings unfavorable to the faithful discharge of their public duties. Their integrity may be proof against improper considerations immediately addressed to themselves, but they are apt to acquire a habit of looking with indifference upon the public interests and of tolerating conduct from which an unpracticed man would revolt. Office is considered a species of property and government rather as a means of promoting individual interests than as an instrument created solely for the service of the people. Corruption in some and in others a perversion of correct feelings and principles divert government from its legitimate ends and make it an engine for the support of the few at the expense of the many.

Jackson understood incentives better than many of the critics who trusted in politically neutral experts. His opposition to the privileges of the Bank of the United States was condemned by academic and financial authorities for reasons similar to his opposition to entrenchment in government employment. He shared the popular belief that "The duties of all public officers are, or at least admit of being made, so plain and simple that men of intelligence may readily qualify themselves for their performance; and I can not but believe that more is lost by the long continuance of men in office than is gained by their experience."

The dozen years preceding Jackson's presidency, including the Era of Good Feelings, have also been called America's "first great era of corruption." Swindles and misbehavior in government were commonplace news. "That scandalous defalcations in our public pecuniary agents, gross misapplications of public money, and an unprecedented laxity in official responsibilities ... suffered under our government for the past six or eight years are faults not to be concealed," the New York *Statesman* reported on August 6, 1822.

It was a question whether dishonesty or laxity was the more serious. "The Treasury, in particular, was deplorably ill-staffed," an observer reported: "a considerable number of the officers ... are old Men and drunkards. Harrison, the First Auditor, I have not yet seen sober." "Other old Treasury men were crooks," guilty of theft or embezzlement. Jackson's investigators found that $500,000 had been taken from the Treasury. "The Registrar, ... who had defaulted for $10,000, had been there since the Revolution." A chronicler of life in the capital reported that "with many leading officials about to be expelled, Washington was gloomy ... – so many families broken up – and those of the first distinction – drawing rooms now empty, dark, dismantled" (Johnson 1991, pp. 906–908).

Biographer Robert Remini suggested that Jackson may in fact be seen as a reformer, "the first American President who can be called such." Jackson called his program "'reform, retrenchment and economy' – by which he hoped to end the Era of Corruption and restore the country and its government to virtue and honesty."[1] Jackson's administration sought to "guarantee the good behavior of civil servants, ... and to do this they sought both to place their own followers in office and – what is more important – to create a system of depersonalized, specialized bureaucratic rule. Far from being the enemies of bureaucracy, the Jacksonians were among its principal architects," James Wilson (1976; also Crenson 1975, ch. 4) suggested.

Only about 10 percent of officeholders were replaced during Jackson's presidency. Less noticed by the history books, Thomas Jefferson anticipated Jackson's attitudes and actions. "I had foreseen years ago," Jefferson wrote upon assuming the presidency after twelve years of Federalist administrations, "that the first Republican President who should come into office after all the places in the government had become exclusively occupied by Federalists would have a dreadful operation to perform.... On him ... was to devolve the office of executioner, that of lopping off," although "I have carried no passion into the execution of this disagreeable duty.

"Out of many thousands of officers in the United States," he wrote, "nine only have been removed for political principle, and twelve for delinquencies chiefly pecuniary. The whole herd have squealed out as if all their throats were cut.... Was it to be imagined that this monopoly of office was still to be continued in the hands of the minority? Does it violate their *equal rights* to assert some rights in the majority also? ... If a due participation of office is a matter of right, how are vacancies to be obtained? Those by death are few; by resignation, none" (*Writings*, x, 271–76).

The Jefferson–Jackson position is strengthened by recognizing that transitory civil servants may carry much information and experience to their government tasks, not to mention loyalty to their political superiors. Furthermore, the methodical behavior sought by regulation is not necessarily superior to the freedom to innovate, although we will see in Chap. 5 that even Jackson's admirers criticized his opposition to the Bank of the United States, some of them contradictorily claiming laissez faire beliefs.[2]

[1]Remini 1981, pp. ix, 15, 192. "The years 1816–28 are generally known as the Era of Good feelings because ... one party ruled the nation.... (Actually there was considerable quarreling and factious bickering within that party.)"

[2]For example, Schlesinger (1945, pp. 115, 218), and Richard Hofstadter (1949, p. 63, discussed by Temin, 1969, p. 16). Catterall (1902, p. 476), was representative of historians

Jackson wished to divest the federal government of nonessential activities "with the hope of reducing [it] to that simple machine which the Constitution created," confined to "preserving peace, affording an uniform currency, maintaining the inviolability of contracts, diffusing intelligence, and discharging unfelt its other superintending functions." He opposed the central government's support of internal improvements "not national in their character" because of the impossibility of general and well-defined principles regarding those "to which the means of the nation may be constitutionally applied."

> Besides the danger to which it exposes Congress of making hasty appropriations to works of the character of which they may be frequently ignorant, it promotes a mischievous and corrupting influence upon elections by holding out to the people the fallacious hope that the success of a certain candidate will make navigable their neighboring creek …, bring commerce to their doors, and increase the value of their property. It thus favors combinations to squander the treasure of the country upon a multitude of local objects, as fatal to just legislation as to the purity of public men. (President Andrew Jackson, *Fourth Annual Message*, Dec. 4, 1832.)

Reform of the civil service remained a public issue after the Civil War, with the chief objects of economy, efficiency, and morality, although, unlike Europe, the last seemed most important in the United States. Honest government was a paramount objective of reformers in the Gilded Age, and they won a victory in the Pendleton Act of January 1883 that is still on the books. Republicans had lost their congressional majorities in the mid-term election of 1882, and feared the political winds that threatened a Democrat victory in 1884. By extending the security of Federal employment, the lame-duck Republican Congress hoped to satisfy reform elements while reducing future Democrat patronage.

U.S. civil service reform in fact had little to do with government administration beyond job security at the lower levels. Fifty years later, the president and Congress began their terms with the Plum Book of 1933, which

when he wrote that "Jackson and his supporters committed an offense against the nation when they destroyed the bank. [F]ew greater enormities are chargeable to politicians than the destruction of the Bank of the United States. It was a machine capable of incalculable service to this country – a service which can be rendered by no bank not similarly organized." Hummel (1978) observed that even some normally inclined to *laissez faire* criticized Jackson's war on the bank listed the federal civil positions for which examinations were not required. There were 100,000, of which 20,000 "were of more than average significance," including assistant secretaries and undersecretaries of departments, and the heads of nearly all agencies at home and abroad. By the end of 1934, Congress had exempted the personnel of almost sixty new agencies from the merit system. In 1936, only about 60 percent of a federal service of 800,000 was on the merit system. The historian was able to say that FDR's "spoils system ... not only provided for partisan gain [but] also served to keep the bureaucratic bonds of custom and habit ... from crystallizing in the more rigid European pattern" (Van Riper 1958, pp. 94, 316, 320, 357). Andrew Jackson could not have said it better.

American culture and politics have produced bureaucracies with rapid turnovers of nonprofessional members less remote from the public than envisioned by Weber and Frankfurter. Many in the higher levels of government agencies move freely between the government and private sectors, most of them identified with and owing their public positions to a political party. Public agencies consist of political appointees for short terms that usually are not fully served. A study of *Bureaucrats and Politicians in Western Democracies* found the two groups uniquely entangled in the United States, where half the senior administrators were temporary, mostly political, appointees (Aberbach et al. 1981; Page 1985). Most responsibilities of the dozens of the frequently changing deputy-, assistant-, and undersecretaries of U.S. government departments appointed by the sitting executive are borne in other countries by permanent civil servants. For example, of the five commissioners of the Securities and Exchange Commission (SEC, which will be discussed in Chap. 4), no more than three of whom may be of the same political party, are appointed to five-year terms which may be repeated, although median service has been about three years.

There may be advantages to this system, although it presents difficulties in the way of stable goals and practices. In May 2017, four months into the Trump administration, the SEC had three members. The politically independent chairman, Jay Clayton, confirmed May 4, was a partner and specialist in mergers and acquisitions for an international law firm and expected by the financial press to encourage initial public offerings and, in accordance with the president's wishes, streamline the capital formation process by reducing regulations (*Fortune*, May 8, 2017).

Changes in personnel, procedures, and policies are frequent. Republican Michael Piwowar, appointed in 2013, joined the other Republican member during the Obama administration in dissenting against some of the majority's rules and enforcement actions (*Wall Street Journal*, November 10, 2014). He also criticized the super-regulator, the Financial Stability Oversight Council, created by the 2010 Dodd-Frank Act, as an "unaccountable capital markets death panel without transparency" (SEC July 15, 2014). Finally, critics compared Clayton to President George W. Bush's 2001 appointment as SEC chairman, Harvey Pitt, who was compelled to resign after fifteen months in office because of too-close ties to the industry, accusations of going easy on Enron and other financial wrong-doers, and statements to the effect that financial and accounting regulations should be softened.

Difficulties in the way of stable policies were exemplified by the Securities Acts Amendments of 1975, which directed the SEC to facilitate a National Market System in which price and volume information in all markets are universally available. "The major regulatory problems in the securities industry," the Senate "Securities Industry Study" of 1973 had proclaimed, "have not by and large been the result of the SEC's lack of authority but rather of its unwillingness [as claimed in the 1930s] to use the powers it already has.... The inherent limitations in allowing an industry to regulate itself [the SEC's policy toward stock exchanges] are well-known: the natural lack of enthusiasm for regulation on the part of the group to be regulated ... because of vested economic interests."

Congress complained that little had been accomplished by the securities acts beyond dead-end studies and the formal end of fixed commissions, which had been routinely violated and were on their way out (Macey and Haddock 1985). In 2001, in his speech on "A vision that endures," Chairman Arthur Levitt restated the SEC's goals and approach. He admitted that "there is no more potent catalyst in America's economy and markets than the indefatigable drive of the individual." On the other hand, "the truly remarkable growth of our markets is rooted firmly in the standards and structures we have created together, and the public confidence they have engendered." He shared the Brandeis-Roosevelt belief that profits follow confidence which follows regulation.

Lest we rely too much on unregulated profit-seeking forces, Levitt continued, "There is no avoiding ... a fundamental dilemma: allowing unfettered market forces to dictate the cost of pricing data is in direct tension with the mandate for market transparency. Put another way, if market forces allow a dominant market to name the price for its data, this also means the market can withhold the data if it does not get its price. Suffice to say, the implications are not only in conflict with Congress' mandate, but wholly unacceptable for America's investors. Too many investors would be forced to price orders in the dark, [and] national best bid and offer could be supplanted by scattered patches of varying prices, visible to only a few."

Rejecting competition but unable to achieve, or even define Congress's directions, however, the SEC and industry groups had devoted their efforts to more studies without settling on a central market system. Merrill Lynch President William Schreyer complained that

> Despite torrents of words and showers of papers on the subject, no one in any position of authority has yet defined what a national market is.... Without consensus, there is no way that the industry can construct facilities necessary to build one. It is somewhat like building a house where the architect, the plumber, the carpenter and the electrician each has his own conception of what the house should look like and performs his tasks without regard to what the others are doing. (Testimony, U.S. House 1979, pp. 68, 74)

"This is not to suggest that the SEC should have dictated the precise details of the technology to be employed," Seligman wrote. It could, however, have pushed for the removal of some of the more anticompetitive rules of the Exchange, such as fixed commissions and prohibitions against institutional membership and Exchange members trading exchange-listed securities over-the-counter. However, during the 1977–81 (Jimmy Carter's presidency) chairmanship of Harold Williams, the SEC ceased to treat competition as "the most important objective of the system," which "was subordinated to the more conservative objective of avoiding disruptions in securities trading." Williams believed the industry should "maintain the initiative in design and implementation of the system," because the SEC was "not well suited by experience or disposition" to serve as "a planner for industry" (Seligman 2003, p. 501; SEC Nov. 30, 1979; Dec. 4, 1980).

The shortages of expertise and clear goals were joined with competition from other branches of government to obstruct the SEC's regulation, as indicated by the excerpt from the newspaper report in the box. The Republican Treasury was apparently seeking to deflect reforms envisioned by the Democratic Congress and the SEC.

Treasury to Begin Study of the Securities Markets

Eileen Shanahan. *New York Times*, Oct. 24, 1973.

WASHINGTON, Oct. 23 – The Treasury Department announced plans today to develop a group of Administration positions – which may or may not be the same as those taken by the Securities and Exchange Commission – on the regulation of the securities markets. The prime mover behind this unusual incursion into the jurisdiction of a regulatory agency is William E. Simon, Deputy Secretary of the Treasury, who was a senior partner in the investment banking concern Salomon Brothers before he joined the Government. Mr. Simon will have "working supervision" of the study, which will be aimed at adoption of Administration policies on regulatory, tax and other matters related to the securities markets. [It] will consist essentially of a series of 10 meetings … with persons representing a cros-section of the securities industry….

At least one member of Congress was immediately critical …: Senator Harrison Williams, New Jersey Democrat and chairman of the Senate Securities Subcommittee. [H]e expressed fears that the Treasury study could delay legislation regarding the securities industry that is already far advanced in both the House and Senate…. "This is no time for the Administration to propose starting all over again. [R]egulatory jurisdiction over the securities industry has been vested in the SEC, an independent regulatory agency established by the Congress." The Administration appears to be planning "to get involved where it has no business."

An SEC official, when asked to comment on the Treasury's announcement, said it had come as no surprise to the agency, which had been consulted as the plans were formulated. He pointed out, however, that the commission will not be bound by anything they do, although he also said that he saw nothing improper in the Administration's attempt to formulate positions on issues that are primarily or solely within the Commission's jurisdiction.

Pressures on NYSE rules increased in the 1960s and 1970s, as its "back-office" crisis revealed its inability to keep up with business, and "monopolistic" trading restrictions such as fixed commissions and limits on members' off-exchange transactions reduced business. The Justice Department and

Democratic congresses pushed for competitive rule changes, resisted by the Republican administration and conservative Exchange members. "Where was the SEC all those years," Paul Samuelson asked of its failure "to promote ... competition and to control private monopoly" during the Senate Banking Subcommittee's 1972 Hearings on "Stock Exchange Commission Rates."

In 1979, the SEC chairman defended the lack of progress toward a National Market System. "I am not about to be the person to come back to Congress and say I am sorry I implemented your program and it blew [up]. The capital markets of this country are too important." The goal of maximum market-maker competition was subordinated to the more conservative objective of avoiding disruptions in securities trading (Seligman 2003, p. 501).

"Americans have coped with the bureaucratic state," Professor Barry Karl (1987) wrote, "by castigating it all the while and attempting to place upon it every limitation of which they could think." They have been willing to accept bureaucracy as long as they could control it. The special place of American bureaucrats has also been served by the special nature of its politicians. American bureaucrats are politicians as well as technicians, and Congressmen are technicians as well as legislators. Congressional committees are more than legislative bodies. Through hearings and oversight, committee members acquire expertise in their fields and try to see that laws are implemented in their interests, or rather the interests of their constituents. The committees and subcommittees "keep a watchful eye" on their agencies. They often have longer service than the agency heads who report to them. The agency heads themselves are required to behave like politicians, balancing forces as they are lobbied by both political parties and the interests they have been assigned to regulate (Aberbach et al. 1981, pp. 94–98; 1990).

The process has been called "government without passing laws," enforced principally by the "power of the purse" (Kirst 1969; Fenno 1966). Subcommittees seek to control agencies, including the formulation and enforcement of regulations, by means of their budgets. For example, in a statement opening the House Financial Services Committee's Hearings on the SEC's Operations and FY2018 Budget Request on November 15, 2016, shortly after the Republican election victories, Chairman Jeb Hensarling advised Mary Jo White, the Democratically appointed SEC Chair, to go slow on the development of the derivative regulations prescribed by the 2010 Dodd-Frank Act:

> I would strongly urge you to respect the results of last week's election and resist the temptation to finalize any regulations, including Dodd-Frank Title VII regulations, in deference to the right of the incoming administration to set its own priorities upon taking office in January.

Reformers believed that in bypassing legislative conflict agencies would end corporate and political influence on regulation. It should be remembered, however, that agencies are typically created to carry out difficult and controversial tasks with the unreliable support of changing legislatures. They in fact add another venue for political conflicts to which they contribute their own ideas and interests (Niskanen 1971; Fiorina and Noll 1978).

Jonathan Macey (2010) listed three sets of incentives motivating the SEC. First, in seeking the approval of Congress and the public, it pursues high profile, popular, and changing issues. This was especially true at the beginning, as we will see, but has continued. Second, as a largely legal agency, it has been interested in maximizing its legal reputation, often at the expense of timeliness and other economic considerations. Third, instead of solving problems, or allowing them to be solved, it has a strong incentive to promote the appearance that the capital markets are in crisis, again a pattern observed from its outset. There is no simple general theory of the many varieties of bureaucratic behavior (Moe 1997).

The Administrative Process in Theory and Practice

The Administrative Process written by James Landis as the New Deal agencies were getting underway was hailed by scholars as a "celebration" of commissions and "the outstanding theoretical elaboration of administrative regulation." Landis was in an unrivalled position to evaluate government agencies. The thirty-nine-year-old Harvard law professor was reputed to be Harvard Law's best student since Louis Brandeis, he had been a law clerk for Justice Brandeis, the youngest-ever full professor at the School, co-author with his former Professor of Administrative Law, Felix Frankfurter, an author of the Securities Act of 1933, member of the first SEC, and its second chairman (Ritchie 1980; Jaffe 1964; McCraw 1975).

Landis began his book by attributing the expansion of government to the inadequacies of older, simpler, forms. "More and more the state was assuming new burdens in order to direct and to define the objectives of the economic forces that invention had released, and to control the new powers that derived from the wealth which those forces had created." They had created "new relationships between the individual, the body economic, and the state."

"At the turn of the nineteenth century," Landis wrote as he explained the rise of the "administrative tribunal," a name he preferred to "bureaucracy," "the functions of government were limited essentially to the prevention of disorder, protection from foreign invasion, the enlargement of national boundaries, the stimulation of international trade, and the creation of a scheme of officials to settle civil disputes." However, citing one of the new industrial problems, the "high level of transportation charges … that discriminated between communities, commodities, and individuals had made the railroads a political issue. The first attempts at direct legislative control of rates and charges proved crude and useless. Such remedies as the common law and the courts afforded depended upon the initiative of aggrieved shippers [and] were more apparent than real because of the costly and uncertain character of the legal actions that had to be pursued. The need for nondiscriminatory and reasonable rates, uniformly applicable, could not be achieved through the intermittent intervention of the judicial process."

"Some federal mechanism of necessity had to be invented if the rudiments of a national railroad policy were to be developed." This was found in 1887 in the Interstate Commerce Commission, although its powers were limited by "political pressures, remnants of laissez faire economics, [and] the moneyed interests of the East.… The necessary powers were granted later when the need for them could no longer be denied." Most important about the ICC, Landis maintained, was that it was the first "deliberate organization of a governmental unit whose single concern was the well-being, in a broad public sense, of a vital and national industry" (Landis 1938, pp. 1–13).

Although it served as a model for later agencies, the ICC was for most of life held in low esteem. "Whether written by a political scientist, an economist, a judge, a general, or a consumer advocate, the post-World War II literature on transportation regulation has been hostile to the ICC," which is held responsible for inefficiencies and inflexibilities which contributed to the downfall of the railroad industry while at the same time failing to protect its consumers (Hoogenboom 1976, pp. 193–94). It was finally eliminated in 1995, and its functions eliminated or transferred.

The ICC has been explained as an instrument sought by the railroads to secure their previously ineffective cartels in pursuit of high and stable rates

(Kolko 1965, pp. 7–44; Chapman 1979). However, "the true significance of the Commerce Act," James Q. Wilson (1976) pointed out, "is not that it allowed public power to be used to make secure private wealth [although it did this] but that it created a federal commission with broadly delegated powers that would have to reconcile conflicting goals (the desires for higher or lower prices) in a political environment characterized by a struggle among organized interests and rapidly changing technology."

Delivering the mail is uncomplicated. The civil service consisted overwhelmingly of the Post Office in the nineteenth century, when Andrew Jackson's opinions regarding sufficient competence and reformers' goals of an honest and politically neutral civil service seemed reasonable. Other agencies with clear and routine missions, such as the storage of data and sending of checks by the Social Security Administration, also have good reputations for performance (Wilson 1989, pp. 99–110).

On the other hand, Wilson pointed out, the ICC was not "the first federal agency with substantial discretionary powers over important matters." The Office of Indian Affairs had coped for many years with the "Indian problem equipped with no clear policy, beset on all sides by passionate arguments and infected with fraud and corruption that seemed impossible to eliminate" until the exhaustion of all "things in Indian possession worth stealing." Much of the problem was the absence of any clear end toward which Indian control was supposed to be directed, whether extermination, relocation, or assimilation (Wilson 1976). Complicated conceptual problems also troubled later agencies, especially those, such as the FTC and SEC, charged with the regulation of markets. This meant the identification of goals, such as consumer and/or producer welfare, and the means of their promotion, competition, or control.

In the case of the ICC, rate regulations were carried out by regional bureaus consisting of representatives of local transportation companies (its powers over railroads were extended to trucking and water transportation). Rates were designed to preserve the status quo, so that no firm was threatened by competitive undercutting. Railroads were thus unable to benefit from their cost advantage in long hauls. Value pricing meant that hay was shipped more cheaply than gold. Companies received rights to carry specific goods, for example, "fruit and vegetable juices" but not "frozen juices," or "machinery" but not "auto parts." Competition was suppressed by limiting firms to particular cities and restricting freight on return trips. Uneconomic, out-of-the-way, routes and empty capacity were required, apparently to preserve service to small cities off the main routes when unregulated carriers might have solved the so-called problem at prices necessary to cover the additional costs (Chapman 1979).

Landis made no mention of competition or the price system, or even of choice (except in pejorative references to "laissez faire"). One might argue, contrary to the Root-Frankfurter-Landis premise, that growing economic complexity increases the difficulties of regulation as well as the benefits of markets (Bordo and James 2013, Introduction). No individual or group could possibly decide satisfactory schedules of rates and routes for a large country undergoing rapid changes in technology and the distributions of population and industry. Unhappiness with the ICC except for the interests seeking its benefits, primarily existing firms resisting change, was inevitable. Similar dissatisfaction with the FTC led Congress to transfer its securities regulation to a new agency (SEC). Nevertheless, Landis felt able to write that

> In the years that followed the creation of the Interstate Commerce Commission, the same problem [industrial ills, including unreasonable rate structures] presented itself at other points in the economic scene. As particular industries, due to lack of effective economic constraints posited problems of abusive tactics with which traditional legal devices ... failed to cope, this new method of control made its appearance. Banking, insurance, utilities, shipping, communications – industries with sicknesses stemming from misdirection as to objective or from failure adequately to meet public needs – all came under the fostering guardianship of the state. The mode of the exercise of that guardianship was the administrative process.

The more agencies the better, Landis felt, because "Efficiency in the processes of governmental regulation is best served by the creation of more rather than less agencies" since multiple agencies allow specialization. This differed from the nineteenth century, when inexpertness in government attained the status of a principle, Landis wrote. "But expertness cannot derive otherwise" (Landis 1938, pp. 13–14, 23–24).

In the 1920s, Frankfurter had encouraged the Commonwealth Fund to study the performance of administrative agencies, the ICC and FTC, in particular, and both were found wanting. Gerald "Henderson thought an expert agency should be able to make factual findings about an industry that a court could not, but the FTC's findings were of 'meager quality'." They lacked factual and conceptual support. Is a loss leader really part of a punishable "intent, purpose and effect of stifling and suppressing competition in interstate commerce?" (Henderson 1924, pp. 116–19). Terms were not defined nor causation explained, although Henderson believed the agency's shortcomings stemmed from inadequate but readily resolved technical qualifications and resources, rather than unsolved and possibly unsolvable conceptual problems.

"The forms of unfair and oppressive competition are myriad," Landis (1938, pp. 18–19), wrote:

> By the time Congress has discovered and defined a dozen, a dozen more will be devised and put into operation. A tribunal should be created, with power to mold and adapt the law to each new situation. Since business and economic problems will be encountered, as well as questions of law, the power should be lodged with a commission composed of eminent lawyers, economists, business men and publicists.

Landis's reference to the greater "efficiency" of bureaucracy, and Weber's "technical superiority," entitle us to ask the meanings of these terms. Webster's Collegiate Dictionary defines "efficiency" as "Effective operation as measured by a comparison of production with cost in energy, time, money, etc."; that is, "production relative to cost." Yet agencies often began without meaningful goals or cost measures. The *Interstate Commerce Act* declared that "rates shall be reasonable and just," and the Federal Trade Commission Act sought to "curb unfair [and] anticompetitive trade practices" (Seligman 2003, pp. 57–58, 416–17). We will see in the next chapter that the SEC's mandate was as broad and loosely defined.

The ICC's solution to the problem of policy, instead of relying on competition in any of its senses, was to dictate rates by what sometimes looked like arbitrary formulas. In 1912, the "tireless" Commissioner Franklin Lane "threw his energy into working out a simple system" of express rates. He allowed

> two classes – general merchandise and foods and beverages – and divided the nation into 950 blocks bounded by each degree of latitude and longitude. For local rates, these blocks were subdivided 16 times. With rates no longer set from point to point but from block to block, [he was proud to reduce] the possible number of rates from over 600 million to less than 345 thousand.

"The ICC also entered 'into the minutiae of billing, routing, and other details' and in all worked 'a revolution and renovation in the methods and rates of express companies'." The post office was so impressed that it applied the system to parcel post (Hoogenboom 1976, pp. 69–70;

Sharfman 1931–37, ii, pp. 69, 78). The factors affecting the costs of services between blocks were many and substantial, including values per unit, weight, fragility, liability to spoilage, dangers and difficulties of handling, competition, numbers of lines and competitors, whose effects on rates can only be determined by their effects on potential carriers and their customers. The main threat to the public welfare envisioned by this system was the entry of carriers attracted by the profit opportunities provided by mispricing. Yet in spite of a rational system of prices and quantities that can only be supplied by markets, even if imperfectly, the agency dictated prices and services in the interests of existing groups unwilling to accept market outcomes.

Landis called opposition to the new agencies "hysterical," stemming from an irrational fear of change. He referred to the dislike of bureaucracy, sometimes called the "fourth branch," as a mystical attachment to the number three and the exultation of inexpertness.[3] Bureaucracy had been made necessary by the inadequacies of "the judicial process, [which] suffers from several basic and more or less unchangeable characteristics" the law professor wrote. One was "its inability to maintain a long-time, uninterrupted interest in a relatively narrow and carefully defined area of economic and social activity." Their general jurisdiction makes "judges jacks-of-all-trades and masters of none," a problem "enhanced under our constitutional system which permits judges to disregard those solutions reached by other governmental agencies, such as the legislative and the administrative, when the solution appears to them unfair, unreasonable, or unwise" (Landis 1938, pp. 30–31, 47).

It is appropriate to point to a logical problem with Landis's point that the judiciary is inadequate to deal with the volume and technical nature of agency business. The workload is not given. Why is it so large? It is true that growth of the judiciary has not matched the regulatory ambitions of

[3] In 1936, the president established a Committee on Administrative Management (chaired by Louis Brownlow) to make recommendations about how he might manage the independent agencies. The Committee pointed out that they had been created one by one over the past 50 years, and threatened to become a headless fourth branch of the Government, not contemplated by the Constitution, nor responsible administratively to the President, Congress, or the Courts. "The president needs help," the Committee reported, and its recommendation for a new Executive Office of the President to oversee the agencies was adopted in the Reorganization Act of 1939, along with the assignment of several agencies to existing departments of government. (Fesler 1987)

Congress, although the latter could be the main problem. More could be left to markets, which in many cases prevail anyway.

Landis shared Charles Hough's regret in the *Harvard Law Review* that lawsuits are usually based on the hope that some court will find something "inexpedient in light of the civilized requirements of the day.…That method of decision makes every case one of fact, and yet under our system produces as precedents the opinions on those facts of a jury of judges, who in all good conscience are necessarily actuated … by mental attitudes or predilections based on heredity, environment, and education, as all other juries are [but not bureaucrats?]. This is truly a most unsatisfactory result from a juridical standpoint" (Landis 1938, pp. 31–32; Hough 1917).

"To these considerations must be added two others," Landis (pp. 33–34) wrote. "The first is the recognition that there are certain fields where the making of law springs less from generalizations and principles drawn from the majestic authority of textbooks and cases, than from a 'practical' judgment" based on all the relevant "political, economic, and social considerations." It was a matter of regret that "judges made rather than discovered the law," especially in the fields of monopoly and labor, where they "too often held economic and social opinions opposed to the ideals of their time," and had made the Sherman Anti-Trust Act of 1890 a dead letter by their narrow interpretations.[4]

"The second consideration may be even more important. It is the fact that the common-law system left too much [to costly] private initiative, [to] the willingness of individuals … to become martyrs to their convictions – [which is] a slow and costly method of making law. To hope for an adequate handling of the problem of allowable trade practices by the sudden emergence of a host of Pyms and Hampdens was too delightfully visionary to be of much practical value. The retaliatory powers of business associates or competitors are today such an immensely powerful force that few persons care to run the risk of its offensive vengeance in the effort to

[4]In 1895, the Supreme Court ruled that the American Sugar Refining Company had not violated the law even though the company controlled about 98 percent of all sugar refining in the United States on the ground that the company's control of manufacture did not constitute a control of trade. Manufacturing was not the commerce specified in the law. On the other hand, the Roosevelt and Taft "trustbusting" administrations used the Act successfully against the Northern Securities Company, Standard Oil, and American Tobacco. The Clayton Antitrust Act of 1914 was passed to make the Sherman Act's provisions against anticompetitive practices more precise.

secure what they might deem to be their legal rights" (Landis 1938, pp. 34–35).[5]

Nor was criminal prosecution a solution. "The traditions of the common law in criminal cases erect … imposing barriers to prosecution," juries are always an uncertain factor, judges may be unsympathetic to the policy of the law, and prosecuting agencies, like courts, lack the necessary single-mindedness of devotion to a specific problem. All these agents "fall substantially short of promoting an enlightened long-term development of law and administration in a particular field."

Traditional law as well as the economic underpinnings of America's rise to greatness were declared irrelevant or at least inadequate—along with legislation, which is often vague and imprecise because of political compromise or the "lack of exact knowledge of the subject." Some had deplored the resulting delegation of congressional power, but in Landis's view that delegation gave agencies desirable flexibility. They sometimes unnecessarily relinquish that flexibility by letting themselves be "lured into rendering interpretive assistance" by defining the subjects of regulation. "The Securities and Exchange Commission made that mistake, in the beginning, by attempting to define 'public offerings.' It soon realized that advantage was being taken of these definitions [and] retreated … from the field, [refusing] to do more than point to the considerations which, it believed, should have primary weight in … differentiating the exempt 'private offering' from the registerable 'public offering'."

The area in which the courts insist that administrative findings of fact cannot be final is an interesting one, Landis complained. "It seems odd, very odd, as a three-judge court has expressed it, that a Constitution which expressly makes findings of fact by a jury of inexperienced laymen, if supported by substantial evidence, conclusive … prohibits Congress making findings of fact by a highly trained and especially qualified administrative agency likewise conclusive." "The inadequacies of [the judicial] process to deal with the rate problems of a national system of railroads led to the institution of administrative agencies." Yet the next thing we know is that the courts have reviewed (taken cases challenging) administrative

[5] John Hampden was a member of Parliament who stood trial in 1637 for his refusal to be taxed for ship money, and was one of the five members (with John Pym) whose attempted unconstitutional arrest by King Charles I in the House of Commons in 1642 sparked the Civil War.

decisions to such an extent that the intentions of legislation have broken down and the regulatory process has been brought into contempt.

Landis had great ambitions for the bureaucracy. "It is obvious," he said, that "the administrative process is not, as some suppose, simply an extension of executive power.... In the grant to it of that full ambit of authority necessary for it ... to plan, to promote, and to police, it presents an assemblage of rights normally exercisable by government as a whole," even thinking "in terms of the economic well-being of an industry." Its power "is in essence the response ... to the demand that government assumes responsibility not merely to maintain ethical levels in the economic relations of the members of society, but to provide for the efficient functioning of the economic processes of the state." Markets and legislatures had become disposable (Landis 1938, pp. 35, 51, 68–69, 83–84, 125, 133, 15–16). How that efficiency was to be achieved was unspecified, although presumably it would be by bureaucratic direction. In any case, agency responsibilities were great, even forbidding. No wonder that when it came to practice, the SEC under Landis was known for its caution.

Landis left his chairmanship of the SEC (1935–37) to become dean of the Harvard Law School (1937–46), although he also served in the Office of Civilian Defense during the war. He was appointed by President Truman to head the Civil Aeronautics Board in 1946, left the next year, acted as a counsel to the Kennedy family, and as special assistant to the president for regulatory policy during John F. Kennedy's administration. The criticisms of the Landis *Report on Regulatory Agencies for the President Elect* (John Kennedy, December 1960) came as something of a bombshell. The *Report* pointed to inadequate personnel and procedures, claimed that commissions had become a drag on the economy, and called for sweeping changes. The Report asserted that "good men can make poor laws workable, poor men will wreak havoc with good laws." For example, the Federal Power Commission would need thirteen years to complete its backlog of cases. It called for presidential support of budgets to assist efficiency as well as an end to White House meddling that put a premium on "lobbying in its worst characteristics."

Donald Ritchie asked why Landis changed his mind about commissions, and answered in terms of revelation through personal experience, especially at the CAB. Landis's positive experiences at the SEC in the 1930s were not typical, Ritchie argued. This was a period during which, in the eyes of many, general economic recovery was at least as important as reform. The securities business, including the New York Stock Exchange, the SEC's main concern, was at a low ebb, and the SEC's regulation was light. It encouraged self-regulation by the Exchange, and the two sides cooperated to smooth their naturally adversarial relations. Landis had the support of his colleagues, and relations were generally diplomatic. There were differences in detail, but most agreed about the importance of restoring the confidence of investors after the depression.

Landis found a different situation in President Harry Truman's Fair Deal and the CAB. He found an inactive commission with a large backlog of cases arising from a lethargy exacerbated by reluctance to improve competition by opening routes to new and competing airlines. Landis often found himself in the minority in CAB votes. Nor did the White House provide any political protection from lobbying. Quite the reverse. The SEC's independence had eroded in the 1930s as finance gained strength and the administration's interest waned. The sides were not as far apart in that situation, however, as the positions of Landis and the airlines regarding competition after World War II.

Landis's hopes for competition, such as more carriers on profitable routes, was not shared by existing airlines or his CAB colleagues. "There is too much competition," complained Eastern Airlines' Eddie Rickenbacker. The industry's lobbying against Landis succeeded when Truman did not reappoint him at the expiration of his term in 1947. Truman felt that Landis (like Marriner Eccles, see below) had given him "a first-class double-crossing." Landis' successor also resigned when Truman used his power over international flights (for national security reasons) to reverse the CAB's denial of a merger favored by Pan-American (Hamby 1995, p. 427; *New York Times*, July 18, 1950).

Landis returned to private practice, and argued lengthy and expensive cases before the CAB, leading him to write to a friend: "Some years ago I wrote a fairly popular book defending the administrative process on the ground that it would be expeditious and less costly than going to court. After this experience and several others with the CAB, I almost feel it a moral duty to revise my estimate of that process made before my acquaintance with the organization" (Ritchie 1980).

At least a few students shared Landis' hopes and disappointments regarding the modern administrative process. Legal historian Wallace Mendelson (1957) agreed that it "is, in essence, our generation's answer to the inadequacy of the judicial and legislative processes." He conceded that "the ability of the Anglo-American legal system to accommodate changing social needs has been one of its major merits." However, like

Landis, he thought accommodations had been "slow and painful," and that common law judges have not gracefully bridged "the transition from medieval to modern culture," causing "a long conflict between the old and the new institutions." The inability of government to accommodate the transformation from a frontier to an urban-industrial society, from competition to oligarchy in large segments of the economy, and from laissez faire to the service state produced the modern administrative process.

> When once it was recognized … that competition was simply not feasible for the control of railroad rates, government regulation became inevitable. But the old system of judicial enforcement of legislative mandates was not adequate for the task. Legislatures discovered that rate regulation involved subtleties far beyond their competence. Their universal response was to delegate such problems to specialized administrative agencies – agencies that either had or could be expected to develop techniques commensurate with the esoteric nature of the work assigned them.

"At first the courts refrained from interference," recognizing "that what constituted 'fair and reasonable' railroad rates was a problem for specialists. But such scruples soon yielded to *laissez-faire*.… To give administrative specialists the final word on railroad and utility rates was deemed incompatible with fundamental property rights [and] that much desired 'rule of law'." Although unable to repeal regulatory legislation, its enemies sought to use legislatures for "their ends via control of administrative personnel and finances and by 'administrative code' provisions for various degrees of judicial supervision of regulatory actions.… In short, administrative law has been … a judicial break or bottleneck, according to one's bias, imposed first by judges and then by legislators upon the administrative process."

Thus, we have an unwieldly combination of the two worlds: agencies together with the continuation (even expansion) of legislative and judicial processes, all providing routes through which interests seek influence. Landis admitted that agencies were even more susceptible to influence from the executive and legislative branches than the judicial (Landis 1938, p. 101). This is particularly true of crisis-driven legislation, whose public support may be short-lived, and even overridden during the implementation process, called "politics by other means" and pursued with the intensity of a "blood sport," as SEC Chairman Arthur Levitt complained (McGarity 2012). Dependence on scandals and imprecision to get bills passed only extends political conflicts, as we see in the experiences of the SEC.

Progressive legal theorists including Frankfurter and Landis had looked forward to an independent, nonpolitical, judicially unreviewed "administrative absolutism," as critics called their position. What they got was the extension of interest-group bargaining to "administrative agencies, and the Progressive claim that administrative agencies pursued science rather than politics became difficult to sustain" (Tushnet 2011).

Regulators, like reformers, are often subject to the nirvana, or *grass-is-greener*, fallacy, in which the an untried zero-cost perfect-information theoretical substitute is expected to be an improvement on actual imperfect market practice.[6] Difficulties cannot be seen in what has not been tried. These idealistic goals—real and professed—of legislation are particularly at risk during the implementation process. "[T]he inherent problem with ... lawmaking moments is just that – they are moments," and subject to the difficulties of collective-behavior. "Indeed, unless the number of individuals in a group is quite small, or unless there is coercion or some other special device [such as a crisis] to make individuals act in their common interest, ***rational self-interested individuals will not act to achieve their common or group interests.***" The costs of regulations borne by firms tend to induce evasions which might negate the intended benefits to be spread over the consumer-public, Mancur Olson pointed out in *The Logic of Collective Action* (p. 2).[7] An agency established to take the consumers' side is inevitably also [perhaps even more] concerned with the industry's welfare.

Practice failed to coincide with theory. In 1976, after a two-year study, the House Subcommittee on Oversight and Investigation reported that "attacks on Federal regulation have driven its image to an historic low." "Critics of the regulatory process had become legion," Ritchie wrote, "and their lists of complaints a familiar litany: the commissions had become

[6] Demsetz (1969) made this point when he took issue with Arrow's (1962) claim that a free-market economy tends to underinvest in research to such an extent that the (full-information, zero-transactions-cost) government must intervene.

[7] McGarity (2012) addressed Dodd-Frank's charge to the Federal Reserve to limit bank charges to retailers for credit- and debit-card transactions ("swipe fees") to what is "reasonable and proportional" to their costs, and indicated a reduction from 44¢ to 12¢. The Fed's decision of 21¢ was overruled in July 2013 by a U.S. district court which said Congress had wanted a much lower fee. The U.S. Court of Appeals for D.C. overturned the district court in March 2014, saying that Dodd-Frank's language was sufficiently ambiguous to give regulators leeway to set a higher fee cap. The U.S. Supreme Court declined an appeal. Michigan democratic Senator Richard Durbin announced that efforts to reduce fees would continue (Reuters, January 20, 2015).

captives of the special interests, promoters of narrow economic purposes, and servants of an entrenched bureaucracy. Every president since Franklin Roosevelt had proposed some form of regulatory reform." It is worthy of notice that the investigative committee was a subcommittee of the House Committee on Interstate and Foreign Commerce, which had been responsible for the Securities Acts of the 1930s, and the House and its committees were still Democratic.

Industry influences on commission memberships and practices have been significant, and sometimes dramatic, since their inceptions. Marriner Eccles believed that Truman did not reappoint him chairman of the Federal Reserve Board in 1948 because A.P. Giannini, head of the Bank of America, complained about Eccles' part in the Fed's actions against the bank's holding company, Transamerica. After years of fruitless discussions with Giannini, the Federal Reserve Board proceeded against Transamerica under Section 7 of the Clayton Act, having determined that its bank acquisitions in California, Oregon, Washington, Nevada, and Arizona had resulted in a substantial lessening of competition and a tendency toward monopoly in banking in this five-state area. The Board ordered Transamerica to divest itself of all its banking interests except Bank of America. The Court of Appeals for the Third Circuit set this order aside, concluding that the Board's findings of fact failed to indicate a Section 7 violation. The Court regarded the "Board's conclusion of a tendency to monopoly in the five-state area" inconsistent with "its own finding that the local community is the true competitive banking area." The Fed's argument was also judged to be weak in the delayed timing of its action as well as in its failure to define competition, which without argument it used interchangeably with size. The Fed's failures in this case were ultimately rewarded when its regulatory powers were expanded by the Bank Holding Company Act of 1956 (Hyman 1976, pp. 322–39; Hamby 1995, pp. 426–27; Neal 1953).

The Federal Power Commission's regulation of the natural gas industry had been too stringent to suit the industry, which opposed the reappointment of FPC Chairman Leland Olds in 1949. He had served on the commission for ten years, and had been reappointed with little difficulty in 1944, but his opponents gathered their forces in 1949. Olds had been an effective opponent of the Kerr bill that would have amended the Natural Gas Act of 1938 "to remove any effective federal regulation of the price of gas moving in inter-state commerce." The Kerr bill (after Senator Robert Kerr of Oklahoma) passed the House but was defeated in the Senate three months before the end of Olds' term, and the industry asked Senator

Lyndon Johnson to see that Olds was not reappointed (Caro 2003, pp. 232–301; Harris 1951). Johnson delivered and, in the process, destroyed Olds' career.

Johnson secured the chairmanship of the subcommittee of the Interstate Commerce Committee that would look into Olds' renomination along with permission to hold hearings on the issue. Johnson's tactic was the communist smear. The House Un-American Activities Committee's Hollywood blacklists had begun in 1946, the Alger Hiss case was underway, and in a few months Senator Joseph McCarthy would announce his list of Communist Party members in the State Department. It was in this atmosphere that a Johnson subcommittee witness produced a selection of writings by Olds, mostly from the 1920s, commenting on domestic and international affairs, some of which—and this was the most telling damnation of Olds—appeared in the *Daily Worker*, which had been one of the eighty newspapers that subscribed to the press service for which he worked. Olds had also once spoken from the same platform as Earl Browder, leader of the American Communist Party, and could not deny unequivocally that he had always opposed public ownership in all its forms.

"Shall we have a commissioner or a commissar?" Johnson asked on the Senate floor. Olds' nomination was defeated 53–15 and the Kerr bill passed the following year, although it was vetoed by President Truman.

Legislatures Again

Congress does not just pass laws and turn them over to the bureaucracy. They sometimes care about the purposes of the laws and wish to see them carried out. "Political analysts have long argued that a key to successful representative government lies in the ability of the legislature to oversee and control the administration of public policy. The power to legislate is largely meaningless if the legislature lacks the ability to ensure proper administration of public policy" (Dodd and Schott 1979, p. 155). As Woodrow Wilson wrote in *Congressional Government*, in 1885, "quite as important as legislation is vigilant oversight of administration":

> It is the proper duty of a representative body to look diligently into every affair of government and to talk much about what it sees. It is meant to be the eyes and the voice, and to embody the wisdom and the will of its constituents. Unless Congress have and use every means of acquainting itself with the acts and disposition of the administrative agents of the government, the country must be helpless to learn how it is being served. (p. 198)

Wilson thought Congress was too intent on legislation and not enough on administration. He believed it should be like a good manager, who not only issues orders but sees that they are carried out (p. 197). This is done to some extent by congressional committees and their specialized subcommittees.

It has been said that "much of the ongoing process of national policy determination ... takes place ... outside the public view in small 'whirlpools' or 'subsystems' of government" made up of congressional subcommittees, agencies, and interest groups. They form relationships and the distinction between policy-maker and expert is blurred. It is not unusual for long-serving subcommittee chairmen, assisted by the subcommittee's staff, to be more expert than the revolving-door agency heads. Moreover "the alliances formed between congressional committees and executive bureaus, and between congressmen and bureaucrats, often run counter to overhead executive control" (Dodd and Schott 1979, pp. 10, 42). What is particularly striking to some is that Congress has not been content merely to outline the administration of statutes. "The novel feature of the attempted relationship," Macmahon wrote in 1943, "is its immediacy." The methods of continuous intervention include (1) the amendment of statutes, (2) congressional investigations, (3) cross-examinations of administrators by standing committees, (4) Senate confirmation of appointees, and (5) staffs with broad assignments. Congress's influences on agencies extend beyond their budgets.

Anything can happen to a law's implementation when people, interests, conditions, and political alignments change. A student of implementation experiences wrote:

> It is hard enough to design public policies and programs that look good on paper. It is harder still to formulate them in words and slogans that resonate pleasingly in the ears of political leaders and the constituencies to which they are responsive. And it is excruciatingly hard to implement them in a way that pleases anyone at all, including the supposed beneficiaries or clients. (Bardach 1977, pp. 1–3)[8]

"It's amazing that federal programs work at all," Aaron Wildavsky and Jeremy Pressman wrote in reference to the failure of the Economic

[8]Failures, according to Bardach, included minority hiring, President Johnson's plan to build model communities on surplus federal land in cities, a model education program, subsidized integration of southern schools under the 1964 Civil Rights Act, and improved community mental health services.

Development Administration's Oakland employment program. Eugene Bardach (1977, pp. 4–5) concluded "that even when [we think] we know what ought to be done, and can get political leaders to mandate it, government is probably ill-suited to do the job." Direction unsupported by self-interest is insufficient, even mischievous. "[G]overnmental strategies are likely to be as complex as the society upon which, and through which, they work," involving subsidiary political considerations that may be inconsistent with the primary goals.

The Future of the Administrative State

The American bureaucracy has always been legally as well as politically and economically controversial. Opponents of the federally chartered Bank of the United States argued that it was illegal because it violated the 10th Amendment of the U.S. Constitution, under which "The powers not delegated to the United States by the Constitution, nor prohibited by it to the States, are reserved to the States respectively, or to the people." The issue came up regarding the first U.S. Bank in 1791, when some members of President Washington's cabinet unsuccessfully urged him to veto the bill chartering the Bank. When the charter of the second U.S. Bank was challenged in the 1819 case of McCulloch v. Maryland (discussed further in Chap. 5), Supreme Court Chief Justice John Marshall, in the course of delivering the unanimous opinion of the Court and using what is called the "doctrine of implied powers," pointed out that Congress possessed the power under the Constitution to "make all laws … necessary and proper" to carry out the specific powers conferred on Congress. This included, he said, "the establishment of the Bank of the U.S. in the course of exercising Congress's power to 'coin money [and] regulate the value thereof'."

The growth of federal agencies during the New Deal led to lawsuits challenging Congress's violation of (1) the Commerce Clause of the Constitution (which limited its regulatory authority to interstate commerce) and (2) the constitutional separation of powers by conferring its legislative powers on the executive. In 1935, in *Schechter Poultry Corp. v. the United States*, the Supreme Court unanimously invalidated the *National Industrial Recovery Act* of 1933 on both these grounds. Schechter sold chickens locally, and locally agreed "codes of fair competition" (mainly wage and price agreements) had unconstitutionally (according to the Supreme Court) been given the force of law (Shlaes 2007, pp. 219–24, 239–43).

The Court reversed its positions later in the decade as the understanding of interstate commerce was extended to indirect effects, and federal regulations expanded into every aspect of American life. The "administrative state" envisioned by Frankfurter and Landis, was well on its way although legal battles over the separation of powers continues. The relative authorities of agencies and the judiciary have not been settled. Some of the controversy stems from the 1984 case of *Chevron v. Natural Resources Defense Council*, in which the Court set forth its test for determining whether to defer to an agency's interpretation of a statute, whether, as critics say, the rule of law or administrative fiat will prevail. In the Court's opinion upholding an interpretation by the Environmental Protection Agency, Justice John Paul Stevens explained "administrative (often called 'Chevron') deference":

> First, always, is the question whether Congress has directly spoken to the precise question at issue. If the intent of Congress is clear, that is the end of the matter; for the court, as well as the agency, must give effect to the unambiguously expressed intent of Congress. If, however, the court determines Congress has not directly addressed the precise question at issue, the court does not simply impose its own construction on the statute.... Rather, if the statute is silent or ambiguous with respect to the specific issue, the question for the court is whether the agency's answer is based on a permissible construction of the statute.

Quite apart from the difficulties of applying Chevron—what's clear to you may be ambiguous to me—a growing portion of the judiciary objects to the rule in principle. In a 2016 concurring opinion in *Gutierrez-Brizuela v. Lynch*, in which the 10th Circuit Court of Appeals overruled a decision of the Board of Immigration Appeals that was contrary to an earlier decision of the Court, Judge Neil Gorsuch (named to the Supreme Court in 2017) nodded to Chevron but ruled that to have upheld the BIA in this instance would have required the court to overrule its own decision about the law in favor of an interpretation of an executive agency.

> There's an elephant in the room with us today. We have studiously attempted to work our way around it and even left it unremarked. But the fact is *Chevron* and *Brand X* permit executive bureaucracies to swallow huge amounts of core judicial and legislative power and concentrate federal power in a way that seems more than a little difficult to square with the Constitution of the framers' design. Maybe the time has come to face the behemoth.

"Precisely to avoid the possibility of allowing politicized decisionmakers to decide cases and controversies about the meaning of existing laws," Gorsuch wrote, "the framers sought to ensure that judicial judgments 'may not lawfully be revised, overturned or refused faith and credit by' the elected branches of government." "Yet this deliberate design, this separation of functions aimed to ensure a neutral decisionmaker for the people's disputes, … is instead subject to revision by a politically accountable branch of government."

Neither Congress nor the judiciary is clear about the powers of the bureaucracy, although some have indicated a desire to clarify the issue in a way that they believe is more consistent with democracy, the rule of law, and the Constitution (Adler 2016). During the Supreme Court's 2014–15 term, Supreme Court Justice Clarence Thomas argued that the principles of the Constitution's separation of powers are incompatible with the system of bureaucratic rule that has been growing since the Progressive Era. "[T]he Constitution does not vest the Federal Government with an undifferentiated 'government power,'" Thomas dissented in *Department of Transportation v. Association of American Railroads.*

On the other hand, the separation of powers, especially those given to or assumed by the elected parts of government, was deplored by Professor Woodrow Wilson in his 1887 essay, "The study of administration," as inefficient and unnecessarily reliant on the "selfish, ignorant, timid, stubborn, or foolish" populace. What was needed was the consolidation of power in the hands of "experts," whose discretion would not be dangerous because it would be exercised responsibly.[9] Charles Cooper (2015) argues that Wilson's vision—desire for efficiency (as opposed to political compromises of the sort found in the Constitution), trust in experts, and distrust of the electorate—is the foundation of the administrative state as sanctioned by the U.S. Supreme Court.

In 1932, in *Crowell v. Benson*, the Court held that, because of their "prompt, continuous, expert, and inexpensive" adjudication, agencies rather than courts can decide disputed issues of fact as long as their factual findings receive minimal judicial oversight and their findings are subject to judicial review. "The Court thus united the judicial, legislative, and executive

[9]Wilson earned a doctorate from Johns Hopkins University in 1886, taught at Cornell, Bryn Mawr, and Wesleyan, moved to Princeton in 1890, where he was president (1902–10) until becoming governor of New Jersey (1911–13) and president of the United States (1913–21).

powers in the 'expert' hands of the administrative state," Cooper wrote, "heedless of Madison's famous warning in Federalist no. 47 that '[T]he accumulation of all powers, legislative, executive, and judiciary, in the same hands … may justly be pronounced the very definition of tyranny'."

Unspecified, however, is the meaning of "expert." Appointments to the SEC, for example, have been partisan and sometimes unrelated to technical understandings of financial markets or institutions. Its staff could if desired have been more economically sophisticated, but that route was not taken, and in any case, decisions are made by the commissioners.

What does this mean for our enquiry into who governs? An effect of the bureaucracy has been to shift political battles from the floors of Congress as interests carry their battles to congressional subcommittees and agencies. Interests may benefit from the administrative state as they are enabled to focus on smaller groups (agencies) further removed from the public. Voters may have less influence on specialist agencies than on their elected representative as interests are released from the necessity of congressional majorities.

Finance has shown many examples of these relations. Everyone is affected by financial regulations, and the majorities necessary for laws are difficult to achieve. The Securities Acts of 1933 and 1934 and the Banking Act of 1933 were made possible by a combination of the Great Depression and a congressional majority supporting a reformist administration during a crisis—similar to the 2010 Dodd-Frank Wall Street Reform and Consumer Protection Act—and the Financial Institutions Deregulation and Monetary Control Act of 1980 was passed under pressure from a court which ruled that bureaucratic violations of the law be ended or made legal by a recalcitrant Congress (Wood and Wood 1985, pp. 61–63).

In all these cases, legislated or regulatory obstructions offered profit opportunities for their violation. Enforcement difficulties also arise from inadequate specifications of laws, such as the 1970 Clean Air Act's directive to the Environmental Protection Agency "to protect the public health," the Agricultural Adjustment Act's directive to the Secretary of Agriculture to make agricultural marketing "orderly" (meaning to fix the prices of unspecified crops at unspecified levels), the Financial Stability Oversight Council's responsibility under the Dodd-Frank Act to identify and regulate banks that are "too big to fail," and the SEC's responsibility to "perfect the mechanisms of a national market system for securities." All these goals (or "wishes") were worthy of study, but none was operational. They gave the agencies free rein, as far as the law-making function of Congress was concerned, although they continued to be subject to congressional subcommittees and the influences of the industries concerned.

Not all agencies can justifiably be accused of exceeding their authorities. Rather, they are compelled by the vague and incomplete assignments of Congress to exercise their own, what amounts to legislative, discretion. This is not just laziness, David Schoenbrod (1993) writes, but part of Congress's program of taking credit for popular objectives, such as clean air, stable and high farm incomes, and low-risk financial markets, while shifting the blame for costly and often ineffective regulations to the agencies. Controversies, lawsuits, and congressional criticisms surround agency decisions while the so-called legislators seek to bask in the sunlight of reforms. They behaved as if they had finished their legislative task after they passed Dodd-Frank in 2010, although five years later nearly half the rules composing the act had yet to be formulated as the agencies negotiated with the interests involved, with little support from a politically changed Congress.

The post-New Deal consensus in favor of the administrative state, the belief that it can be reconciled with the Constitution and the rule of law, may be in decline. We saw this above in institutional terms among conservatives. "At the same time, the decline of faith in administrative agencies among progressives and liberals reveals that both sides are dissatisfied with the way that bureaucracy functions" (Postell 2017, p. 319). These considerations increase the uncertainty of the roles of agencies, although we will see at least in the cases of the SEC and the Federal Reserve that it may not matter much because their influences have been less than often supposed.

References

Aberbach, Joel D., Robert D. Putnam, and Bert A. Rockman. 1981. *Bureaucrats and Politicians in Western Democracies.* Cambridge: Harvard University Press.

———. 1990. *Keeping a Watchful Eye: The Politics of Congressional Oversight.* New York: Brookings.

Adler, Jonathan H. 2016. Should Chevron be Reconsidered? A Federal Judge Thinks So. *Washington Post*, August 24.

Arrow, Kenneth T. 1962. Economic Welfare and the Allocation of Resources for Investment. In *The Rate and Direction of Inventive Activity.* Princeton: Princeton University Press.

Bardach, Eugene. 1977. *The Implementation Game: What Happens after a Bill Becomes Law?* Cambridge: MIT Press.

Bordo, Michael, and Harold James. 2013. *The Economic Challenge. Learning from Crises.* Cambridge: Cambridge University Press.

Burke, Edmund. 1790. *Reflections on the Revolution in France*, ed. E. J. Payne, *Selected Works*. Clarendon Press. (Liberty Fund, 1999).

Caro, Robert. 2003. *The Years of Lyndon Johnson. Master of the Senate*. New York: Knopf.

Catterall, Ralph C.H. 1902. *The Second Bank of the United States*. Chicago: University of Chicago Press.

Chapman, Stephen. 1979. The ICC and the Truckers, in Peters and Nelson. *The Culture of Bureaucracy*.

Coase, Ronald H. 1960. The Problem of Social Cost. *The Journal of Law and Economics*, October.

———. 1964. The Regulated Industries: Discussion. *American Economic Review*, May.

Cooper, Charles J. 2015. Confronting the Administrative State. *National Affairs*, Fall.

Crenson, Matthew A. 1975. *The Federal Machine: Beginnings of Bureaucracy in Jacksonian America*. Baltimore: Johns Hopkins University Press.

Demsetz, Harold. 1969. Information and Efficiency. *Journal of Law and Economics*, April, 1–22.

Dodd, Lawrence C., and Richard L. Schott. 1979. *Congress and the Administrative State*. New York: Wiley.

Fenno, Richard. 1966. *The Power of the Purse. Appropriations Politics in Congress*. Boston: Little, Brown.

Fesler, James W. 1987. The Brownlow Committee Fifty Years Later. *Public Administration Review*, August.

Fiorina, Morris, and Roger Noll. 1978. Voters, Bureaucrats, and Legislators: A Rational Choice Perspective on the Growth of Bureaucracy. *Journal of Public Economics*, June.

Frankfurter, Felix. 1927. The Task of Administrative Law. *University of Pennsylvania Law Review*, May.

———. 1930. *The Public and its Government*. Boston: Beacon Press.

———. 1936. The Young Men Go to Washington. *Fortune*, January.

Godwin, William. 1798. *An Enquiry Concerning Political Justice and its Influence on Morals and Happiness*, 3rd. G.G. and J. Robinson (rep. F.E.L. Priestley, ed., 1946, Toronto: University of Toronto Press).

Hamby, Alonzo L. 1995. *Man of the People. A Life of Harry S. Truman*. New York: Oxford University Press.

Harris, Joseph P. 1951. The Senatorial Rejection of Leland Olds: A Case Study. *American Political Science Review*, September.

Hayek, F.A. 1945. The Use of Knowledge in Society. *American Economic Review*, September.

———. 1960. *The Constitution of Liberty*. Chicago: University of Chicago Press.

———. 1973, 1976,1979. *Law, Legislation, and Liberty*. Chicago: University of Chicago Press.

Henderson, Gerald C. 1924. *The Federal Trade Commission: A Study in Administrative Law and Procedures.* New Haven: Yale University. Press.
Hofstadter, Richard. 1949. *The American Political Tradition.* New York: Knopf.
Holmes, Oliver W., Jr. 1881. *The Common Law.* Boston: Little, Brown.
Hoogenboom, Ari and Olive. 1976. *A History of the ICC.* New York: Norton.
Hough, Charles M. 1917. Covert Legislation and the Constitution. *Harvard Law Rev*, 801–811.
Hummel, Jeffrey. 1978. The Jacksonians, Banking, and Economic Theory: A Reinterpretation. *Journal of Libertarian Studies* 2: 151–165.
Hyman, Sidney. 1976. *Marriner S. Eccles.* Stanford Graduate School of Business.
Isaacson, Walter, and Evan Thomas. 2012. *The Wise Men. Six Friends and the World They Made.* New York: Simon and Schuster.
Jaffe, Louis L. 1964. James Landis and the Administrative Process. *Harvard Law Review*, December.
Jefferson, Thomas. 1903–1907. *Writings*, ed. A.A. Lipscomb and A.E. Bergh. Washington, DC: Jefferson Memorial Foundation.
Jenkins, John A. 1978. The Revolving Door Between Government and the Law Firms, in Peters and Nelson. *Culture of Bureaucracy.*
Johnson, Paul. 1991. *The Birth of the Modern.* New York: Harper.
Karl, Barry D. 1987. The American Bureaucrat: A History of a Sheep in Wolves' Clothing. *Public Administration Review*, January–February.
Kirst, Michael W. 1969. *Government Without Passing Laws.* Chapel Hill: University of North Carolina Press.
Kolko, Gabriel. 1965. *Railroads and Regulation, 1877–1916.* Princeton: Princeton University Press.
Landis, James M. 1938. *The Administrative Process.* New Haven: Yale University Press.
———. 1960. Report on Regulatory Agencies to the President Elect, December.
Macey, Jonathan R. 2010. The Distorting Incentives Facing the U.S. Securities and Exchange Commission. *Harvard Journal of Law and Public Policy*, Spring.
Macey, Jonathan, and David D. Haddock. 1985. Shirking at the SEC: The Failure of the National Market System. *University of Illinois Law Review.*
Macmahon, Arthur W. 1943. Congressional Oversight of Administration. *Political Science Quarterly*, June.
McCraw, Thomas K. 1975. Regulation in America. A Review Article. *Business History Review*, Summer.
McGarity, Thomas O. 2012. Administrative Law as Blood Sport. *Duke Law Journal,* May.
Mendelsohn, Wallace. 1957. Mr. Justice Frankfurter on Administrative Law. *Journal of Politics*, August.
Moe, Terry M. 1997. The Positive Theory of Public Bureaucracy. In *Perspectives in Public Choice: A Handbook*, ed. D. Mueller. Cambridge: Cambridge University Press.

Neal, Phil C. 1953. The Clayton Act and the Transamerica Case. *Stanford Law Review*, February.
Niskanen, William A. 1971. *Bureaucracy and Representative Government*. New York: Aldine-Atherton.
Olson, Mancur, Jr. 1965. *The Logic of Collective Action*. Cambridge: Harvard University Press.
Page, Edward C. 1985. *Political Authority and Bureaucratic Power. A Comparative Analysis*. Nashville: University of Tennessee Press.
Peters, Charles, and Michael Nelson, eds. 1979. *The Culture of Bureaucracy*. New York: Holt, Rinehart and Winston.
Postell, Joseph. 2017. *Bureaucracy in America. The Administrative State's Challenge to Constitutional Government*. Columbia: University of Missouri Press.
Remini, Robert V. 1981. *Andrew Jackson. The Course of American Freedom, 1822–32*. New York: Harper & Row.
Ritchie, Donald A. 1980. Reforming the Regulatory Process: Why James Landis Changed his Mind. *Business History Review*, Autumn.
Root, Elihu. 1912. Judicial Decisions and Public Feeling: Presidential Address Before the New York State Bar Association. In *Addresses on Government and Citizenship*, ed. Robert Bacon and James Scott. Cambridge: Harvard University Press.
Schlesinger, Arthur M., Jr. 1945. *The Age of Jackson*. Boston: Little, Brown.
Schoenbrod, David. 1993. *Power without Responsibility. How Congress Abuses the People Through Delegation*. New Haven: Yale University Press.
Securities and Exchange Commission (SEC). Reports and Speeches. Washington, DC.
Seligman, Joel. 2003. *The Transformation of Wall Street. A History of the Securities and Exchange Commission and Modern Corporate Finance*. 3rd ed. New York: Wolters Kluwer.
Sharfman, I. Leo. 1931–37. *The Interstate Commerce Commission*. Vol. 4. New York: Commonwealth Fund.
Shlaes, Amity. 2007. *The Forgotten Man. A New History of the Great Depression*. New York: HarperCollins.
Smith, Adam. 1776. *An Enquiry into the Nature and Causes of the Wealth of Nations*. London: Strahan and Cadell. (Random House 1937).
Sowell, Thomas. 1987. *A Conflict of Visions*. New York: William Morrow.
Temin, Peter. 1969. *The Jacksonian Economy*. New York: Norton.
Tushnet, Mark. 2011. Administrative Law in the 1930s: The Supreme Court's Accommodation of Progressive Theory. *Duke Law Journal*, April.
U.S. House of Representatives. 1976. *Federal Regulation and Regulatory Reform*, Subcommittee on Oversight and Investigation, 94th Cong., 2nd sess.
———. 1979. *Progress Toward the Development of a National Market System*: Joint Hearings Before the Subcommittee on Oversight and Investigations and the Subcommittee on Consumer Protection and Finance, 96th Congress, 1st sess.

U.S. Senate. 1972. *Stock Exchange Commission Rates*, Hearings, Banking Subcommittee, 92nd Congress, 2nd sess.

———. 1973. *Securities Industry Study*, Report No. 865. 93rd Cong., 2nd sess.

Van Riper, Paul P. 1958. *History of the U.S. Civil Service*. Evanston: Row, Peterson.

Weber, Max. 1922. *Economy and Society*, trans. E. Fischoff, et al., ed. G. Roth and C. Wittich. London: Bedminister Press, 1968.

———. 1946. *Essays in Sociology*, ed. H. Gerth and C. Mills. New York: Oxford University Press.

———. 1947. *The Theory of Social and Economic Organization*, trans. by A.M. Henderson and T. Parsons. New York: Free Press of Glencoe.

Wildavsky, Aaron, and Jeffrey L. Pressman. 1979. *Implementation: How Great Expectations in Washington are Dashed in Oakland*. 3rd ed. Oakland: University of California Press.

Williamson, Oliver E. 1973. Markets and Hierarchies: Some Elementary Considerations. *American Economic Review*, May.

———. 1975. *Markets and Hierarchies*. New York: Macmillan.

Wilson, Woodrow. 1885. *Congressional Government*. Boston: Houghton, Mifflin. (with Introduction by Walter Lippman, World Publishing Co.).

———. 1887. The Study of Administration. *Political Science Quarterly*, June.

Wilson, James Q. 1976. The Rise of the Bureaucratic State. In *The American Commonwealth*, ed. Nathan Glazer and Irving Kristol. New York: Basic Books.

———. 1989. *Bureaucracy. What Government Agencies Do and Why They Do It*. New York: Basic Books.

Wood, John H., and Norma L. Wood. 1985. *Financial Markets*. San Diego: Harcourt Brace Jovanovich.

CHAPTER 4

The NYSE and the SEC

You gentlemen are making a great mistake.... The Exchange is a perfect institution.
—Richard Whitney to Ferdinand Pecora and John Flynn (Senate investigators), February 1934.

Exchanges have always administered their affairs in much the same manner as private clubs. For a business so vested with the public interest, this traditional method has become archaic.... It is essential no element of the casino be allowed to intrude and that all such elements be obliterated.
—SEC Chairman William O. Douglas, November 23, 1937.

The Securities and Exchange Commission is an agency established by the federal government in 1934 to interpret and enforce securities laws for the protection of investors; maintain fair, orderly, and efficient markets; and facilitate capital formation. This chapter describes the SEC's origins and early experiences, especially its relations with the New York Stock Exchange and its first full-time president, William McChesney Martin, Jr. Its impacts on the securities markets will be seen to depend especially on the knowledge and relative political strengths of reformers and private interests.

J. H. Wood, *Who Governs?*, Palgrave Studies in American Economic History, https://doi.org/10.1007/978-3-030-33083-5_4

The New York Stock Exchange

Membership, Traders, and Markets There were nearly three dozen securities exchanges in the country in 1934, but the Securities Exchange Act of that year was aimed principally at the New York Stock Exchange, known simply as "the Exchange." The New York Stock and Exchange Board had been organized nearly 150 years earlier outside 68 Wall Street under a buttonwood tree, when 24 brokers agreed to deal with each other on specified terms:

> We the Subscribers, Brokers for the Purchase and Sale of the Public Stock, do hereby solemnly promise and pledge ourselves to each other, that we will not buy or sell from this day for any person whatsoever, any kind of Public Stock, at a rate less than one quarter of one percent Commission on the Specie value and that we will give preference to each other in our Negotiations. In Testimony whereof we have set our hands this 17th day of May at New York, 1792.

Bids on securities were taken in order by the chairman in a "call market." The principal developments in organization and practice during the next 140 years were the increase in membership to a fixed 1375 that were bought and sold competitively and continuous trading through dealer/specialists of hundreds then thousands of listed securities. Listing required information about company assets, liabilities, earnings, voting rights, and other information "adequate for an investor to form his own opinion intelligently concerning the value of the securities," in the words of a student in the 1920s. Requirements were not much different from those later required by the securities acts (Meeker 1930, p. 96; Seligman 2003, pp. 46–47).

Listing was neither a guarantee against loss nor a recommendation by the Exchange. Unfortunate exceptions to this rule were the United States Liberty Bonds patriotically promoted by the Exchange at below-market interest rates during World War I (Meeker 1930, p. 96). Those redeeming their investments before maturity suffered further losses as interest rates rose after the war. More lost when Congress defaulted on its bond gold clauses in 1933 (Wood 2005, pp. 216–18). The federal government was among the most irresponsible securities issuers in the years before the securities acts, although that did not prevent it from condemning private borrowers.

Fig. 4.1 Daily trading volume on the NYSE, 1900–1970 (thousands of shares). (Source: Based on data from NYSE Factbooks)

The prices of seats, as memberships had been called since the days when members sat in regular places for the roll calls of securities to be traded, varied with their expected values, which depended on business (Fig. 4.1). Memberships fell from $600,000 at the height of the twenties bull market to $90,000 in 1932 and $10,000 in 1941. They did not recover 1920s values until the 1980s, but had reached $4 million in 2005, just before memberships were converted to shares (NYSE *Fact Books*). Members included approximately 300 specialists posting bid and ask prices, 170 floor traders who traded for their own accounts, and floor brokers and representatives of broker-dealer firms executing orders from the public.

The primary function of a stock exchange specialist/dealer is to *make markets*—that is, to be ready to buy and sell at stated bid and ask prices—in assigned securities. Considered beneficial to market liquidity, they acquire envied information in the course of their work, particularly knowledge of current and future supplies and demands as revealed by orders. Specialists also traded for their own accounts, but were not supposed to use their privileged information for their own benefit, and were expected to stabilize markets by trading against the tide.

The Exchange was proud of the quality of its market, particularly the small *spreads* between bid and asked prices as well as *price continuity* in the form of small differences between successive prices. Active trading in widely held issues meant ready transactions at smoothly changing prices.

Critics were not so sure, testifying to the Pecora committee that specialists were unnecessary and abused their privileges to the detriment of investors. The same was true of floor traders, Tommy Corcoran, New Deal advisor and an author of the Securities Acts, testified (U.S. Senate 1934, pp. 19–20; U.S. House 1934, p. 124):

> They take no chances. They take no position against the market. They simply follow the market the way sea birds follow a ship, following the trend and picking up what they can on the way. They sense the market and follow the pools, whether the market is long or short .... They serve no purpose, in the long run, to make the market any better for the investor on the outside, but rather because they are quick and on the inside, they help to accentuate the swings of pools. They are naturally pool operators.

The much-maligned pools were groups which manipulated prices, such as Joseph Kennedy and his associates who in 1933 bid up the price of Libby-Owens-Ford stock before jumping in masse and letting innocents take the fall, earning "Kennedy ... the distinction of leading the last legal pool in stock-market history" (Sobel 1975, pp. 19–20; Goodwin 1987, Ch 26).

Corcoran did not explain what made the markets the floor traders followed. We acquire some understanding of the differences between Corcoran's world and the Exchange when we realize the latter was in the business of making markets in return for commissions and spreads, whereas Corcoran thought buyers and sellers were sufficient. William McChesney Martin, Jr., whom we will meet shortly and was at the NYSE between 1931 and 1941, believed that markets came from private initiatives which ought to be encouraged. Corcoran overlooked the primary reason for the Exchange, which was to make markets, a service supplied in the hope of gains.

President of the Exchange between 1938 and 1941, Martin carried his education there to his later chairmanship of the Federal Reserve, where he tried to see that the Fed interfered with securities markets as little as possible. A Federal Reserve Board study committee which he had initiated painted a picture of a well-functioning market,

> which possesses *depth* when there are orders, either actual orders or orders that can be readily uncovered, both above and below the market. The market has *breadth* when these orders are in volume and come from widely

> divergent investor groups. It is *resilient* when new orders pour promptly into the market to take advantage of sharp and unexpected fluctuations in prices. (Federal Reserve Board 1952, p. 265)

Martin and his colleagues differed from the regulators in their belief that these market characteristics benefitted from the professional, profit-seeking, and sometimes speculative behavior of traders on the exchange.

Governance The Exchange's constitution limited its Governing Commission to members. The president was part-time, unsalaried, and rotating. (NYSE presidents and SEC chairmen are listed in Table 4.1.) The brokerage firms dealing with the public owned 52 percent of NYSE seats but occupied less than a third of the 40 places on the Governing Commission. Their influence was further limited by the requirement that only floor members could serve on the Governing Commission, giving rise to the "anomalous condition," the SEC observed, that only the "less influential partners of large firms … are eligible for participation in the administration of exchanges" (U.S. House of Representatives 1935).

The Governing Commission had an annual turnover of one-fourth, elected by Exchange members from a slate chosen by a five-member nominating committee. These procedures led to Exchange governance by a few in the manner, William Douglas said, of a private club. Governance and trading practices were about to become matters of negotiation between the traditional NYSE and the new SEC.

The Securities Exchange Act of 1934

President Roosevelt expressed a popular view when he wrote Senator Duncan Fletcher, chairman of the Banking and Currency Committee, that "unregulated speculation in securities [was] one of the most important contributing factors in the artificial and unwarranted 'boom' which had so much to do with the terrible conditions in the years following 1929." He believed stock exchanges had been part of the problem. The Democratic platform and the candidate had promised to address the problem. FDR wrote Fletcher that he wanted legislation to prevent "the use of the exchanges for purely speculative operations" by setting brokers' margin loan requirements "so high that speculation … will of necessity be drastically curtailed," prevent "insofar as possible manipulation of prices to the detriment of actual investors," and give "the government … definite

Table 4.1 The NYSE and SEC, 1930–51

NYSE presidents	*SEC chairmen*	*Events*
Richard Whitney 1930–35	Joseph Kennedy 7/34–9/35	Great Depression, Securities Act of 1933, Securities Exchange Act of 1934, SEC Kennedy was a businessman, politician, financier; head of the Maritime Commission and ambassador to the United Kingdom after leaving the SEC. Whitney came from a wealthy, banking background, was a model prisoner for three years at Sing Sing, and afterward lived a quiet life as a farmer and businessman.
Charles Gay 5/35–2/38	James Landis 9/35–9/37	May 1935, eight members (office partners of member firms) elected to NYSE Governing Committee, raising the number from 42 to 50. Dec. 1935, supervisory Committee on Customers' created. Landis was a Harvard law professor, head of government agencies, and advisor to presidents, including John F. Kennedy. Gay was a close associate and supporter of Whitney at the NYSE.
Wm. McC. Martin, Jr. 7/38–3/41	William Douglas 9/37–4/39 Jerome Frank 5/39–4/41	Martin came to NYSE in May 1931 as A.G. Edwards' floor broker; elected to NYSE Board of Governors 1935; member and secretary of Conway Committee, Dec. 1937 to Jan. 1938; U.S. Army, lend-lease, Export-Import Bank, Undersecretary of the Treasury, 1941–51; Chairman Board of Governors of the Federal Reserve System, 1951–70. Douglas went from Sterling Professor of Law at Yale to the SEC during the New Deal, succeeded Brandeis on the Supreme Court, where he became the longest-serving justice ever at 36 years. Frank was a practicing attorney and legal scholar before joining the New Deal; left in 1941 to become a judge until his death in 1951.
Emil Schram 1941–51	Edward Eicher 4/41–1/42	World War II; SEC moved to Philadelphia for duration of the war. Schram went from Indiana farm management to the National Drainage Association to the Reconstruction Finance Corporation in 1933 before succeeding Martin at the NYSE.
	Ganson Purcell 1/42–6/46	Former congressman Eicher served as interim head of SEC before leaving for a judgeship. Purcell served on the SEC from the beginning, was a protégé of Douglas, and left in 1946 under President Truman's displeasure.

powers of supervision over exchanges [so] that the government itself will be able to correct abuses which may arise in the future" (Roosevelt, March 26, 1934; Seligman 2003, p. 586).

In the meantime, the president found it necessary to defend the 1933 Act. In the summer of 1933, the Pecora hearings were in recess, the Morgan inquiry was past, Mitchell was found not guilty of tax evasion, and the Hundred Days were gone. Shouted down for weeks, Wall Street's opposition to the Securities Act began to be heard. Some had begun to worry as much about the Act's short-term impact on the recovery of an economy still in depression as about financial reform in the long term.

In August, corporate lawyer Arthur Dean wrote in *Fortune* that he expected the law to be "drastically amended at the next session" because of its complexity and severe civil liability sections, which were such "as to render financing exceedingly difficult, if not actually impossible." He feared the Act would "seriously retard economic recovery ... result in unemployment because corporations may be forced to make drastic economies and to suspend the payment of dividends in order to obtain necessary working capital," make it difficult for "new and speculative corporations [to obtain] long-term capital," increase the cost of selling securities for all corporations, and discourage underwriters from helping issue securities, thus forcing American corporations to go abroad for capital. He sympathized with the purposes of the law, but felt it was "hardly necessary to burn down the house to exterminate vermin."

Roosevelt denied that there would be significant changes in the 1933 Act, and pressed for an exchange bill with "teeth in it" (U.S. House 1934, p. 2). In February 1934, he sent a message to Congress formally recommending legislation to regulate the exchanges. At the same time, Fletcher and Congressman Rayburn jointly introduced a bill drawn up by Ben Cohen from a draft given to him by Pecora (U.S. Congress, *CR* 1934, pp. 2264–72, 2378). It proposed to segregate brokers and dealers and outlaw pools, wash sales, matched orders, and short sales.

A *wash sale*, often for tax purposes, is the sale of a security at a loss and purchase of the same or substantially identical security shortly before or after. An example of *matched orders* is the purchase and sale of the same security by an individual or group to give the impression of unusual trading activity in the security. A typical *short sale* involves selling a borrowed security with the expectation of buying it back at a lower price in the future; it is a bet on a price fall. A *broker* represents a buyer or a seller whereas a *dealer* buys and sells to maximize his returns; can the same person, as a broker, represent (try to get the best price for) a customer and at the same time, as a dealer, try to get the best price for himself?

Landis advised more leniency but Cohen agreed with Pecora that a reform bill should ask for more stringency than Congress was likely to enact in order to make room for compromise (*The New York Times* February 4, 1934; Landis 1959). They were in for a surprise when a *Times* headline announced a DRASTIC STOCK MARKET BILL (February 10, 1934). Securities exchanges were required to register with the Federal Trade Commission, which was empowered to overrule their regulations. In addition, the bill proscribed nine specific market manipulations, including wash sales, matched orders, or otherwise creating a "false and misleading appearance of active trading" in a security, or "disseminating false or misleading information to influence investors to buy or sell a security."[1]

Section 6 forbade brokers to lend investors margin credit more than 80 percent of the lowest price of a security during the preceding three years or 40 percent of current prices. The FTC could mandate more severe loan limits if "appropriate in the public interest or for the protection of investors." Giving the FTC the authority to set loan limits reflected New Dealers' doubts that the Federal Reserve was sufficiently independent of Wall Street.

Section 10 revolutionized the membership. Floor traders were to be abolished. "The only interest the public has in a stock exchange," Corcoran had written, "is that it should be a place where the outside public can buy and sell its stocks. There is no public interest to be served by giving an inside seat to a small group of men who are trading for their own account." Specialists were barred from trading for their own accounts, replaced by exchange officers who would perform the functions of specialists but not for their own accounts. Brokerage houses were prohibited from acting as dealers or underwriters. Lending to investors on margin was restricted. Virtually every avenue of profits was obstructed. "Rarely was a statutory proposal so well calculated to unite its opposition."

A feature of this bill, in common with previous federal legislation directed at markets, including the creation of the Federal Trade Commission,

[1] The Wash Sale Rule defines a *wash sale* as one in which an individual sells a security at a loss, and within 30 days before or after this sale, buys a substantially identical stock or security, or acquires a contract or option to do so. A *matched order* is an order placed with a broker to buy a specified stock at a price above the market price with the intention of immediately selling the stock through another broker at the same price to give the appearance of active trading in the stock.

was its naïve understanding of markets, which have to be made. Suppliers and demanders need market-makers, if not floor traders and specialists, then something else, which Corcoran and company had not proposed.

Exchange-listed firms were required to file registration statements like those required by the 1933 act for new securities, update them periodically, and hold corporate elections for stockholder empowerment. The last provision was a step toward federal regulation of corporate governance (Seligman 2003, pp. 85–87; U.S. House 1934, pp. 1–15, 94, 123–40).

The growing opposition included more than a few hundred specialists and floor brokers at the NYSE. Society's permanent anti-banker feeling had been aroused, but had peaked and was running into the interests dependent on existing financial practices. There was a difference between arousing feelings toward bankers in the abstract and actually interfering with credit. Much of the initial popular and press support of stock exchange legislation in general was evaporating before specifics.

The Exchange's Whitney launched a counter-attack four days after the Fletcher-Rayburn bill was introduced when he met with representatives of thirty brokerage firms. The next day he wrote every member of the exchange that the bill would "have very disastrous consequences to the stock market." A similar letter was sent to the presidents of corporations listed on the Exchange, emphasizing the "serious" effects the bill would have on their firms and their directors, officers, and shareholders.

The 46,000 New York City brokerage house employees were organized to protest the bill, and the city's brokerage firms communicated the message to their own and correspondent offices throughout the country. "Are your employees alive to the fact that with the passage of the bill, a great many of them will be out of employment." One firm took out ads in Washington papers accompanied by the Declaration of Independence to protest "the apparent 'New Deal' philosophy that engaging in a business for profit is unlawful."

Members of Congress were deluged with letters, telephone calls, and telegrams. "Day by day," presidential advisor Raymond Moley complained in the April issue of *Today*, "the ranks of the newspaper supporters of the bill have thinned." Roosevelt's successor as governor of New York, Herbert Lehman (former partner and son of a founder of the Lehman Brothers financial firm), wrote the president that the state was counting on $40 million in stock transaction taxes in 1934–35, and hoped the interests of the Exchange "will be given careful and sympathetic consideration" (Seligman 2003, p. 589; de Bedts 1964, p. 67). Pecora's hearings into alcohol stock manipulations surrounding Congress's vote to repeal prohibition the previous year, timed to coincide with the introduction of the bill to the committees, received little notice.

The opposition was also effective in the House and Senate hearings on the Fletcher-Rayburn bill in February and March. Whitney was impressive on the witness stand when he testified that the Exchange was not opposed to regulation, but the bill as it stood gave the FTC the power to "actually … supervise and manage all stock exchanges [and] establish indirectly a form of nationalization of business and industry which has hitherto been alien to the American theory of Federal Government." Even if the FTC exercised its powers with restraint, the stringent provisions in the bill would "destroy the free and open market for securities." The rigidity of the proposed margin requirements would reduce liquidity, and the rule barring specialists from trading for their own accounts would allow erratic fluctuations in stock prices heretofore prevented by specialists' purchasing and selling shares to ensure orderly price movements (U.S. Senate 1934, pp. 6582–85, 6625; U.S. House 1934, pp. 152–215).

Opposition to the bill was not limited to Wall Street. It was national, and included small exchanges and firms toward which the public was more sympathetic than to Wall Street. On five successive House hearing days, representatives of twenty-four local exchanges echoed Whitney's testimony. The Cincinnati Stock Exchange's W.D. Gradison feared the bill would "eliminate from existence" most regional exchanges, which the San Francisco Stock Exchange's president said would make "the cost of capital to small firms … almost prohibitive." Several complained that the bill so focused on the NYSE that it failed to consider that the smaller exchanges could not afford the segregation of brokers and dealers and its other attacks on profits.

The case against the bill was further strengthened by the private circulation of rules of fair practice and expressions of willingness to accept regulation in the form of a stock exchange coordinating authority with private as well as public representation. This included Dean Witter appearing on behalf of 204 Pacific coast dealers, the United States Chamber of Commerce, the National Association of Manufacturers, the Investment Bankers Association, the usually politically liberal investment banking firm of Lehman Brothers, and several more investment houses. The president's cousin Archibald Roosevelt stated on behalf of the New York City Municipal Bond Dealers Committee that "if the bill goes through as it is, we will be put out of business" (*Newsweek* March 17, 1934; Seligman 2003, p. 88).

A blow came in the defection of the large and formerly cooperative broker E.A. Pierce & Co. (to become through merger in 1940 part of Merrill Lynch, Pierce, Fenner & Beane), which closed ranks with Whitney, terming the bill "destruction" and testifying that the margin provisions alone would result in forced liquidations of several hundred million dollars' worth of stock (U.S. House 1934, pp. 312–15; Seligman 2003, p. 92). Support from within the administration also wavered. Assistant Secretary of Commerce John Dickinson opposed the removal of control over credit for stock margin loans from the Federal Reserve (U.S. House 1934, pp. 508–11, 543; Seligman 2003, p. 92).

The bill's future darkened when on March 5, the Senate majority leader announced: "As to whether the Stock Exchange Regulation Bill may be ready for disposition during this session of Congress, no assurance can be given." It was resuscitated two days later, however, by a White House announcement that the president expected a bill in the current session. After meeting with Roosevelt, the senator revised his earlier statement by saying "the bill would be simplified as much as practicable (*The New York Times*, March 6, 9, 1934; Seligman 2003, p. 93)."

Faced with the possibility of his first major legislative defeat, Roosevelt assumed direction of the bill with the assistance of Landis in place of the less compromising Pecora. Landis, Cohen, and Corcoran met with the Treasury and the Federal Reserve Board, which had opposed the bill. Margin requirements were returned to the Fed, and the new regulations were put off until 1939. Ten versions of the bill were drafted between March 4 and March 19. Section 10 was revised to allow members of regional exchanges to act as both brokers and dealers, but directing the FTC "to make a study of the feasibility ... of the complete divorcement of the functions." State banks, denied the power to lend money to brokers for margin in the original draft, were now given that power "in localities where there are no [Federal Reserve] member banks or to meet emergency needs." The Treasury and the Federal Reserve, after all, are essentially partners with Wall Street in the efficient functioning of securities markets.

Roosevelt also accepted amendments to the 1933 Securities Act which limited recoverable damages to those resulting from misrepresentations or omissions in registration statements, limit underwriters' liability to the extent of participation in a securities issue, allow courts to assess full costs against unmeritorious claims, and shorten the Act's statute of limitations. He was willing to make every significant change sought by critics except buyers' proof of reliance on the registration statement. Roosevelt and

Landis met with leading investment bankers to consider revisions. Many of them and their successors later served in Roosevelt's and subsequent administrations, including Winthrop Aldrich (Chase National Bank, war relief, ambassador to the UK) Robert Lovett (Brown Brothers Harriman, assistant secretary of war, secretary of defense), and Averill Harriman (Brown Brothers Harriman, lend-lease, ambassador to the USSR) (Parrish 1970, pp. 195–97; Seligman 2003, p. 94).

It is ironic that the Federal Reserve, whose fluctuating monetary policies had been the overriding cause of the Great Depression, and had failed as a bank regulator during a period (1920–33) in which bank suspensions reduced their number from 30,000 to 13,000, carried so much political weight and was able to expand its powers—an experience repeated the next century. After the Fed's easy money had fed the housing boom, and its clamp-down and interferences with market adjustments worsened the downturn, the Dodd-Frank Act of 2009 expanded its powers, including the creation of rules for compliance with real estate appraisal standards, developing alternatives to credit ratings, creating procedures for securities holding company registrations, fashioning new reporting requirements for S&L holding companies, and regulating escrow account requirements. The Fed chairman now sits on the Financial Stability Oversight Council created by Dodd-Frank, which makes the Fed partly responsible for identifying firms that pose a threat to U.S. financial stability and for developing rules and regulations for them. The Fed now supervises living wills and stress tests for these "systemically important financial institutions" (Michel 2014).

The revised Fletcher-Rayburn bill was introduced into the House on March 19, and for the first time Roosevelt came out publicly for the bill. He worried that "a more definite and more highly organized drive is being made against effective [stock exchange] legislation … than against any similar recommendation made by me during the past year. … I do not see how any of us could afford to have [the bill] weakened in any shape, manner, or form" (U.S. Senate 1934, pp. 7577–78).

The opposition was unmoved. Whitney and the regional exchanges indicated that they could support the bill only if it was altered to create a new federal stock exchange commission in place of the FTC's enforcement of the act, grant the Federal Reserve discretion in setting margins, and leave specialists, floor traders, and corporate elections alone (Roosevelt 1934). These changes were made, and in addition, the Federal Reserve Board's discretion to alter margin requirements was increased and the provision barring insiders' stock purchases and sales at a profit within six months was dropped. The House passed the revised bill, with Landis's amendments to the 1933 act, on May 4, followed by the Senate on May 12. (Seligman 2003, pp. 97–9; Parrish 1970, pp. 137–36).

It "was a marvel of irresolution," Professor Joel Seligman wrote. "On most controversial substantive issues, Congress had been stalemated. Rather than providing the new commission with clear mandates, the legislators had granted the agency authority to study conflicts and approve or issue rules ... in the public interest or for the protection of investors." Whether Roosevelt got an act "with teeth in it" would depend on the new commission, which would in turn depend on the support of Congress and the executive, and the cooperation of the securities industry, especially the NYSE. "The political processes that produced the jerry-built statute were allowed to continue" (Seligman 2003, pp. 99–100).

Forced to defend the watered-down bill, an angry Rayburn complained of "the most vicious and persistent lobby that any of us have ever known in Washington." He condemned opposition letters as coerced or forgeries (CR, April 30, 1934, pp. 7693–96, and May 4, 1934, p. 8116).

One of the reasons for the substitution of the SEC for the FTC was Exchange and business dislike of the latter, which had been an ally of the New Deal. Also, attempts to influence it required competition with multiple FTC constituencies. An agency like the SEC which focused on the securities industry might be more amenable to Wall Street. In the event, Roosevelt appointed the FTC's most progressive member, Landis, to the SEC, along with the Wall Street veteran, Joseph Kennedy, as chairman (Khademian 1992, p. 34; Phillips and Zecher 1981).

The Securities and Exchange Commission

The SEC was (and is) headed by five commissioners appointed by the president to staggered five-year terms, no more than three belonging to any political party. The president also chooses the chairman. The breadth of the SEC's jurisdiction combined with the vagueness of its powers required all—more than all—the talents and energies of its commissioners. Looking back after a half century, Seligman wrote (2003, p. 416):

> By requiring the same agency to regulate public utility holding companies, the investment company industry [added after 1934], all national securities markets, all interstate broker-dealers, as well as corporate disclosure, corporate governance, accounting and trust indenture requirements for [business firms], Congress created an extraordinarily broad mandate that all but ensured that significant portions of it would be largely ignored.

The SEC's competence, interests, and budget have compelled it to focus narrowly on company reporting in line with the law, to the neglect of economics and accounting principles. They are proud of their standing as the second-best legal staff in Washington, but regulatory costs, as opposed to "fairness," have been disregarded. Even the narrow and fairly well-defined program for the reform of stock-exchange trading has made little headway.

This was not a problem at the beginning because the task of the first commission, as the president and the chairman saw it, was political—to persuade the securities industry to accept the law as an aid to investor confidence rather than to resist it as a costly impediment. Many were surprised by the appointment of securities manipulator and Democratic fundraiser Joseph Kennedy (1934–35) as the first SEC chairman—a fox to guard the henhouse—but its purpose was to secure the cooperation of business and end the "capital strike." Instead of pressing for trading reforms, Kennedy and his assistants "packed their suitcases like travelling salesmen" to meet with investment bankers and corporate counsels to persuade them of the convenience and advantages of the new system (Seligman 2003, p. 115).

Nor did his successor push for change. The Landis (1935–37) commission preferred not to use its rule-making authority unless the probable effects were understood. It was devoted rather to study, and took the Exchange's side against reformers on issues such as the segregation of broker and dealer functions and the trading of unlisted securities, pending further study.

The Man Who Got Things Done

> Under Joe [Kennedy] the gains made toward protecting the rights of investors through President Roosevelt's legislative program were consolidated. Under Jim [Landis] we were taught how to get things done. And we're now going to go ahead and get them done. (William O. Douglas, press conference, Sept. 22, 1937.)

The pace picked up with the elevation of Commissioner William O. Douglas to the chairmanship. Douglas had taken leave from his position as a Yale law professor to join the New Deal in July 1934, as an investigator for the SEC, was appointed a commissioner in January 1936, and became the SEC's third chairman in September 1937 (until April 1939). He was young (born in 1898), energetic, ideological, ambitious, and hostile to business and "the goddamn bankers." He was to become, at age 40, the youngest (and longest serving, 1939–75) U.S. Supreme Court justice. Douglas was known for his advocacy of individual (especially first amendment) rights and the idiosyncrasies of his decisions. He tended not to cite legal texts nor did he value judicial consistency. It is ironic that he headed the agency of which his principal opponent on the Court, Felix Frankfurter, had been a founder. Justice Frankfurter, who favored judicial restraint, was often at odds with "Wild Bill" and his unsystematic views (Tomlins 2005, pp. 475–76; Murphy 2003, pp. 106–107).

Tired of waiting for the NYSE to reform itself according to guidelines suggested by the SEC in 1935, the new chairman threw down the gauntlet. The principle of self-regulation was not working. Negotiations had broken down and the NYSE had complained of over-regulation in its *Annual Report*. It had better move or the SEC would make it move by issuing the necessary regulations, Douglas warned. He called on the Exchange to reform itself in almost all aspects of its organization and functions. In the past, he claimed, the NYSE had served the needs and desires of its members, especially the specialists and private traders; it was, in effect, a "private club." Now it would have to serve the investors instead, and this would require changes. Private traders should be eliminated, specialists should be obliged to meet new and stringent standards of behavior, and the entire "NYSE administration itself should be scrapped, for it had always reflected the will of powerful specialists and investment bankers." There "should be a new administration, with a paid president and staff, independent of the floor, with power over it. The president should be selected by a board, which would include public as well as private members – government officials, educators, and recognized men of character." Their "first order of business … would be to put bans on short selling and trading on margin, since both encouraged gambling, and so were not what Douglas considered in the public interest. [O]dd-lot dealers – houses that specialized in serving individuals who traded in less than 100 share units – were badly in need of regulation, and perhaps had always worked to cheat small investors" (*The New York Times*, November 24, 1937; Sobel 1975, pp. 31–32).

Douglas believed the SEC might overcome the New Deal's loss of momentum. Roosevelt was in the process of taking his greatest political defeat in the court-packing case and Congress was growing more conservative (Patterson 1967). The president suffered embarrassing defeats in campaigns against conservative Democrat senators in 1938, what would become a severe recession had begun in May 1937, and war drums were beating in Europe and Asia. Douglas could count on little support from the otherwise engaged administration or Congress, and finance, whose profits were still low, had regrouped.

Also operating against regulation, and would continue to do so after the establishment of the Securities and Exchange Commission, was the fragile situation of the financial industry. "Grass was growing on Wall Street," it was said, as business continued to decline. Leading members of the Exchange, supported by banker Winthrop Aldrich, blamed the 1937 stock collapse on SEC regulations that had impaired the efficiency of the stock market, rendering it able to absorb "a greatly reduced volume of sales only with very serious breaks in prices" (*New York Times*, October 15, 1937; Seligman 2003, p. 159). In fact, the 1930s were the most volatile decade in the Exchange's history (Fig. 4.3), sometimes attributed to the policy shocks of the New Deal.

Douglas's goals were nevertheless ambitious, most important, changing the Exchange from a competitive marketplace of profit-seeking traders to a government-operated collection of order-takers. The pro-regulators' response to criticisms was that the best way to restore its business was to improve confidence in the Exchange.

"Douglas's chairmanship of the SEC was to prove one of the few bright spots in the New Deal's waning years," Seligman wrote. His assistant Abe Fortas (also a future Supreme Court justice) said that Douglas's greatest achievement as chairman was to change business attitudes toward the SEC. "Douglas was primarily responsible for completing the acceptance of public responsibility by financial institutions, for persuading a reluctant Wall Street that it was an appropriate subject for legal mandates." "He set and enforced standards for Wall Street which ushered the financial community into a new age of social responsibility." He "domesticated" Wall Street, it was enthusiastically claimed, although even domestic creatures often get their way. With Martin's help, Wall Street learned to play the new game to its own advantage (Seligman 2003, p. 159; Fortas 1975).

It is true that Douglas managed several changes in the NYSE's governance during his chairmanship, but neither those nor his public attacks on them had much effect on practices. It seems that changes in the Exchange's governance left unaltered its views of the best (most profitable) trading methods. Why should it? It was still an institution of profit-seekers. The Exchange yielded to the SEC on (what turned out to be) cosmetic (organizational) issues while holding firm on those that mattered to profits. We will see how much Wall Street gave up, how much Douglas actually got done.

Douglas, Conway, and Whitney Whitney's reaction to the SEC's program provoked a breach in the NYSE's position. The commission-house trade association endorsed the SEC, Whitney backed down, and the Exchange's governing board added eight brokerage-house partners. Whitney chose not to run for the presidency, although associate and close friend, Charles Gay, took his place and the Old Guard continued its dominance.

FDR made concessions, including naming an NYSE member to the SEC, and Douglas's threat to alter trading rules directly unless the NYSE was reorganized along democratic lines and the internal split in the organization further produced conciliation on the Exchange. Gay promised, "in the friendliest spirit, and in the firm belief that cooperation between the Exchange and the Commission is essential," to appoint a committee "to study this whole matter," although it turned out to be limited to the "organization and administration of the Exchange." The membership of the Conway Committee (chaired by Carle Conway, chairman of the board of Continental Can) was announced on December 10, 1937, and it reported on January 27, 1938.

As an indication of the kind of rules that would be imposed if the committee did not recommend substantial reorganization, the SEC required that short sales be limited to a price above the last price—"on an uptick," which has continued despite continuous protests by the financial industry and the lack of evidence of adverse effects (Macey et al. 1989). The Committee's report was a nearly complete adoption of the SEC's earlier recommendations, including a full-time paid president and a Board of Governors with outside members, and limitations on floor traders and specialists so that the governing majority would be commission-house brokers. Douglas and the SEC deferred their rule-making authority in favor of their preferred governance, presumably in the belief that this would be the easiest or most effective path to operating changes in the public interest. Self-regulation held out hopes for peace with effectiveness, although only the former was (partially) achieved.

Then the Whitney scandal broke. In March 1938, Richard Whitney and Co. announced its bankruptcy, and it was found that to offset his failed investments, Whitney had embezzled securities belonging to the NYSE Gratuity Fund, of which he was custodian, $105,000 from a trust fund established by his late father-in-law, and $153,200 from the New York Yacht Club, of which he was treasurer. He pleaded guilty to indictments of grand larceny by the New York County district attorney and the New York State attorney-general.

"It was as if the floor had dropped out from under Wall Street." The unmasking of its personification cast a "sense of gloom ... in the faces of the people I was meeting," an SEC lawyer said. "They knew Douglas was preparing to buck, and they knew now that he was going to be successful" (Seligman 2003, p. 168). "They have delivered themselves into my hands," Douglas said. "Not Dick Whitney! Not Dick Whitney!" the president, close to tears, said of his friend and fellow Groton graduate when Douglas told him the news (Douglas 1974, pp. 289–90).

The story darkened further when it became known that Whitney's problems had been known or suspected by many on the Street, including his brother and other J.P. Morgan partners. The SEC conducted hearings for fourteen days between April and June 1938, with most of its attention on the knowledge or complicity of Exchange members. "He was broke and borrowing all over the street," but none of the fifty-two witnesses admitted to suspicions of misconduct, even though fellow trustees were aware of missing funds. No one reported these possibilities of embezzlement to responsible authorities, nor, Jack Morgan volunteered, would he have done so even had he known.

For the press, "The end of Richard Whitney was the end of the Old Guard also." Even so, "Douglas's campaign against the Old Guard continued for the balance of his term as chairman." The U.S. Justice Department ignored the SEC's request that it investigate those suspected of helping Whitney conceal his activities. I don't know why they "cast our reports into the dustbin," Douglas lamented: "Somewhere in the background was a powerful figure with money and political connections" (Alsop and Kintner 1938; Seligman 2003, p. 171; Douglas 1974, pp. 302–303).

Douglas persuaded the SEC to remind the Exchange Board of Governors of its power "to suspend any member adjudged guilty of any act ... detrimental to the interest or welfare of the Exchange." Douglas's friend and mentor at the Yale Law School, and now president of the University of Chicago and one of the reformed Board's public members, Robert Hutchins, moved that it hold a public hearing into the conduct of three members whose testimony during the Whitney hearings he found "incredible." He was voted down 27–1, and promptly resigned (Seligman 2003, p. 172).

Most of the Board felt "the actions of these persons were really in the interest of the Exchange rather than detrimental to it and, in fact, that it would have been much more to the interest of the Exchange if the persons involved had been more successful in their attempts at secrecy and the whole matter had been kept from the public and quietly hushed up." Douglas exploded at the "Whitney white-wash," and prepared a statement which accused the Exchange of being unwilling to police itself, considered reopening the Whitney hearings, and proposed new legislation to prevent the repetition of such a white-wash. However, such a statement would have discredited the governance which the SEC had promoted, and instead it issued a brief reassurance that "the action on the Whitney case has not caused a change in the cooperative program which we launched," although "the problem of better coordination and allocation of the policing and disciplinary functions between the Exchange and the Commission" might be "constructively explored" (Seligman 2003, p. 173).

William McChesney Martin, Jr.

Douglas used the Whitney scandal to take a more active role in choosing the Exchange's first full-time president. The SEC had issued a press release that it neither sponsored anyone nor claimed the right of approval of the president, but on March 19, Douglas announced that the Commission looked with disfavor on "the retention in the government of the Exchange ... representatives of the group which was formerly in control." A revival of confidence in the stock market was needed, and the new Board's search committee indicated that they wanted a symbol of the probity that Judge Kenesaw Mountain Landis had brought to baseball after the 1919 "Black Sox" scandal (Seligman 2003, p. 174).

They found a good fit in 31-year-old William McChesney Martin, Jr., Yale graduate and floor broker for the respected St. Louis firm A.G. Edwards & Sons since 1931. Untarnished by the shady dealings of the 1920s, active participant in the reform movement, and a representative of out-of-town members, Martin could not be cleaner or less Old Guard, and his moderation and hard work had earned him the trust of both sides. Gay had named him to the Conway Committee, where he acted as secretary and wrote much of the Report. He was named interim president, and in July 1938, became the first full-time president of the Exchange (*New York Times*, April 12, 1938; May 14; July 1; Sobel 1975, p. 55; *Fortune*,

Aug. 1938; *Time*, Aug. 15, 1938; Flynn 1938, pp. 11, 41–42; *Business Week*, July 9, 1938).

During the search, after a meeting with Exchange representatives, Douglas threw an arm over Martin's shoulders and exclaimed, "Here's a fellow I can really work with," a sentiment corroborated by the new Exchange president's statement: "The days of the Exchange as a private business are past." It "is a public service institution [that] will be operated as a public business." "I suggest that, for any who fear too much government intervention, the correction lies in themselves and their own deeds." To avoid the SEC's imposition of rules, the Exchange would have to "demonstrate by action [that] it would be unnecessary for government to interfere," Martin said (Seligman 2003, p. 175).

Martin was a publicist's dream. He did not smoke, drink, or gamble, even on stocks, and the article which accompanied his picture on *Time*'s 8/15/38 cover was entitled *Mr. Chocolate* after his penchant for hot chocolate following his regular attendance at Broadway musicals, in the cheap seats, of course, before finishing the day by calling his father in St. Louis.

> He startled the Exchange first by leaving the door of his tawny-paneled office open to anyone who wanted to see him—a change from the days when Richard Whitney sat there in regal isolation. He irked crusty conservatives by letting photographers attend his first board meeting and also take pictures on the floor during trading hours. But chiefly he astonishes his broker associates by eating at the Automat, living at the Yale Club, spurning an automobile as too expensive, preferring to study or sit in a theatre balcony to splurging at some swank Long Island resort.

He was 100 percent in agreement with Douglas's desires to establish: (1) a depository for customers' funds now kept helter-skelter in brokerage houses; (2) a trial segregation of broker-dealer functions; (3) an assumption by the Exchange of full policing duties so the SEC will not have to patrol Wall Street; (4) plans for increasing the volume of bond trading on the floor; and (5) a possible rearrangement of commissions.

"He has pressed steadily along the line he announced when he took office," it was noted: "Our duty is plain. We must do everything in our power to provide as safe and as efficient a market for the nation's securities as can be devised." He ended a sixty-year-old relation with the Exchange's lawyers because they were too closely identified in the public mind with Richard Whitney's resistance to reform. "He jammed through the SEC's short-selling rule. He inaugurated a series of round-table talks with the SEC to affirm publicly the partnership between himself and Douglas."

"Whether Martin can continue to deliver the goods, he himself is the last to say. There still remains a large body of opposition. But by this time even the dullest floor trader must realize that even if Bill Martin cannot complete the job, Bill Douglas can," *Time* concluded.

Fine words, but what did they mean? Martin as president wanted the NYSE and SEC to get along in the public interest, but how and when, if at all, does that interfere with private interests? We have seen Douglas's skepticism of the profit system. The increasingly difficult Douglas-Martin relation might be understood if we explore the economic views of the latter.

Martin was born in St. Louis in 1906. His lawyer/banker father helped found the Federal Reserve System, and was the first chairman of the Board of Directors and Federal Reserve Agent of the Federal Reserve Bank of St. Louis, serving as its president 1929–41. Junior remembered trips with his father and local bankers down dusty, rutted roads to farms, where "he saw his father sweating in the blistering sun and often overheard him talking earnestly about the importance of studying new agricultural techniques and expressing his concern about excessive borrowing by overly optimistic farmers"—particularly during the farm depression following the wartime boom that left many deeply in debt. Such experiences were also part of family history. The assets of his grandfather's firm, the McChesney & Martin Grain Company of Lexington, Kentucky, had been auctioned as partial payment of debt left from the panic of 1893, after they had borrowed heavily to finance inventory during the preceding boom.

Martin majored in English at Yale, but also took courses in economics, and after moving to New York, studied for a year or so for a Ph.D. in finance at Columbia. He helped organize an economic seminar and a journal, *Economic Forum*, at the New School for Social Research. He had worked after college as a bank examiner for the Federal Reserve Bank of St. Louis, where he learned more about bank risks, and in November 1928, joined the St. Louis brokerage firm, A. G. Edwards & Sons. Its managing director, Martin's uncle, Albert N. Edwards, encouraged him: "It's not a very complicated business and you can find out whether you like it." Martin got off to a good start, initiating a one-man research department, but within a year, although its own losses were manageable, Edwards' staff was working night and day on the fall-out of the crash.

Sent East as Edwards' representative on the NYSE, Martin saw more suffering caused by the crash and the Great Depression. The catastrophe affected different people differently, not uncommonly affirming conservative views, especially among bankers steeped in the virtues of individual prudence and institutional stability, as well as the inevitability of busts after booms, especially those produced by easy money (Bremner 2004, pp. 7–21).

We will see evidence of such a model during Martin's time at the Federal Reserve, where his speeches and policy statements indicated belief in the efficacy of free markets. No particular view of economic policy comes out of the *Economic Forum*, which was written by economists from across the policy spectrum although the frontispiece of the last volume of the first year (Fall 1933) presents a view similar to Martin's statements and actions as president of the NYSE.

> With this issue the *Economic Forum* completes its first year. The year is best symbolized as having ushered in the New Deal. In the main, the New Deal objectives are brilliantly conceived, but in translating them into action the original version became blurred. [I]t has become enervating and stifling with its heavy yoke of static regulations unrelieved by counter-balancing levitating effects.

The paper by co-editor Joseph Mead in the same issue, "Amend the Securities Act!" called it "too hasty," "too repetitive," and "representative of thought which is out of sympathy with American competitive and democratic principles. It may destroy what it should merely regulate. Every fair-minded person is in sympathy with the president's statement to Congress that every issue of securities should be accompanied by full publicity" to ensure honest dealing. However, the sections of the Act that entitle investors to sue directors, brokers, and others (who bear the burden of proof) for absent or incorrect information threaten to discourage markets.

Martin expressed his views of some of the effects of government actions in an "Address on unemployment" to a University of Chicago seminar (1935a). "I would like to open the meeting with the assertion that the Roosevelt administration has so far made no material indentation in the ranks of the unemployed, and on the basis on which it is proceeding, can never hope to make any material progress.... Unemployment arises," he said, "because while the supply of labor grows more or less steadily, the demand for labor, [while also] growing, varies incessantly as to its character, volume, and distribution. These variations are due very largely to trade fluctuations and" changes in the direction of production.

He rejected the socialist criticism of existing institutions, as well as the possibility of guaranteed work. Rather, "the practical answer ... must take the form of reducing the pain of unemployment to relative insignificance." He recommended labor exchanges to help match workers with shifting jobs and "making the supply of labor capable of waiting for the demand" by an insurance program. "It is perfectly obvious that the average man or woman cannot through saving average his or her income over their life time through any other means than insurance," meaning unemployment insurance into which he had paid. Martin showed a sophisticated appreciation of what was later called permanent income, with government help to overcome inadequacies in the private capital market. He thought the new Social Security System might be altered along these lines, although he warned of the effects of government relief on effort. We are "breaking down the competitive system ... we are no longer attempting to reward people according to merit."

Martin's views were common before Keynes—an efficient free-market system tending toward full employment, which might be helped by a little, with an emphasis on "little," government help in overcoming frictions. Many views were changed by the Great Depression and Keynes's *General Theory*, in which downturns might be long and without tendencies to recover. Martin would have to deal with these views as chairman of the Fed, but he remained a classical economist increasingly surrounded by Keynesians.

His sympathies with unregulated competition extended to finance, and he shared with other members of the Exchange a strong belief in the social benefits along with the private advantages of its long-standing practices which Douglas and the SEC thought, and still think, were fit only for a private club of gamblers. Price declines are unpopular, but if a change in information suggests a fall in a stock's value, efficiency benefits from practices which facilitate the fall. This includes short sales, about which controversy is still active.

On September 19, 2008, the SEC issued a temporary ban on short sales of 799 financial stocks. A poll of corporate executives found that 75 percent approved, and a professor of corporate law said it was "kind of a time-out." "In a time of crisis, the dangers of doing too little are far greater than the dangers of doing too much." In fact, the ban "failed to slow the decline," which ended after the two-week ban was lifted. "Similarly, following the downgrade of the U.S. sovereign credit rating in 2011 – another notable period of market stress – stocks subject to short-selling restrictions performed worse than stocks free of such restraints" (Battalio et al. 2012; Beber and Pagano 2013).

Martin's own position had been presented in a 1932 paper entitled "The present agitation over short selling." "To the careful student of finance," he began, "the recent agitation against short selling appears only as discouraging evidence that economic education remains decidedly limited. The bursting of every speculative bubble in recent history has produced similar stories, and is a sad commentary on human nature that mankind seldom admits guilt and through rationalization always discovers a scapegoat," such as the "much publicized activities of the New York Stock Exchange."

This is in the spirit of Adam Smith's comparison of popular criticisms of grain speculations "to the popular terrors and suspicions of witchcraft. The unfortunate wretches accused of this latter crime were not more innocent of the misfortunes imputed to them, than those who have been accused of changing grain prices" (1776, p. 500).

"The Stock Exchange is a visible reflection of" the factory and the farm, "not they a reflection of its energy," Martin said. "High wages do not produce prosperity, as President Hoover has endeavored to make us believe; on the other hand, prosperity is the only thing that can make for high wages. And similarly, it is putting the cart before the horse to talk about higher stock prices leading to good business."

"Neither the bull nor the bear can alter basic values over a period of time.... [S]peculators are followers, not leaders, who attempt to sense the direction of markets." They sometimes assist market adjustments, and sometimes interfere with them, but their importance is exaggerated. "If we were to destroy all the instruments that can occasionally be misused, there would be little of the machine age remaining."

Instead of wasting "our energies attacking ghosts such as short sellers," we should face squarely the fundamental causes of economic volatility and the associated "human misery" (referring to the Federal Reserve's monetary policy), namely the "excessive and unwarranted grants of credit. [W]hen we are able to devise a means of controlling credit within reasonable limits we will not worry about such straw men as short sellers and will have a sounder prosperity than before."

Martin suggested in a talk on "Government and business, friends or enemies?" (1935b) that government supervision is sometimes necessary to the protection of business and the public. An example is the SEC, with which the NYSE wishes to cooperate "fully for the protection of the public. Its function, however, is supervising and not operating, and it is asking too much of human nature to think that man can draw such an instrument as the Securities Exchange Act … in a way that is perfect." The SEC should therefore go slow, be a friend, allow the brokerage business time "to catch its breath" and study the possibility of improvements.

Martin and his colleagues also tried to persuade the SEC not to interfere with Exchange specialists, who were obliged to pursue a "course of dealings reasonably calculated to contribute to the maintenance of price stability and to the minimizing of the effects of temporary disparity between supply and demand, immediate or reasonably to be anticipated." Specialists had been criticized by an SEC study for not always trading against market movements, but an NYSE study pointed out that "In the process of adjusting inventory to changing market conditions, the specialists properly may buy in rising markets and sell in declining ones. Such purchases may, for example, be designed to acquire inventory for … resale at anticipated higher levels".

A conservative must be careful in a world of reform. Avoid name-calling, Martin, Sr. advised his son in March 1940 (St. Louis Fed archives). "It seems to me that you are safe in following the general line of your public utterances about the SEC; in other words, it should be administered for the nourishment, protection, and sustenance of not only the public but of business in general, for unless business prospers the public will not prosper. Regulation within bounds is not wholly undesirable, but … must be constructive and cooperative or regulations will fail of their purpose. A regulation is a general statement of a rule of conduct, but it is not control, and when it becomes control it ceases to be regulation and becomes management." The SEC "should be courteous enough to give the Exchange credit for honestly endeavoring to make a public market in which the public is sure of fair treatment in the exercise of its judgment. As you have stated, neither Government nor the Exchange can … keep a man from suffering from wrong judgment. The minute it holds itself out as doing such a thing it is deceiving the public; in other words, the SEC can be a help so long as it stays on its side of the line." Do not get "sucked in" by any political group, especially in a year of national politics. Do not say "anything that could be construed as asking help from" any political person or group. Martin had gone public in a radio speech protesting the temper of the SEC and its efforts at control by indirection.

Remaining on Douglas's agenda were the elements making the NYSE a casino for which he could see no public purpose. The Exchange properly understood, he believed, was a public utility whose *raison d'etre* was public service. It ought to consist of brokers executing orders for the public.

Dealers (market-makers) were suspect because they were too interested in profit. It was not a place for the production of information because that was taken care of by legislated reporting requirements. The idea that the competitive price system is itself an information machine was foreign to his thinking.

Douglas wanted the elimination or restriction of floor traders, as well as separation of the broker and dealer functions. How could a dealer be a broker without conflict of interest? He was not persuaded by arguments of floor traders' and specialists' contributions to price formation and liquidity. He also wanted the separation of broker and customer accounts in the form of an independent trust corporation. Martin had agreed that a central depository was desirable, and in what was to become his standard procedure, formed a well-publicized study group.

The SEC contended that extensive studies lay behind its recommendations, but though authorized by the 1934 Act to promulgate rules, it did not wish to push too rapidly or unilaterally. It hoped and expected the Exchange to apply them, using a later term, "with all deliberate speed." Douglas relied on self-regulation, with the Commission issuing directions only if the Exchange failed to act.

Douglas had gotten pretty much what he wanted in the way of the NYSE's organization and hoped for action by the reformed Board. However, the new representation proved as conservative as the old, and even the composition of the Board of Governors was reverting to its former dominance by floor members. Whatever the reasons for the Exchange's practices, whether they lay in its interests or custom, they were turning out to be insensitive to organization.

Highly publicized round-table conferences gave the SEC and NYSE "another opportunity to display their new friendship, and they posed for pictures showing them smiling at one another, shaking hands, and engaging in thoughtful conversation." "The day of the crackdown is over," Douglas said. "The honeymoon is over," Martin told reporters. "Now I'll have to produce."

More meaningful to those looking for real change was the 15-point agenda for reform announced by Martin on October 31. The points were primarily concerned with the supervision and integrity of Exchange members through audits, reports, and studies of various kinds. Douglas called it a good beginning, and it was well received by the press, but Martin appeared to believe it was also the end. It was not a plan for action. Most of it had already been approved by the Governing Council, although member firms indicated resistance to even modest changes in supervision unless tied to decreased controls (Sobel 1975, pp. 56, 59). Nowhere was there mention of the trading floor: of specialists, floor traders, or the segregation of broker and dealer functions.

The End of Reform

Much of the slowdown of the SEC's regulatory push may be explained by the weakening of political support for reform in general as well as growing resistance from the regulated sector. Douglas was also tired. He may have felt that he had done all he could, or that the reconstituted NYSE might actually begin to move. In any case, his increasingly conciliatory behavior toward the Exchange, including his failure to discipline those involved in the Whitney affair, had begun to erode his support in the liberal media. "The latest reform era in the New York Stock Exchange has, like its predecessors, gone up in smoke," said *The New Republic* as 1938 drew to a close. "Is the SEC so anxious to fraternize with President 'Bill' Martin of the Exchange that it is willing to shut its eyes to fact which disturbs the carefully built-up picture of a 'reformed' Stock Exchange," *The Nation* added. Two months later, Douglas left for the Supreme Court, disappointing his associates at the SEC preparing for future battles with Wall Street (Murphy 2003, pp. 162, 172).

Martin still felt the squeeze between profit-starved Exchange members who believed they had given up too much, and Douglas's successor in May 1939, Jerome Frank, who believed they had not begun to give. Steve Axilrod (2009, p. 25), an advisor to Martin at the Fed, remembers that his Uncle Ben, a specialist on the NYSE, described Martin as "de guy who sold us down de river to the SEC."

Frank was known as a brilliant lawyer and legal philosopher who had come to Washington in the early days of the New Deal as, with Frankfurter's help, General Counsel of the Agricultural Adjustment Administration. "In his fiery two-year career at the AAA, Frank fought the meatpackers and processors to protect consumers, finally losing his job by pressing too hard for legal rights for sharecroppers." He served various government departments the next two years, and in December 1937, at Douglas's request, was appointed SEC commissioner "to countervail the appointment of investment banker John Hanes," whose appointment itself, as a member of the NYSE, "was recognized as a conciliatory gesture (Seligman 2003, pp.160, 216)."

Chairman Frank and his associates renewed the push for action by the Exchange, and the fireworks the next couple of years were due to Frank's unwillingness to accept the end of reform. On May 15, 1939, a letter from Ganson Purcell, director of the SEC's Trading and Exchange Division, reminded Martin of his November 1938 meeting with Douglas on various matters, such as rules regarding floor traders to be adopted by the Exchange. These had grown out of an earlier suggested rule sent to exchanges for comment in April 1938. "You said (at the November meeting) you would lay it before the Board of Governors. I heard from you in December that it was under consideration. In view of the fact that it is nearly six months since our conference," Purcell wrote, "I am long overdue in making a report to the Commission concerning the Exchange's action on this rule. I wonder if you could let me know in the near future what the Exchange proposes to do with respect to this rule so that I may make a report to the Commission regarding the subject."

On June 21, Purcell again reminded Martin of his need for a report, and "In the event that my letter of May 15 should not have reached you I am enclosing a copy thereof, and I would very much appreciate as early a reply as you can conveniently make" (This and the following correspondence are from the Missouri History Museum, Martin papers, box 1).

Martin announced another study in reply. In July he appointed a special committee, called the Public Examining Board, "to make a study of the broad problem of customer protection," as had been suggested by Frank. He transmitted the Board's report to the membership on September 1, and urged members "to give immediate and careful study to these recommendations, in order that such action, based on them, as may be deemed desirable in the public interest, may be taken as promptly as practicable."

This report "marks, in a sense," Martin said, "the completion of a broad program which was begun more than 18 months ago with the formation of the Conway Committee to outline the reorganization of the Exchange. More specifically, this study of consumer protection rounds out the particular program which we announced in cooperation with the SEC in October 1938. The reorganization of an institution this size would have been, in itself, a major task. But the addition to this of the special program that was developed jointly with the SEC as a result of the Whitney failure has made extraordinary demands on the time and energies of the management and staff of the Exchange. Moreover, it has also added to already burdensome overhead costs [during a time when the] low volume of transactions and reduced listings have resulted in a serious loss of income to the Exchange and to its member firms." From now on, Martin assured his constituency, the "Exchange management intends … to devote itself to the problems which are pressing," particularly, "the preservation of the market itself [and] the rebuilding of our business." There was nothing about trading rules.

The round-table meetings ended, Martin largely ignored the SEC, and his relations with Frank, such as they were, became confrontational. Martin's notes on his meeting with Frank on September 15, 1939, records that he had gone to Washington to tell the SEC chairman how much the Exchange had accomplished, but Frank opened the meeting by telling Martin he had something for him, and pointed to a corner of the room, in which there was a box labeled "Dynamite." Martin turned to the Exchange's grievances. He had promised full cooperation when Frank assumed the SEC's chairmanship, but had lately heard through the "grapevine" that Frank had abandoned the round-table (negotiated self-regulation), and was planning the direct imposition of rules regarding floor trading and a brokers' bank. This was coming "at a peculiarly bad time for my [Martin's] administration … inasmuch as the completion of the program worked out jointly was nearing the end [which Frank did not admit], and the low volume of business was causing serious dissatisfaction in my own community with any steps for changes, regardless of whether they had been agreed to the previous October or not. [T]his was a human factor which anyone with intelligence would recognize."

The NYSE was tired of serving as a "guinea pig" for the industry. Rules imposed on it were ignored by other exchanges, Martin said. Some of "my fellows were saying that if the Exchange had a man with guts the way the New York Curb had and the Chicago exchange, they wouldn't have to put in any of these rules." They were considering backing an opponent for the presidency.

Frank had gone public in his criticisms, suggesting duplicity and time-wasting by Martin, but the end of the meeting was a "friendly discussion" of various questions, including "service charges and commissions. I [Martin] told him that … a Committee … was going into the question, [which] in my judgment [was] the biggest single political issue in the Street and … there was no simple solution to this matter in a democratic organization. Under a Hitler regime [using the language of New Deal critics] it would be easy."

SECURITIES AND EXCHANGE COMMISSION
WASHINGTON
July 6, 1940

Honorable William McC. Martin
President, New York Stock Exchange
Dear Bill:
It was fine to see you again [at] the delightful dinner given by [financial services co.] Case, Pomeroy in honor of Commissioner Pike.

Your remarks ... were enlightening and entertaining as always, but I was somewhat intrigued by your expression of regret that the Commission did not give more time to the problems of the Stock Exchange. It is true that we have recently avoided bothering you while the war market commanded full attention. There comes to my mind, however, that as long ago as early in March we were promised a reasonably prompt report on the deliberations of your public examining board. Speaking for at least one member of the Commission, I would welcome the chance to devote some more time to matters affecting the Exchange if you would cooperate by giving us the opportunity.

Sincerely yours, Edward C. Eicher, Commissioner

The exchange between Martin and Commissioner Eicher initiated by the letter (in the box) highlights the different ideas of the Exchange's problems. "The thing we are most worried about," Martin replied on July 9, was the "lack of business." He gave assurance of his "full cooperation, [but] I have been having a great deal of trouble working things out down here. [F]idelity insurance and the reserve fund have become more and more complex the further we have gone in attempting to develop them.... The speeding up of the war and the resultant dislocations have made it difficult to crystallize sentiment in the brokerage business."

> What I referred to specifically in my desire to have the Commission spend more time on our problems was the necessity for all of us to study carefully means of maintaining and improving markets. I thoroughly appreciate the desirability of placing all reasonable safeguards to minimize the chances of customers losing money through methods of doing business by broker.

"[T]he accomplishment of the SEC working with the Stock Exchange in achieving the joint [really rather weak set of recommendations and proposed studies by the Exchange, the reverse of a call to action] program of October 26, 1938 have been little short of amazing.... In other words, so far as the Exchange is concerned, I am largely of the opinion that our first major goal has been practically achieved."

"We can never, of course," Martin continued, denying the purpose of the Securities Acts, "prevent dishonesty by rules or regulation."

> [I]f you down on the Commission could be as close to the picture as I am, since we are both motivated by the desire to serve the public rather than merely to please the brokers, you would come to the conclusion that our attention should be turned more toward helping build up markets than ... providing more safeguards for customers. It would be a terrible thing for the standard of living of the people of this country if our stock market should be reduced to a totalitarian affair.

Resenting the criticism, the commissioner replied:

> It is impossible for me to see any excuse for further delay. I am also unable to understand how a response to my question has anything to do with reducing the stock market to a totalitarian affair. Indeed, it might well be said that a proper regard for the safety of investors will do much to prevent the discontent of the middle class that is one of the most effective implements employed by those with totalitarian ideas (Martin papers).

On February 28, 1940, the Exchange announced that it would enforce its Rule 390 against "multiple trading," that is, the prohibition against members trading NYSE stocks on other exchanges, which had been part of the Buttonwood Agreement. The SEC's response was critical but restrained until after the November elections. In late November, the Commission formally requested that the rule be changed, but according to the *New York Times* (December 28, 1940) was "flouted again by [the] Exchange."

The Commission scheduled a hearing to decide whether it should invoke its so-far unused power to order an exchange to change its rules, and in October 1941, ordered the NYSE to rescind its probation against members trading NYSE-listed securities on other exchanges. This was supported by the regional exchanges, who could not survive by only trading local securities, and the Big Board complied (Seligman 2003, pp. 233–34).

The Exchange's prohibition against members' trading Exchange-listed securities over-the-counter still stood, however, in order, they said "to preserve and maintain the depth and liquidity of the auction market" [the Exchange], so that customers could be assured of "the fairest market ... in which all orders are entitled to an execution based on the best price available." Its revised Rule 390, by which members had to get permission from the exchange's management before conducting trades on listed securities anywhere other than the trading floor was not abandoned until 2000, after many years of criticisms of monopoly practices and interferences with the new electronic markets (Seligman 2003, p. 384; Kam et al. 2003).

Returning to 1940, the SEC's activism had run out of steam. It had lost the government's and public's interest and support, and the financial press had begun to suggest that it was staffed by political appointees with little knowledge of the industry they were supposed to regulate (Sobel 1975, p. 90). In March 1941, Martin received a draft notice and announced his resignation from the presidency. He sent a departing shot in his farewell speech. He had wanted the Securities and Exchange Act. His quarrel was with its administration. He did not deny that the commissioners were "men of good will, but they are ignorant. Knowledge of the law, of the intricacies of this bill or that bill is not adequate." He believed, however, that the pendulum of public opinion would swing back toward a free market (*New York Times*, March 6, 1941; Seligman 2003, pp. 234–35).

Frank left for a federal judgeship in April 1941. The modesty of his accomplishment at the SEC despite his brilliance and hard work has been attributed to his inexperience in government. He was one of those recruited for the "New Deal [in the] conviction that intelligence could move the world, [which] was ready to be moved," only to find that knowledge, specifically of the workings of the financial markets, was also necessary. It was not enough to want to protect innocent investors from embezzlers and pool operators (Sobel 1975, p. 84). On Frank's behalf, however, some of his lack of progress must be laid at the door of politics, specifically the declining pressures for reform as Wall Street recovered its political influence, the conservative backlash had gained strength, and the administration's attentions had turned elsewhere.

"The Exchange quickly took steps to repair its tattered relationship with the SEC," Seligman wrote, "by appointing as its new president [New Deal stalwart] Jesse Jones's protégé and hand-picked successor as Reconstruction Finance Corporation chairman, Emil Schram," an Indiana drainage expert who came to Washington to take charge of similar work at the Reconstruction

Finance Corporation and proved an effective administrator. "He knew little about securities markets, but well understood that he had been hired to harmonize the relationship between the Exchange and Washington. 'It is illogical,' he urged in his June 1941 maiden address as Exchange president, 'to suppose that the Securities and Exchange Commission is intent upon either the destruction of the Exchange or the strangulation of security markets … cooperation must be the keynote of the hour'." Three weeks later he informed the SEC that the Exchange would not dispute its rule against prohibitions of members' off-exchange trading (Seligman 2003, p. 237; Sobel 1975, pp. 108–109).

The administration met the Exchange half way by promoting Commissioner Edward Eicher, former Iowa railroad attorney and congressman, who had indicated a preference for the bench, to the chairmanship (Sobel 1975, p. 91). Eicher got his judgeship in nine months, and SEC staff member Ganson Purcell, who had succeeded Frank on the Commission, became chairman in 1942. He was "an able bureaucrat," who had risen through the ranks of the SEC. "The Commission passed beyond politics to administration, [entering] an age of bureaucracy," Robert Sobel wrote. "Not for another generation would the Commission be a moving force in lower Manhattan" (Sobel 1975, p. 92).

The SEC and the NYSE After 1941

Martin left under pressure. No one was happy with him. The SEC was frustrated and business on the Exchange was at its lowest level in two decades (Fig. 4.1), although he had accomplished or overseen a good deal. He had preserved NYSE trading practices, giving up little to reform. Of the changes in reporting and governance desired by the SEC, the former had mostly been accomplished before 1929, and the latter mattered little for trading. Conflicting views continued, but were held largely in abeyance during the war. As a "nonessential agency" the SEC was moved from an overcrowded Washington to Philadelphia in March 1942. Its enforcement activities were not wanted in a nation at war dedicated to maximum production.

The approach of the end of the war brought a flurry of activity in the Commission. A January 1945 staff study made a case for prohibiting Exchange members from trading solely for their own accounts because of the alleged advantages floor traders enjoyed over public customers, and their tendency to "give rise to excessive speculation, resulting in sudden and unreasonable fluctuations in the price of securities." The Exchange was opposed and President Schram threatened to appeal to Congress.

Nevertheless, the SEC voted to abolish floor traders on August 8, although two weeks later, Chairman Purcell told an SEC meeting that the White House had ordered the vote rescinded. No reason was given, but it was guessed that the administration regarded the dispute as a diversion from the war effort. By spring 1946, Purcell's situation was tenuous. President Truman considered Douglas, Purcell's mentor, a political rival, and Purcell resigned effective June 1946 (Seligman 2003, pp. 214, 238–40).

Criticisms of the SEC diminished with the economy's improvement and the stock boom of the 1950s. The Commission even became a selling point, a sort of Good Housekeeping Seal of investor protection (as was said in the last chapter), without, of course, ending resistance to real reform. The importance of Roosevelt's 100 days is exaggerated. "[T]he inherent problem with [crisis-driven] lawmaking moments is just that – they are moments," and unless the political forces which joined to pass the law continue, its application will be different from its original intentions (McGarity 2012; Bardach 1977; Pressman and Wildavsky 1984).

Table 4.2 shows the fall in the size of the SEC between 1939 and the 1950s (the price level doubled during the period). Neither Truman nor Eisenhower were reformers, and both were dedicated to balanced budgets that were constantly threatened by military spending. Government activities lacking political support bore the brunt of budget pressures, and investors were happy with the postwar rise in stock prices. (The Dow quadrupled between 1945 and 1960, and rose another two-thirds before it peaked in 1966; Fig. 4.2). When Truman was asked in a December 1945 press conference about the active stock market, he replied, "I have had so many things to think about that I haven't looked at the stock market because I have never been interested in the stock market personally" (Peterson 1985, p. 227).

The SEC's rule-making and enforcement activities were slight. It was able to inspect the books of less than a quarter of the nation's broker-dealers annually. SEC Chairman Ralph Demmler (1953–55), Republican

Table 4.2 SEC appropriations and employment

Fiscal year ending June 30	*Appropriations $000s*	*Total employment*	*Employment in regional offices*
1939	4872	1576	327
1946	4694	1176	325
1953	5.245	773	268
1955	4813	699	251

Source: SEC Annual Reports

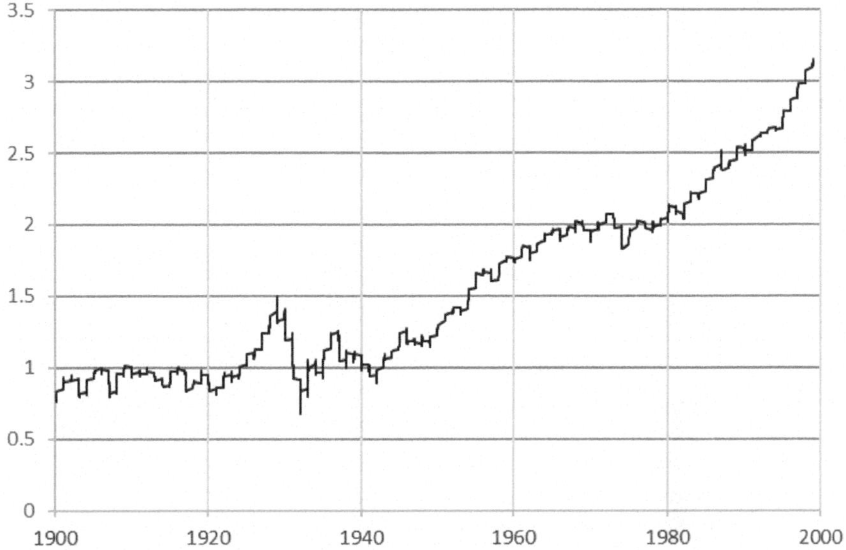

Fig. 4.2 S&P 500 Stock Index (logs), 1900–1999. (Source: Based on data from Shiller 2015)

and corporate lawyer, affirmed that "the principles behind the Acts which the Commission administers are basically sound," but noted "that there are many representative, responsible and informed people who think that the Commission in certain areas has from time to time gone beyond its statutory powers in an excess of regulatory zeal; that it has been dominated by its staff; that both staff and Commission have sometimes been high-handed, and that the Commission has been careless of other peoples' time and money in imposing on issuers and underwriters useless and duplicative paper work" (Seligman 2003, pp. 269–70).

The 1960s saw attempts to resuscitate the Exchange, although President Lyndon Johnson, who did not want to weaken political support for more important items on his agenda, told a meeting of heads of regulatory agencies on December 3, 1963, that they should be more concerned with cooperation than control. The SEC accepted the structure of the NYSE, including such anti-competitive practices as fixed commissions and the exclusion of institutions from Exchange membership so they could not bypass existing brokers. It was only when the Justice Department came on the scene in 1968 that competitive commissions and less restrictive memberships were allowed (Seligman 2003, pp. 352–411).

Martin complained that the SEC was picking on the NYSE, but one of its effects has been the elimination of much of the Exchange's competition. U.S. stock exchanges have fallen from about three dozen before 1933 to a number less than the fingers of one hand as they have closed or been taken over partly because of the costs of regulation, such as the Intermountain Stock Exchange described in the box.

Exchange in Utah Will End 90 Years of Trading

Bruce Ingersoll, Staff Reporter of the *Wall Street Journal*, 4/23/86

WASHINGTON – The Intermountain Stock Exchange, one of Salt Lake City's last vestiges of frontier finance, will close its doors Oct. 31, the Securities and Exchange Commission said. After SEC inspectors found numerous "deficiencies" in the exchange's self-regulation system and threatened enforcement action, the exchange's members voted unanimously to go out of business.

The 90-year-old auction market for mostly mining stocks has one employee, a part-time secretary, and is open for one hour a day.... The trading floor is in the front of a downtown brokerage house ... and 28 stocks are listed. "If anybody has any trades, they call me and I act as floor broker," said Woolley, the exchange's president. "I then call the newspapers with the quotes and sales." The exchange reported a dollar volume of $26,000 in August, with 55,000 shares traded, the latest figures given by the SEC. "That might constitute two block trades for all we know," Alton Harvey, an SEC attorney, said yesterday.

Until a few years ago, the exchange was housed in a grand, turn-of-the-century building, and it flourished whenever silver and gold prices boomed. Spectators used to pack the galleries to watch a mob of traders as the exchange's official called out stocks for trading in alphabetical order. "My uncle was one of the founders," says the 74-year-old Mr. Woolley. "My dad was a broker and I started trading in 1931."

But the exchange ... "effectively ceased operating" as a call exchange since its building was sold and it moved to Mr. Woolley's office, according to an SEC letter to the exchange. In January, the agency ... gave the exchange an ultimatum: Hire a self-regulation staff to oversee the 23 members' activities, or risk an enforcement action that could result in revocation of the exchange's SEC registration. "They wanted us to pattern ourselves after the New York Stock Exchange," said Mr. Woolley. "There's no way we could do it without raising our dues to a ridiculous level. It's a sad thing."

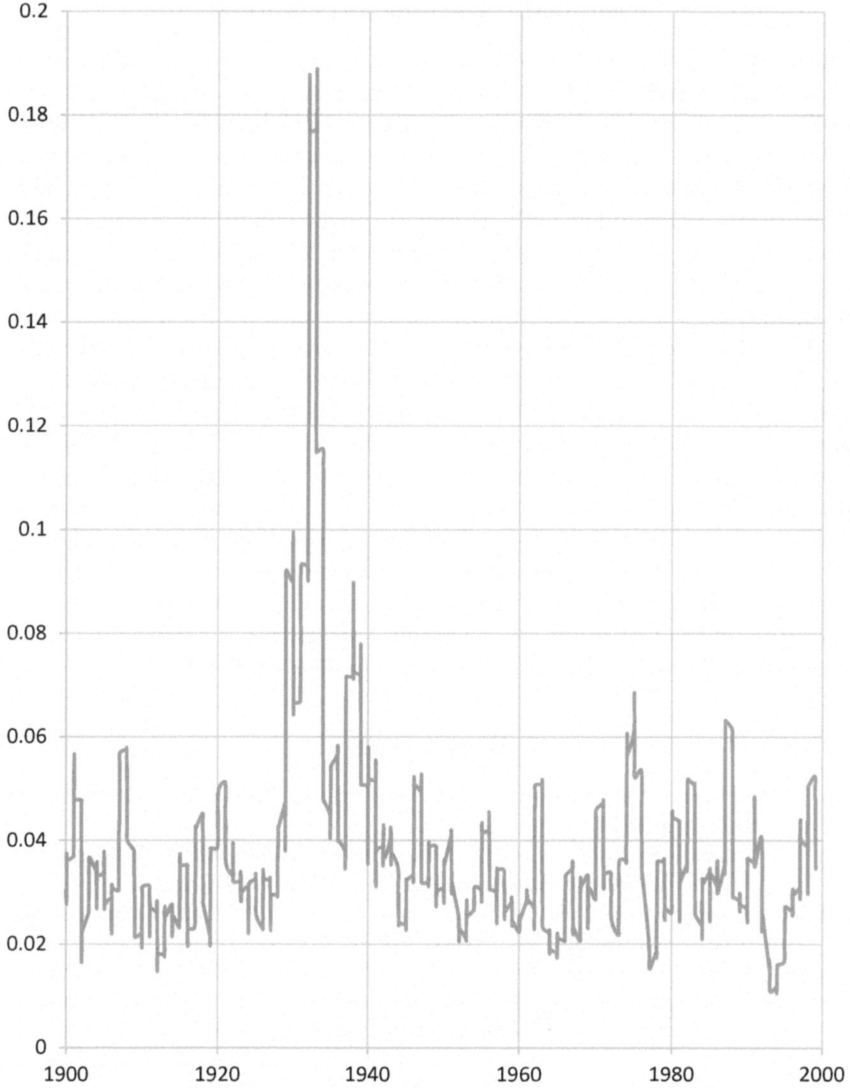

Fig. 4.3 Twelve-month moving average of standard deviations of U.S. stock returns, 1900–2000. (Source: Data from Shiller 2015)

What Really Affects the Stock Market?

Martin was right when he said that stock prices are determined by business, which benefits from stability. Looking at the index of S&P500 stocks in Fig. 4.2, we see three periods of significant stock increases since 1900—1920–29, 1946–65, and 1981–99—which were also periods of prosperity with price stability. The stock market has not been fond of inflation. The three rises corresponded with periods of price stability following significant inflations: during and immediately after World Wars I and II, and after the Great Inflation of the 1970s initiated by government deficit financing.

There has been no trend in the volatility of stock prices since the 1860s, as we see in Fig. 4.3. The outliers of the 1930s were products of the Great Depression and its recovery. The stock market boomed between July 1932 and July 1933, but crashed in July, at the end of FDR's 100 days. It boomed again, only to crash again toward the end of the decade as the economy was buffeted by the social security tax, the taxation of undistributed corporate profits, and a fall in money resulting from the Federal Reserve's doubling of commercial bank reserve requirements. Perhaps the best thing the government (including its agencies) could have done for investors, instead of going after greedy bankers, was to behave itself by means of more stable fiscal and monetary policies of its own

References

Alsop, Joseph, and Robert Kintner. 1938. The Battle of the Market Place. *Saturday Evening Post*, June 11, p. 9.

Axilrod, Stephen A. 2009. *Inside the Fed. Monetary Policy and Its Management, Martin Through Greenspan to Bernanke*. Cambridge: MIT Press.

Bardach, Eugene. 1977. *The Implementation Game: What Happens after a Bill Becomes Law?* Cambridge: MIT Press.

Battalio, Robert H., Hamid Mehran, and Paul H. Schultz. 2012. Market Declines: What is Accomplished by Banning Short-Selling? Federal Reserve Bank of New York. *Current Issues in Economics and Finance*, No. 5.

Beber, Alessandro, and Marco Pagano. 2013. Short-Selling Bans Around the World: Evidence from the 2007–09 Crisis. *Journal of Finance* 68: 343–381.

Bremner, Robert P. 2004. *Chairman of the Fed. William McChesney Martin, Jr. and the Creation of the Modern American Financial System*. New Haven: Yale University Press.

de Bedts, Ralph F. 1964. *The New Deal's SEC. The Formative Years*. New York: Columbia University Press.

Douglas, William O. 1974. *Go East Young Man*. New York: Random House.
Federal Reserve Board. 1952. *Report of the Ad Hoc Subcommittee on the Government Securities Market*. Washington, DC.
Flynn, John T. 1938. The Lamb of Wall Street. *Colliers*, July 30.
Fortas, Abe. 1975. William O. Douglas: An Appreciation, *Indiana Law Journal* 51: 3–4.
Goodwin, Doris K. 1987. *The Fitzgeralds and the Kennedys*. New York: St. Martin's.
Kam, Tai-Kong, Venkatesh Panchapagesan, and Daniel G. Weaver. 2003. Competition Among Markets: The Repeal of Rule 390. *Journal of Banking and Finance* 27: 1711–1736.
Khademian, Anne K. 1992. *The SEC and Capital Regulation. The politics of expertise*. Pittsburgh: University of Pittsburgh Press.
Landis, James M. 1959. The Legislative History of the Securities Act of 1933. *George Washington Law Review* 28: 29–49.
Macey, Jonathan R., Mark Mitchell, and Jeffry Netter. 1989. Restrictions on Short Sales: An Analysis of the Uptick Rule and Its Role in View of the October 1987 Stock Market Crash. *Cornell Law Review* 74: 799–835.
Martin, William McC Jr. 1932. The Present Agitation Over Short Selling, Commonweal. (Federal Reserve Bank of St. Louis, Federal Reserve Archival System of Economic Research (FRASER)).
———. 1935a. Address on Unemployment, University of Chicago. (Federal Reserve Bank of St. Louis, Federal Reserve Archival System of Economic Research (FRASER)).
———. 1935b. Government and Business. Friends or Enemies, Missouri History Museum, Martin papers, Box 9.
McGarity, Thomas O. 2012. Administrative Law as Blood Sport. *Duke Law Journal* 61: 1671–1762.
Meeker, J. Edward. 1930. *The Work of the Stock Exchange*. New York: Ronald Press.
Michel, Norbert. 2014. Dodd-Frank's Expansion of Fed Power: A Historical Perspective. *Cato Journal* 34: 557–567.
Murphy, Bruce A. 2003. *Wild Bill. The Legend and Life of William O. Douglas*. New York: Random House.
New York Stock Exchange. *Fact Book*, Annual.
Parrish, M.E. 1970. *Securities Regulation and the New Deal*. New Haven: Yale University Press.
Patterson, James T. 1967. *Congressional Conservatism and the New Deal*. Lexington: University of Kentucky Press.
Peterson, Gale E. 1985. *President Harry S. Truman and the Independent Regulatory Commissions, 1945–52*. New York: Garland.
Phillips, Susan M., and J. Richard Zecher. 1981. *The SEC and the Public Interest*. Cambridge: MIT Press.

Pressman, Jeffrey L., and Aaron Wildavsky. 1984. *Implementation: How Great Expectations in Washington are Dashed in Oakland*. Oakland: University of California Press.

Roosevelt Papers. 1933–45. *Official File*. Hyde Park: FDR Presidential Library and Museum.

Seligman, Joel. 2003. *The Transformation of Wall Street. A History of the Securities and Exchange Commission and Modern Corporate Finance*. 3rd ed. New York: Wolters Kluwer.

Shiller, Robert. 2015. *Irrational Exuberance*. Princeton: Princeton University Press.

Sobel, Robert. 1975. *N.Y.S.E. A History of the New York Stock Exchange, 1935–75*. New York: Weybright and Talley.

Tomlins, Christopher L. 2005. *The United States Supreme Court*. Boston: Houghton Mifflin.

U.S. House of Representatives. 1934. *Stock Exchange Practices Hearings*. Commerce Committee. 73rd Cong., 2nd sess.

———. 1935. *Report on the Government of Securities Exchanges*. Doc. No. 85, 74th Cong., 1st sess.

U.S. Senate. 1934. *Stock Exchange Practices. Report No. 1455*, 73rd Cong., 2nd sess.

Wood, John H. 2005. *A History of Central Banking in Great Britain and the United States*. Cambridge: Cambridge University Press.

CHAPTER 5

Central Banking in the United States

The Congress shall have power to coin Money, regulate the Value thereof, and of foreign Coin, and fix the Standard of Weights and Measures.
—*U.S. Constitution*, Article I, Section 8.

An act to provide for the establishment of Federal reserve banks, to furnish an elastic currency, to afford means of rediscounting commercial paper, to establish a more effective supervision of banking in the United States, and for other purposes.
—*Federal Reserve Act*, Preamble, Dec. 23, 1913.

Money, Banking, and Central Banking

This chapter explores the bureaucracies established by Congress to exercise its monetary powers (see above), and so lays the groundwork for beginning to understand the conduct of the Federal Reserve during the years 1951–70 when our friend William McChesney Martin, Jr., was its chairman. Congress's monetary agencies have taken different forms, such as the Banks of the United States during the early years of the republic, the U.S. Treasury for 80 years, including most of the nineteenth century, and the Federal Reserve since 1913, but their conduct and goals, although not invariable, have shown considerable continuity.

This chapter is based on Wood (2005, Ch. 6–8; 2015, Ch. 3–5).

J. H. Wood, *Who Governs?*, Palgrave Studies in American Economic History, https://doi.org/10.1007/978-3-030-33083-5_5

However, their consequences in terms of price and monetary stability have been mixed. Inflation and instability have been the usual outcomes of conflicts and compromises between governments, finance (especially banks), the official monetary agencies, and the public, which in elections has shown its dislike of inflation, even though it might have liked the previous expansionary policies which produced the inflations (Fair 1978).

The 1913 dollar was worth 4¢ a century later. Someone who paid $100 for a 25-year U.S. bond in 1945 would have redeemed it for less than $50 in real terms as the purchasing power of the dollar halved (the annual rate of inflation was 2.8 percent) during the life of the bond. Annual inflation of the Consumer Price Index averaged 7.9 percent between 1970 and 1982, 3.3 percent between 1982 and 1998, and 2.4 percent during Martin's tenure, which was special, although not dramatically so.

Monetary policy has always been a political variable. Banks and finance in general usually want stability, which limits uncertainty. The high interest rates of borrowing for investment during boom times are difficult to maintain when inflation slows or reverses, depressing the profits of borrowers and their banks. Governments, on the other hand, are often attracted to deficit financing, especially with the low interest rates that can be arranged by central banks, which is politically less costly than taxation but results in inflation. Legislatures have repeatedly pledged respect for the independence of the money-creating monetary authorities, pledges that have often been broken. Several examples are given below. Furthermore, America's frequent financial crises reveal that banks and others in finance have often jumped on speculative bandwagons.

Volatile inflation loses its mystery when it is understood as an outcome of the fluctuating political powers of competing forces. For example, in the commercially developed western world (Europe and North America), price levels were about the same in 1914 as in 1815 (although there was a jump during the American Civil War, which the government financed by printing large quantities of currency). The more developed northeastern United States, led by J.P. Morgan, Senator Nelson Aldridge, and associates, defeated populists led by William Jennings Bryan in elections during which the monetary standard—gold, meaning sound money and stable prices, versus the cheaper and declining silver—was the primary issue (see below). The inflations before and after this mainly steady-price century arose from the government's need for cash arising from policies which the taxpayers were unwilling to support or for which politicians were afraid to ask.

Those twentieth-century needs arose initially and in the largest amounts from World Wars I and II and the nearly continuous inflation since then from the smaller Cold War and succeeding wars along with expanding government services. The Federal Reserve's assignments in its originating 1913 act were primarily price and financial stability, and its statements and behavior indicate that these assignments have been taken seriously. There has been little genuine belief at the Fed in the *dual* mandate (price-output) trade-off. They have generally believed that booms must be followed by busts. Furthermore, the easy money and government deficits during recessions ought to be balanced out by the opposite during economic expansions. If so, the 14-fold increase in prices since 1945 must be the result of fluctuating pressures on the Fed, with the government's needs generally prevailing. The battles between the Fed under Martin and five presidents, discussed in the next chapter, might contribute to an understanding of President Trump's similar recent battle with the so-called independent Fed (Wood 2005, pp. 2–4).

This argument assumes that the price level is determined by the stock of money relative to output and that the former is governed by the Fed, which determines bank reserves by its open-market purchases. The data strongly support these relations so that we may confidently say that the Fed determines the price level (Friedman and Schwartz 1963). So, to understand money and prices, we must understand what determines the Fed, which, is certainly not independent. We will see that the forces determining money prices preceded the Fed, whose greater effects than its predecessors have arisen from its greater powers.

Countries' monetary authorities, the ultimate sources of bank reserves and money, have come to be called central banks even if they are not banks. They derive their name from the Bank of England, which since the eighteenth century has been at the center of the English and then British banking systems. It was a bankers' bank. Its reserve took the form of gold, and it loaned money, mainly in the form of Bank of England notes (currency), which other banks held as reserves. It was a true central bank, and in the event of monetary shortages, other banks expected the "Bank" to be the "lender of last resort" (Baring 1797; Bagehot 1873).

The Banks of the United States (1791–1811 and 1816–36) were also sources of accommodation, although they did not have the time or support necessary for the status earned by the Bank of England. The Federal Reserve, on the other hand, is not a bank. Banks compete for (mainly deposit) funds, which they lend and hope to profit from the interest and cost spread between loans and deposits. The Fed, on the other hand, prints its nearly costless bank reserves and does no business with the public, which was a condition imposed on the Federal Reserve Act to gain the acceptance of the banking community. Nor was the Treasury strictly a central bank, although it was an important source of bank reserves.

The great difference between the money-creating powers of these institutions stemmed from the gold standard, which required that paper money be backed by gold. That constraint ended in the 1930s, but considerable monetary discretion had existed before then in the form of the variable reserve ratios (gold/paper currency) of the monetary authorities and banks (Barro 1979; Eichengreen 1992).

Which brings us to banks. Central banks of course engage the economy through banks. The American monetary system has undergone many technical and regulatory changes, but the primary practices and purposes of its dominant, commercial banking, institutions have persisted. First, these banks have always been the principal creators and movers of money, without which economic activity would be very difficult, and they also have been in the forefront of the transfer of resources from savers to investors, enabling economic growth. The two activities are connected as savers invest in commercial bank deposits, which make up most of the money stock and enable banks to lend for investment and consumption.

Notice the dominance of the deposit and loan categories in the bank balance sheets in Table 5.1—from 1837 to 2000. Banks have been enabled by technology to engage in a variety of often complex derivatives and other activities, but we see from these balance sheets that their principal (loan and deposit) activities have persisted. They differed little in 2000 from 1837. Part of this continuity may be explained by the inflexibility of regulation which inhibited the development of banks.

By enabling (financing) new combinations, the banker "is not so much primarily a middleman in the commodity 'purchasing power' as a *producer* of this commodity," Joseph Schumpeter wrote in his classic *Theory of Economic Development* (p. 74). Since reserve funds and savings "flow to him, and the total demand for free purchasing power, whether existing or to be created, concentrates on him, he has either replaced private capitalists or become their agent; he has himself become the capitalist par excellence. He stands between those who wish to form new combinations and the possessors of productive means. He is essentially a phenomenon of development.... He makes possible the carrying out of new connected combinations, authorizes people, in the name of society as it were, to form them. He is the ephor [overseer] of the exchange society."

Table 5.1 Aggregate U.S. commercial bank balance sheets, 1925–2000; New York State Chartered Banks, 1837 (billion $, June)

1950				*1970*			
Assets		*Liabilities*		*Assets*		*Liabilities*	
R	17	93	DD	R	27	189	DD
L	38	29	TD	L	241	157	TD
I	65	...	B	I	95	18	B
O	14	1	O	O	67	33	O
	134	10	K		420	33	K
		133				420	

1925				*2000*			
Assets		*Liabilities*		*Assets*		*Liabilities*	
R	3	22	DD	R	269	617	DD
L	21	10	TD	L	3724	3043	TD
I	9	1	B	I	1305	1201	B
O	6	1	O	O	607	569	O
	39	5	K		5905	475	K
		39				5905	

1837 (NY)			
Assets		*Liabilities*	
R	4	33	D+N
L	61	25	O
I	3	37	K
O	27	95	
	95		

Sources: Federal Reserve, ***Banking and Monetary Statistics, 1914–41*** (see pp. 61–71 for definitions) and *1941–76;* Fenstermaker, ***American Commercial Banking***, pp. 218–19

Sample: Federal Reserve member banks, 1925–70; all commercial banks, 2000

Definitions: *R* bank reserves in cash and on deposit with the Fed, *L* Loans, *I* investments (mainly U.S. bonds), *O* other assets (mainly balances with other banks and bank premises and other real estate), and owed to foreign branches *DD* demand deposits until 1980, thereafter transactions accounts, *TD* time deposits of nontransaction accounts, *B* bank borrowings from the Fed, *K* capital accounts, *D&N* deposits and notes. The liabilities column includes capital accounts

Banks make up the majority of financial institutions in the early stages of development and are joined by a growing variety of financial activities as incomes, savings, and investments grow. For example, banks held 71 percent of the assets of all American financial institutions in 1860, with thrift institutions (mostly Savings and Loan Associations) and insurance companies holding the rest. The bank share fell below 40 percent in the late 1950s, as pension funds and insurance and investment companies (mostly mutual funds) grew, and has stayed above 30 percent (Saunders and Cornett 2012, p. 18).

Martin's period at the Fed saw the end of an unusual period for banks. Banks are first and foremost lenders, with their "investments" (mainly U.S. bonds) serving as "secondary reserves," ready to be sold for funds to make loans (Wood 1975). Notice the dominance of L over I in 1925. Then came the Great Depression, during which loan demands fell drastically, followed by World War II, during which government demands were financed considerably by government bonds. It was not until the 1960s that the loan-investment ratio recovered its pre-depression values. In the meantime, Martin was privileged to deal with less than normally risky banks. Looking further at these balance sheets, the rising time-to-demand deposit ratios between 1950 and 1970 were also consequences of the expanding economy, inflation, and technology. Time deposits pay interest, which was rising, and also were more easily convertible into demand deposits. Increasing bank borrowing from the Fed was also indicative of rising demands for finance. A 2000 portfolio is included to show the continuation, and indeed acceleration, of these trends. In fact, these bland balance sheets understate bank risks.

Because of their roles in the money (payments) process, banks are even more important to the economy than these financial industry shares might suggest. Everyone keeps money in banks and so conducts their business through banks. Changes in bank behavior, therefore, self-induced or because of outside, possibly regulatory, pressure exert leveraged effects on the economy (Wood 1970). The importance of banks has also been maintained by growing fees from off-balance-sheet activities, such as loan commitments, letters of credit, loan sales, and derivatives (Saunders and Cornett 2012, pp. 383–87).

A cost of banking, however, has been its fragility, derived chiefly from the mismatch of its liability to redeem its deposits on demand and the longer maturity of its assets. It is fundamentally illiquid, although less so than some other institutions. Its greatest asset, therefore, is its credibility. Loss of confidence in the solvency of a bank is self-fulfilling as depositors demand their money *now*, before the bank is able to sell its assets for fair market value.

Banking's importance to individuals and the economy has inspired numerous regulations intended to maintain their solvency. The United States is considered a relatively competitive economy, but its regulatory restraints on finance have been extensive. An effect has been the persistence of the banking structure as regulators have sought to preserve the tried and true, and to discourage innovation. There are few, if any, industries whose activities are as similar between the nineteenth and twenty-first centuries (Table 5.1).

American bank regulation must be judged a failure in light of the frequent (world-leading) bank failures throughout its history. The only successful (financial panic and bank-failure free) period lasted from the mid-1930s, after the massive failures of the Great Depression (1929–33), to the inflation of the 1970s. This was attributable to the combination of a record period of farm prosperity (most bank failures have been those of small banks in agricultural areas) and the unusually conservative bank portfolios discussed above. Bank loans/(loans + bonds) were 72 percent in mid-1929, 21 percent in 1945, 61 percent in 1960, and 70 percent in 1970 (*Historical Statistics of the U.S.*, Series 590, 593). Banks did not significantly raise their risks until the acceleration of inflation after Martin's tenure.

Martin may have been lucky in the period of his chairmanship, when large bank solvency did not demand a large share of the Fed's attention. He was not, unlike some of his successors, called on to bail out banks or the financial sector, although he may have been partly responsible for his own good fortune through his contributions to price stability.

Martin's job as chairman of the Board of Governors of the Federal Reserve System, which he occupied longer than anyone else, April 1951 through January 1970, was similar in several respects to his presidency of the New York Stock Exchange.[1] An obvious difference was that in the earlier position he represented the regulated whereas in the latter he was a regulator. Perhaps the chief similarity was his support of liberal values and free markets, demonstrated, as we have seen, by his resistance to New Deal securities restrictions, and later by his promotion of a competitive monetary system as opposed to its manipulation for political purposes. His ideas dominated his offices. He wanted both the SEC and the Fed to stay out of the way of market forces. Ideas sometimes matter even in bureaucracies.

[1] Marriner Eccles (1934–48) and Alan Greenspan (1987–2006) also served for long periods. Paul Volcker (1979–87), Arthur Burns (1970–78), and Ben Bernanke (2006–14) were chairmen about eight years each. Eccles was an ordinary member of the Board 1948–51. There were six chairmen during the Board's first 20 years.

Table 5.2 Timeline of American money and finance, 1790–1950

1790–91	Federal government assumption of state debts and creation of Bank of U.S.
1811	End of Bank of U.S.
1812–15	War of 1812
1816	Creation of second Bank of U.S.
1819	Panic and depression
1832	Jackson vetoes renewal of Bank of U.S.'s charter
1837	Panic and depression
1846	Adoption of the Independent Treasury
1861–65	Civil War and suspension of gold convertibility
1879	Resumption of gold standard
1890–93	Passage and repeal of Silver Purchase Act
1900	Formal adoption of the gold standard
1907	Panic and depression
1913	Creation of the Federal Reserve
1914–20	The Great War and world inflation
1929–33	The Great Depression
1938–45	World War II
1951	Treasury—Federal Reserve Accord

The next chapter reviews Chairman Martin's battles over monetary policies with Congress, presidents, and economists. The present chapter develops the history of the monetary environment, particularly public preferences and the ideas and institutions within which the conflicts have occurred. The Federal Reserve was a new institution but it developed from existing interests and forces that are still with us. A timeline of significant American monetary events is given in Table 5.2.

The Banks of the United States

> Whereas it is conceived that the establishment of a bank for the United States...will be very conducive to the successful conducting of the national finances; will tend to give facility to the obtaining of loans, for the use of Government, ... and will be productive of considerable advantage to trade and industry in general: Therefore, *be it enacted*, etc. That a Bank of the United States shall be established. (*Annals of Congress*, Feb. 25, 1791.)

The First Bank The first Secretary of the Treasury, Alexander Hamilton (1789–95), advocated the federal government's support of the new country's industry, trade, and finance, including the establishment of a national bank.

Table 5.3 Congressional votes for and against national banks[a]

	All	*NE*[a]	*SE*[a]	*Other Slave*[b]	*NWT*[c]	*W*[d]	
1791	39–19	33–1	6–18				House
							Senate[e]
1811	64–65	44–25	18–34	2–5	0–1		House
	17–17[f]	9–7	7–5	1–3	0–2		Senate
1816	80–71	35–43	34–21	3–2	8–5		House
	22–12	8–7	7–4	6–0	1–1		Senate
1832	107–82	65–28	20–34	12–15	10–5		House
	28–20	14–4	4–8	5–7	5–1		Senate
1841	127–98	61–43	28–31	18–16	20–8		House
	26–23	11–7	7–3	4–9	4–4		Senate
1913[g]	287–85	59–35	39–1	74–11	75–9	40–29	House
	54–34	6–10	10–2	14–2	4–6	20–14	Senate
1927	Yeas and nays not taken; 1/24/27.						House
	Accepted with other amendments without separate vote.						Senate

Source: Wood, *Central Banking in a Democracy*, p. 32

[a]Original 13 states and ME and VT, above and below the Mason-Dixon Line
[b]KY, TN, LA, MO, MS, AL, AK, FL, TX, WV
[c]Northwest Territory: OH, IN, IL, MI, WI
[d]Others (all west of the Mississippi River)
[e]Senate proceedings not published
[f]Vice-president broke tie vote against the Bank
[g]FR charter for 20 years (FR Act, Sec. 4), extended indefinitely in 1927 by McFadden Banking Act, Sec. 18. *Sources: Annals of Congress, Congressional Globe, Congressional Record. Dates of votes.* 1791: H 2/8 S 2/14. 1811: H 1/24 S 2/20; 1816 H 3/14 S 4/13; 1832: H 7/3 S 6/11. 1841: H 8/6 S 7/28. 1913: H 9/18 S 12/19

Congress voted (Table 5.3) a twenty-year charter for the bank, with capital of ten million dollars, of which the U.S. Government might supply two million. The Bank's notes were acceptable as payments to the United States.

There were to be twenty-five directors, chosen for one-year terms by and from the stockholders, who would in turn choose the Bank's president from among their number. Only citizens of the United States were eligible to be directors, and not more than three-fourths "shall be eligible for the next succeeding year." The Bank "may sell any part of the public debt whereof its stock shall be composed, but shall not be at liberty to purchase any public debt whatsoever," and may not lend more than 100,000 dollars to the Government of the United States, more than 50,000 dollars to any particular State, or to "any foreign prince or state unless previously authorized by a law of the United States."

These provisions largely followed the Bank of England, which was privately owned to limit abuses arising from government control, discouraged cliques by requiring management turnover, and limited the government's use of the Bank to circumvent the legislature's fiscal control. These restrictions had been weakly enforced. Retiring directors tended to be reinstated as soon as they were eligible and the Bank, like banks everywhere, was unable to resist government pressures for finance, especially in wartime. In fact, the Bank of England was founded in 1694 as part of a deal which included a low-interest loan to the government. This problem was less severe in the early United States, which was not at war during the lives of the Banks of the United States and coincided with the frugal administrations of Jefferson (1801–1809) and Jackson (1829–37).

Table 5.4 shows that the federal government was often in surplus during its first half century, exceptions being the War of 1812 and the early years of the republic, when the largest outlay was interest on the debt inherited from the Confederation. The rise in debt in 1803 was due to the Louisiana purchase for $15,000,000, much of which was paid immediately from cash and surplus. The purchase took advantage of the excellent credit rating which Hamilton's fiscal policy had earned for the country. The budget's components were variable and not easily explained by general principles. Tariffs, military spending, and the federal financing of internal improvements were controversial and partisan, affected by Henry Clay's American system, the nullification movement in the South brought on by tariffs, and Jefferson's belief that military preparedness promoted its use. There were no substantial long-term commitments like modern entitlements. Even the civil list, the financing of government, was changeable in the new country (Dewey 1922, pp. 95–121).

The Banks of the United States were controversial. John Marshall in his *Life of George Washington* observed that Hamilton's economic plans, especially for a national bank, "made a deep impression" on the national debate over the nature of the new government, "and contributed, not inconsiderably, to … those distinct … parties, which, in their long and dubious conflict for power, have since shaken the United States to their centre" (Marshall 1807, V, iv, p. 244).

James Madison opposed the U.S. Bank in the House of Representatives because it "did not make so good a bargain for the public as was due to its interests. The charter to the Bank of England had been granted only for eleven years, and was paid for by a loan to the Government on terms bet-

Table 5.4 Federal government budgets, 1791–1836

	Receipts					Outlays					
	Total	Customs	Internal rev.[b]	Sales of public lands	Other	Total	Military[c]	Int. on public debt	Other[d]	Surplus	Public debt[e]
Washington											
1791[a]	4419	4399	0	0	19	4269	810	2349	1110	150	77,228
1792	3670	3443	209	0	18	5080	1210	3202	668	−1414	80,359
1793	4653	4255	338	0	60	4482	1210	2772	500	171	78,427
1794	5432	4801	274	0	357	6991	2781	3490	719	−1559	80,748
1795	6115	5588	338	0	188	7540	2961	3189	1390	−1425	83,762
1796	8378	6568	475	5	1329	5727	1636	3195	896	2651	82,064
J. Adams											
1797	8689	7550	575	84	480	6134	1514	3300	1320	2555	79,229
1798	7900	7106	644	12	138	7677	3496	3053	1127	224	78,409
1799	7547	6610	779	0	157	9666	5420	3186	1060	−2120	82,976
1800	10,849	9081	809	[f]	958	10,786	6074	3375	1338	63	83,038
Jefferson											
1801	12,935	10,751	1048	168	969	9395	3958	4413	1123	3541	80,713
1802	14,996	12,438	622	189	1747	7862	2190	4125	1557	7134	77,055
1803	11,064	10,479	215	166	204	7852	2100	3849	1903	3212	86,427
1804	11,826	11,099	51	488	189	8719	2145	4267	2308	3107	82,312
1805	13,561	12,936	22	540	62	10,506	2393	4149	3965	3054	75,723
1806	15,569	14,668	20	765	107	9804	2956	3723	3124	5756	69,218
1807	16,398	15,846	13	466	73	8354	3082	3370	1903	8044	65,196
1808	17,061	16,364	8	648	41	9932	4868	3428	1636	7128	57,023

(*continued*)

Table 5.4 (continued)

	Receipts					Outlays					
	Total	Customs	Internal rev.[b]	Sales of public lands	Other	Total	Military[c]	Int. on public debt	Other[d]	Surplus	Public debt[e]
Madison											
1809	7773	7296	4	442	31	10,281	5862	2866	1553	−2507	53,173
1810	9384	8583	7	697	96	8157	4032	2845	1279	1228	48,006
1811	14,424	13,313	2	1040	68	8058	4074	2466	1519	6365	45,210
1812	9801	8959	5	710	127	20,281	15,868	2451	1961	−10,480	55,963
1813	14,340	13,225	5	836	275	31,682	26,166	3599	1897	−17,341	81,488
1814	11,182	5999	1663	1136	2384	34,721	27,752	4593	2376	−23,539	99,834
1815	15,729	7283	4678	1288	2480	32,708	22,524	5755	3429	−16,979	127,335
1816	47,678	36,307	5125	1718	4528	20,587	20,109	7213	3264	17,091	123,492
Monroe											
1817	33,099	26,283	2678	1991	2147	21,844	11,616	6389	3839	11,255	103,467
1818	21,585	17,176	955	2607	847	19,825	9468	6016	4341	1760	95,530
1819	24,603	20,284	230	3274	816	21,464	12,770	5164	3530	3140	91,016
1820	17,881	15,006	106	1636	1133	18,261	10,216	5126	2908	−380	89,987
1821	14,573	13,004	69	1213	287	15,811	8023	5087	2700	−1237	93,547
1822	20,232	17,590	68	1804	771	15,000	7248	5173	2543	5232	90,876
1823	20,541	19,088	34	917	501	14,707	7382	4923	2402	5834	90,270
1824	19,381	17,878	35	984	484	20,327	7745	4997	7586	−945	83,788
J.Q.Adams											
1825	21,841	20,099	26	1216	500	15,857	8018	4367	3472	5984	81,054
1826	25,260	23,341	22	1394	504	17,036	9719	3973	3343	8225	73,987
1827	22,966	19,172	20	1496	1738	16,139	9879	3486	3474	6827	67,475
1828	24,764	23,206	17	1018	523	16,395	8916	3099	4381	8369	58,421

Jackson											
1829	24,828	22,682	15	1517	1614	15,203	8983	2543	3677	9624	48,565
1830	24,844	21,922	12	2329	581	15,143	9369	1914	3860	9701	39,123
1831	28,527	24,224	7	3211	1084	15,248	9869	1384	3995	13,279	24,322
1832	31,866	28,465	12	2623	766	17,289	10,586	773	5930	14,577	7012
1833	33,948	29,033	3	3968	945	23,018	15,174	304	7519	10,931	4760
1834	21,792	16,215	4	4858	715	18,628	13,016	202	5409	3164	38
1835	35,430	19,391	10	14,758	1270	17,573	11,579	58	5936	17,857	38
1836	50,827	23,410	[f]	24,877	2539	30,868	20,860	0	10,008	19,959	337

Historical Statistics of the U.S., Series Y

[a]1789–91

[b]Mostly excise (whiskey) taxes plus direct taxes (on carriages, sugar, licenses on distillers, stamp duties, auctions) for War of 1812 (Dewey 138–41)

[c]Army and navy establishments and pensions

[d]Includes Indian affairs, rivers and canals, civil list

[e]end of year

[f]less than $500

ter than could be elsewhere got. Every renewal of the charter had, in like manner, been purchased; in some instances at a very high price (Cong. Annals, February 2, 1791)."

Madison also doubted the Bank's legality. The Constitution of the United States was a limiting document in which "particular powers" were granted to the central government, "leaving the general mass in other hands." It did not mention banks, nor did Congress' explicit financial powers under the Constitution (to lay and collect taxes, and borrow and coin money and regulate the value thereof) make a national bank "necessary and proper," he argued.

Nevertheless, the bill chartering the Bank passed. The House vote was 39–19, with 34 of 35 representatives from above the Mason-Dixon Line in favor compared with 5 of 23 Southerners. (Senate votes were not yet recorded.) Against the advice of Attorney-General Edmund Randolph, and Secretary of State Thomas Jefferson, both Virginians who believed the Bank was unconstitutional, President Washington signed the bill. He preferred the advice of Hamilton, who thought it sufficient that a national bank had a "natural relation" to the powers of collecting taxes, regulating trade, and providing for the common defense. "Now it appears to the Secretary of the Treasury that this general principle is inherent in the very definition of Government ...; namely, that every power vested in a Government ... includes, by force of the term, a right to employ all the means requisite and fairly applicable to the attainment of the ends of such power and which are not precluded by restrictions and exceptions specified in the constitution or not immoral, or not contrary to the essential ends of political society."

The most straightforward and powerful arguments in the debate were undoubtedly those of the economically sophisticated (contrary to Hamilton's opinion) Jefferson, who clearly had studied Adam Smith. "[E]xisting banks," he wrote, "will, without a doubt, enter into arrangements for lending their agency, and the more favorable, as there will be a competition among them for it; whereas the bill delivers us up bound to the national bank, who are free to refuse all arrangements but on their own terms." The Treasury already conducts its business, by means of existing banks. "This expedient alone suffices to prevent the existence of that necessity which may justify the assumption of a non-enumerated power as a means for carrying into effect an enumerated one. The thing may be done, and has been done, and well done, without this assumption, [which], therefore, does not stand in that degree of *necessity*, which can honestly justify it."[2]

Jefferson's argument fits with George Selgin and Lawrence White's "A fiscal theory of government's role in money," which contends that instead of market inadequacies, or failures, as Hamilton would have it, central banks and many other monetary arrangements have been imposed by governments seeking finance. This, in combination with many bank regulations, Charles Calomiris and Stephen Haber (2014) argue, such as the inflexibilities of reserve requirements and forced home loans, have produced a banking system that is "fragile by design."

Nevertheless, Hamilton's view prevailed in the short term, and also in the long term when in 1819, in reference to the second Bank of the U.S., Supreme Court Chief Justice Marshall enunciated the doctrine of implied powers.

> The government which has a right to do an act, and has imposed on it the duty of performing that act, must, according to the dictates of reason, be allowed to select the means; and those who contend that it may not select any appropriate means, that one particular mode of effecting the object is excepted, take upon themselves the burden of establishing that exception. (*McCulloch v. Maryland*, U.S. Supreme Court, 1819.)[3]

The Bank earned reputations for safety and efficiency. It exercised its legislated advantage over the state banks by means of branches in Boston, New York, Baltimore, and Charleston within a few months of opening the main office in Philadelphia in December 1791, which helped it become an efficient fiscal agent for the government. It also financed state banks by holding their notes, although also sometimes behaving like a modern central bank "by pressing them for payment of the notes and checks received against them," and thereby exercising "general restraint upon the banking system" (Hammond 1957, p. 198; Holdsworth 1910, p. 42; Nettels 1962, pp. 118–20, 300–301).

[2] See, Krooss (1969, pp. 273–306) and Clarke and Hall (1832, Ch 2), for Washington's concerns and advice.

[3] Maryland imposed a tax on the notes of out-of-state banks (the only one was the Baltimore branch of the Bank of the United States) during a recession in which the unpopular Bank was contracting the currency. The head of the Baltimore branch was James McCulloch, who refused to pay the tax.)

The Bank financed federal government deficits in its early years and even joined in speculations on the bonds issued in connection with the federal assumption of State and Continental Congress debts. Sharp price rises were followed by collapses during the Panics of 1791 and 1792, and all banks, including the Bank of the United States, "which had recklessly overexpanded its credit creation when it first opened," were in on the verge of closing their doors.

Hamilton's Treasury came to the rescue when it entered the market for securities and offered to lend money on good collateral (government bonds valued at par) at a high interest rate, to be repaid when times, hopefully not very far away, returned to normal. The restoration of the ability to meet debts achieved its purpose, and the economy was "barely fazed." Richard Sylla, Robert Wright, and David Cowen, in "Alexander Hamilton, Central Banker: Crisis Management during the U.S. Financial Panic of 1792," point out that Hamilton's "uncommonly creative" plan anticipated Walter Bagehot's famous rule set forth in *Lombard Street* in 1873: in panic circumstances, rushes for cash, the lender of last resort (the Bank of England in his case) should make loans on good collateral at a very high rate of interest.

Bagehot's rule is often cited but has not been seriously followed by the Federal Reserve, which instead subsidizes favored misbehaving or unlucky banks at low interest rates even when cash is not scarce. Nor can it be in a paper-money economy (Kaufman 1991, p. 53).

Although the Bank's charter, like that of the Bank of England, had prescribed limits to its lending to the government, the temptations for abuse were too great to resist. Congress was unwilling to levy taxes sufficient to cover even routine expenses, and deficits rose with Indian wars and threatened hostilities with Britain and France. "Thus it appears," John Holdsworth (1910, pp. 4–5; also Gibbs 1846, pp. 187–288) wrote,

> that the Bank of the United States accommodated the Government whenever called upon and continued the loans to suit its convenience.... This indebtedness ... amounted to $6,200,000 at the close of the year 1795, ... nearly two-thirds of the entire capital of the bank. The bank naturally became restive and impatient; the loan of so large a proportion of its funds crippled its services to commerce and manufactures and made it difficult to "facilitate the financial operations of the Government by temporary loans."

The government was forced to turn elsewhere, such as bond issues and selling its Bank stock, "rendered necessary by the stupid failure of Congress to provide adequate revenues by resort to taxation, or its desire to embarrass the administration" (Holdsworth 1910, p. 49; Gibbs 1846, p. 348). Jefferson's surpluses relieved the problem. The national debt fell despite the large loan for the Louisiana purchase, but Treasury Secretary Albert Gallatin (1801–1814) still found the Bank useful. Its "affairs ... have been wisely and skillfully managed," he reported to Congress in support of the Bank's continuation:

> The numerous banks now established, under the authority of the several States, might, it is true, afford considerable assistance to Government in its fiscal operations. There is none, however, which could effect the transmission of public moneys with the same facility, and to the same extent, as the Bank of the United States is enabled to do through its several branches.

The Bank applied for the early renewal of its charter in 1808, but Gallatin delayed its consideration until after the disapproving Jefferson's retirement. Notwithstanding Gallatin's recommendation and the country's disagreements with Great Britain which suggested a need for war finance, renewal of the Bank's charter was narrowly defeated in Congress. Its supporters and opponents had changed since its founding. Some of the business interests previously in search of finance now resented the Bank's competition and restraint. The country's three banks in 1791 had increased to ninety in 1811. A major stockholder of the Bank, Stephen Girard, bought the Philadelphia office "virtually on the hoof, acquiring all at once the staff ... and the building" (Hammond 1957, pp. 145, 226). Some agrarians had become reconciled to banking but resented federal interference. Kentucky Congressman Richard Johnson argued that the Bank "would contract very much the circulation of the state bank notes, and would in many other respects come in collision with state rights" (Walters 1957, p. 238; Nettels 1962, p. 301; Clarke and Hall 1832, p. 232).

The Second Bank The opposition of the Republican administration to domestic taxes even after the declaration of war in June 1812, became a problem when the Federalist financial interests of the Northeast refused to support government bond issues. "Public credit began to fail ... and it became necessary to take bids below par," financial historian Davis Dewey wrote. Subscriptions were received at 12 percent discount, then 20 percent, and as the war progressed, in State bank notes worth 65 percent in specie. "The total loss to the government in disposing of its loans during the war period 1812–16 was enormous. [I]n 1830 the committee of ways of means of the House estimated that for loans … over $80,000,000 the treasury received but $34,000,000 as measured in specie" (Dewey 1922, p. 134). These are some of the costs of an unpopular war.

The number of Banks and their circulations nearly tripled during the war, and their metallic reserve ratio fell from 42 percent to 28 percent. The British attacks on Washington and Baltimore in August 1814, provoked a run on the specie in the weakened state banks and a general suspension of convertibility. There was some belated resort to domestic taxes, but not enough to make up for diminished customs receipts. The national debt, which had been reduced from $83 million to $45 million between 1800 and 1811, reached its pre-Civil War peak of $127 million in 1815, financed largely by depreciated State bank notes.

Madison, now president (1809–17), had developed a more favorable view of a national bank, which might restore "the benefits of a national currency," as well as, in Secretary of the Treasury A.J. Dallas's proposal, assist the government. Congress shared the administration's desire for a national bank, but not to the same degree, and substituted its own more modest bank, which Madison vetoed because its capital was insufficient "to produce, in favor of the public credit any considerable or lasting elevation of the market price [and] it must be kept in view that the sole inducement to such a grant [of a bank charter] would be the prospect of substantial aids to its pecuniary means at the present crisis" (Clarke and Hall 1832, p. 609).

"The objection of Congress to the original plan," Bray Hammond wrote, "had been that the Bank had too much of the Government in it. President Madison's objection was that in the Bank proposed by Congress the Government was left out" (Hammond 1957, p. 232). The compromise agreed in April 1816, reflected sound-money interests tempered by the government's desire for a line of credit. Its capital would be $35,000,000, compared with $10,000,000 for the first Bank and the $50,000,000 desired by Madison, with government loans limited to $500,000, compared with $100,000 for the first Bank.

The government was not the only important force behind the Bank. "While many men played their parts in the agitation for a second national bank," Raymond Walters (1945) wrote, "the real leadership was exercised by a half-dozen men," including the financiers John Jacob Astor, David Parish, Stephen Girard, and Jacob Barker, who foresaw participations in the issue of the Bank's stock and improvements in government security prices, as well as, patriotically, more adequate financing of the country's war effort.

Speaking for the Bank bill in the House of Representatives, John Calhoun turned the earlier constitutional objection around. The Constitution in fact required an agency to regulate the currency. "No one could doubt that" the power (and responsibility) "to coin money [and] regulate the value thereof" meant "that the money of the United States was intended to be placed entirely under the control of Congress." However, it now consisted principally of paper currency which had been allowed to develop in a way that defied the Constitution. "By a sort of under-current, [in a] revolution of the currency, ... the power of Congress to regulate the money of the country had caved in, and upon its ruins had sprung up those institutions which now exercised the right of making money for and in the United States."

"In point of fact," Speaker Henry Clay added, "the regulation of the general currency is in the hands of the state Governments, or, which is the same thing, of the banks created by them." It was "incumbent upon Congress to recover ... control." Although the direct regulation of the state banks was impracticable, a sound currency might be regained by the restraining influence of a national bank.

Daniel Webster, who would become a counsel for the second Bank of the United States, including the *McCulloch v. Maryland* case, opposed its creation. The war was over and all that was needed to restore the value and stability of the currency was its compulsory redemption. He proposed that the government accept payment only in coin or redeemable bank notes, and keep no deposits in "any bank which shall not pay its notes, when demanded, in the lawful money of the United States" (Clarke and Hall 1832, pp. 630–34, 669–72, 681–82; *Annals of Congress*, April 30, 1816). Webster's resolution and, with some redundancy, the second Bank's 20-year charter were approved in April 1816, when the later Great Triumvirate of the Senate were members of the House

"The Bank began business in the midst of temptations on every hand to over-extend itself," joining the postwar speculation that it was supposed to control and almost failing along with numerous state banks when the bubble burst. There was little control of the Bank's branches, several of which created obligations beyond the abilities of other branches to redeem them. It survived only with the help of the U.S. Treasury, but at the end of the decade was in a position to force the general resumption of convertibility (Hammond 1957, pp. 256–59).

Under pressure from the Treasury, the Bank began to require its claims on state banks to be redeemed in specie, inducing falls in bank credit, money, and prices, which with the fall in exports to Europe, contributed to the Panic of 1819 and the depression of 1819–21. The Bank's "grim efforts" to collect its debts aroused a popular hatred that "was never extinguished," Hammond wrote. "The Bank was saved and the people were ruined," Jackson's bank-hating advisor William Gouge observed during the debate over its renewal. Maryland was one of several states which had attempted to tax the Bank. After all, the state banks had to pay state taxes. In September 1819, six months after *McCulloch* vs. *Maryland*, an agent of Ohio's state auditor leaped over the counter of the U.S. Bank's Chillicothe office and seized funds regarded by the State as its due (Hammond 1957, pp. 259, 267; Gouge 1833, p. 110).

The Bank's fortunes turned up during the prosperous 1820s, and some have claimed that it was the first conscious central bank. "Not only did it expand [credit] while reserves fell" during the gold drain of 1831, Richard Timberlake (1993, pp. 38–39) wrote, "but it practiced forbearance in presenting notes of other banks for redemption." In 1825, on the other hand, the Bank sought self-protection by contracting credit while the country was losing specie. Explanations of the Bank's behavior have varied between its sometimes stabilizing influence and critics' claim that it was a monopolistic predator. In fact, the Bank's credit tended to vary with that of the state banks, expanding in good times (reducing its reserve ratio) and contracting in hard times, but more conservatively, typical of large suppliers seeking market stability, like U.S. Steel in the twentieth century and Saudi Arabia today (Highfield et al. 1991).

The primary force ending the Bank was President Jackson's conviction that it was unconstitutional, supported by his general dislike of federal government activities. Added to these were the Bank's lack of friends. The state banks resented its competition and restraint, there was a popular fear of its power, and it was no longer needed to finance a deficit or stabilize the currency. Clay had opposed the Bank's renewal in 1811, but had learned "that war cannot be carried on without the aid of banks." However, "Times have changed," Missouri Senator Thomas "Old Bullion" Benton declared in 1831. "The war made the bank; peace will unmake it" (Wood 2006; Clay, *Cong. Globe*, July 15, 1841; Krooss 1969, p. 736).

This was a powerful point. Even Jackson might have tolerated the Bank if war finance had been needed. The English did not go so far, but some of the privileges and powers of the Bank of England were withdrawn during the years following the Battle of Waterloo (Wood 2005, pp. 60–88).

The peacetime usefulness of the U.S. Bank as a central bank, that is, its contribution to stability, was disputed at the time, and later, but any judgment of its performance depends on the time period chosen and especially on the fiscal behavior of the government. The Bank's unhappiest period, its early years, when it was thrust into the inconvertibility and speculation left by the war, were not of its own making, but of the government's fiscal policy. The war had been financed by bonds sold for unrestrained State bank paper, and the Bank was expected to restore a gold-backed currency. A good part, maybe most, of the blame for its initial ineptness and then the crushing deflation should be laid at the door of the federal government. Madison et al. wanted a central bank to pull them out of the hole they had dug by their political cowardice. Not for the first time.

During the 1830s, however, the primary criticism of the Bank was not what it had done but what it could do. When Bank President Nicholas Biddle defended the Bank against the charge of hostility toward the state banks by claiming that it had often relieved them when they might "have been destroyed by an exertion of the power of the Bank," "This is enough," Senator Benton exclaimed, "Proof enough for all who are unwilling to see a moneyed oligarchy established in this land, and the entire Union subjected to its sovereign will. The power to destroy all other banks is admitted and declared; the inclination to do so is known to all rational beings to reside with the power! Policy may restrain the destroying faculties for the present; but they exist; and will come forth when interest prompts and policy permits" (Krooss 1969, pp. 698–737).

The Bank's charter would not elapse until 1836, but Jackson's opponents in Congress made it a campaign issue by voting for its extension in 1832. Jackson took up the gauntlet by vetoing the act, and after his vindication by reelection n, began the withdrawal of government deposits from the Bank.

The anti-Jacksonians hoped to restore the Bank during the Whig administration of William Henry Harrison, elected in 1840. In a public debate in Springfield in 1839, Illinois politician Abraham Lincoln spoke for a Bank as opposed to the Treasury as a repository of public funds. The latter would "reduce the quantity of money in circulation," especially since "the revenue is to be collected in specie," which is the basis of the paper circulation. On the other hand, a bank will pay for the opportunity to keep the public money, which "will be more secure in a national bank than in the hands of individuals, as proposed in the subtreasury"—not because bank officers are necessarily more honest than other men but because, unlike subtreasurers, "the interest of the bank is on the side of its duty" (Lincoln 1907, i, pp. 29–60). However, the Democratic vice-president, John Tyler, who had succeeded to the presidency upon Harrison's death after 31 days in office, vetoed the Bank bill, and a national bank had to wait until 1913.

We have seen that historians condemned Jackson's destruction of the Bank, but it was not missed by the economy. The popular story that its decline allowed excessive state bank expansions and a speculative boom which precipitated the Panic of 1837 and the ensuing depression is unsupported by evidence. In fact, bank reserve ratios remained strong and their credit expansions followed inflows of capital, especially from Great Britain, and specie. "Since the reserve ratio did not fall below its previous level after the removal of the government deposits from the Second Bank," Peter Temin concluded, "the explanation that sees the 'freeing' of the state banks … as the genesis of the inflation must be rejected." The end of the American inflation came in 1837, with the increase in the Bank of England's discount rate as it reacted to a loss of gold, and the fall in the price of cotton which came with reduced British demand (Temin 1969, pp. 71–81, 138–47).

In fact, the end of the Bank was followed by what has been called America's First Great Moderation—a recession-free, 16-year period from 1841 to 1856, the longest economic expansion in U.S. history: with high rates of economic growth and private capital formation, and low financial and macroeconomic volatility, despite, Joseph Davis and Marc Weidenmier (2016), write, "a low level of government spending and the absence of a central bank." The economy's performance resembled that of the Second Great Moderation of 1984–2007. It was led "by a surge in durable goods production," supported by the adoption of general purpose technologies (ships, railroads, and the telegraph), increased financial-market integration, immigration, western expansion, the absence of major international conflict, and low and stable tariff rates. The development of financial markets, reflected in falling interest rate differentials between cities, took advantage of the telegraph, new modes of transportation, and the spread of correspondent banking.

The Independent Treasury

Be it enacted ... Sec. 6. That the Treasurer of the United States ... and all public officials ... are hereby required to keep safely, without loaning, using, [or] depositing in banks ... all the public money collected by them ... till the same is ordered by the proper department or officer of the Government to be transferred or paid out....

Sec. 18. That on January 1, 1847, and thereafter, all duties, taxes, sales of public lands, debts, and sums of money accruing or becoming due to the United States ... shall be paid in gold or silver coin only, or in treasury notes....

That on April 1, 1847, and thereafter, every officer or agent engaged in making disbursements on account of the United States ... shall make all payments in gold and silver coin, or in treasury notes if the creditor agrees to receive said notes. (*Independent Treasury Act*, Aug. 6, 1846.)

The end of the Bank of the United States required the federal government to find a new depository or depositories, which, as between 1811 and 1816, had to be the state banks. It fell to the Secretary of the Treasury to select the banks, and in 1836, Congress directed that all states and territories contain depositories. The Act of June 1836 to *Regulate the Deposits of Public Money* ordered that the federal surplus to be distributed among the states "in proportion to their respective representation in the Senate and House of Representatives of the United States," a process which ended the next year when the surplus turned to deficit.

The panic and bank suspensions of 1837, led the new president, Martin Van Buren, to call a special session of Congress for September 4, before which he advocated the separation of government from the banks, that it collect, keep, and disburse its own funds. This was intended to separate public funds from the risks of banking, lessen the volatility of the currency, and remove the choice of depositories, the so-called pet banks, from the realm of politics. The end of the Second Bank and Panic of 1837 had already brought the Independent Treasury system into effect, but it was not until after almost three years of debate that Van Buren's plan was narrowly formalized by Congress in June 1840 (Kinley 1910, pp. 26–37; Hammond 1957, pp. 419–21). It was criticized in the Senate by Daniel Webster:

> The use of money is in the exchange. It is designed to circulate, not to be hoarded. All the Government should have to do with it is to receive it today, that it may pay it away tomorrow. It should not receive it before it needs it, and it should part with it as soon as it owes it. To keep it – that is, to detain it, to hold it back from general use, to hoard it, is a conception belonging to barbarous times and barbarous Governments (*Cong. Globe*, March 12, 1838).

The Independent Treasury was repealed in 1841 by the Whig Congress in preparation for a third United States Bank, which, however, was vetoed by the democrat John Tyler, who had succeeded to the presidency upon the early death of President William Henry Harrison. "The subject" resumed "the old weary round of discussion in Congress," until early in the administration of former Jackson supporter, President James Polk. The Independent Treasury was reestablished by a vote along party lines in 1846, and it managed the federal government's cash until the coming of the Federal Reserve (Kinley 1910, p. 50).

Despite its inconsistent, even irrational, formal construction, the Treasury's monetary performance between 1846 and 1914 compares favorably with the Federal Reserve's that succeeded it. I say "irrational" because the requirement that the Independent Treasury accumulate or dispose of gold according to the dictates of the budgetary balance might not have been consistent with the monetary standard's fixed gold value of the dollar. The stability of the dollar under the Independent Treasury was due to the intelligence and sensitivity of secretaries who manipulated, even violated, laws which rigidly followed would have been self-defeating.

The system exposed the monetary base to shocks from federal budgets, although it also contained an element of automatic stabilization. Prosperity and inflation might restrain money and credit by the government's accumulation of specie through rising excise and customs receipts. On the other hand, there was a long-term deflationary effect because of the government's tendency to run surpluses. During the last quarter of the century, Treasury cash balances varied between \$50 million and \$250 million compared with an average monetary base of \$1 billion, and a good part of its stabilizing operations of sometimes doubtful legality included what we now call open-market operations.

An early illustration of the Treasury's monetary discretion was reported by Secretary James Guthrie in 1853. Funds "still continuing to accumulate in the Treasury,"

> apprehensions were entertained that a contraction of discounts by the city banks of New York ... might have an injurious influence on financial and commercial operations. With a view, therefore, to give public assurance that money would not be permitted to accumulate in the Treasury, a public offer was made on the 30th of July to redeem ... $5 million of the loans of 1847 and 1848.

Secretary Howell Cobb behaved similarly after the Panic of 1857, but not without limit, and worried that the market had become too dependent. He defended the Treasury's halt to debt purchases in the 1857 *Treasury Report*:

> There are many persons who seem to think that it is the duty of the Government to provide relief in all cases of trouble and distress [and that] it not only can, but ought to relieve them.

The Mexican War was financed in a straightforward manner. The national debt rose from $16 million to $63 million between 1846 and 1849, but government issues were placed at par. "This success may well be compared" Dewey wrote, "with the financiering of the War of 1812, when loans ... were sold with difficulty and at a discount." The more recent "ease of the treasury was due not so much to a wiser intelligence as to the great increase in the wealth of the country and to the advance in government credit.... More significant than any other tribute to the credit of the government was the fact that the loan was subscribed for in specie – the first loan subscribed for on this basis since the foundation of the government" (Dewey 1922, pp. 255–56).

The government's deficits were limited to the market's confidence in its ability and willingness to repay. Particular problems during the War of 1812 had been the war's unpopularity in large sections of the country, especially New England, which threatened secession and refused to buy government securities, along with the government's reluctance or inability to raise taxes. Congress approved the declaration of war in 1812 by the narrowest margin in history, 60 percent of the House after a four-day closed session. No Federalist voted for the war.

There was considerable opposition to the Mexican War by those who saw its purpose as the expansion of slave territory, including Congressman Abraham Lincoln, whose "spot resolutions" demanded that President Polk provide Congress with the spot upon which blood was spilt on American soil, as he had claimed when asking Congress for a declaration of war. Henry Thoreau's essay on *Civil Disobedience* and his refusal to pay taxes were aimed especially at the Mexican War. Nevertheless, Congress voted overwhelmingly for the war.

The Civil War saw greatly increased taxes. The autobiography of John Sherman, member and sometimes chairman of the Senate Finance Committee includes the following anecdote:

> So sweeping were the [tax] provisions that it was frequently a matter of joke as well as comment. Some one remarked to [fellow committee member, Vermont] Senator Collamer that everything was taxed except coffins. He rejoined: 'Don't say that to Sherman or he will have them on the tax list before night!' (1895, i, p. 304)

Even so, the large deficits exceeded the Treasury's credit, and it suspended the gold convertibility of the dollar at the end of 1861. The interest rates required to sell government bonds were high, and Congress turned to inconvertible legal-tender currency (the greenbacks).

It also arranged for a system of "national banks" chartered by the Comptroller of the Currency, an agency of the U.S. Treasury created for the purpose. The National Bank Act of 1863 was a war measure, a device for promoting the demand for federal government debt, which permitted national banks to count greenbacks as reserves and issue currency (national bank notes) secured by government bonds. The spread of national banks was less than desired as most banks preferred state charters. In 1865, Congress levied a 10-percent tax on state bank notes, which caused a change in the ratio of national to state banks from 467/1089 to 1294/349. With the growth of payment by check encouraged by the law, however, most banks returned to state charters—70 percent by 1914—where they have remained (*Historical Statistics*, X634, X580).

The *National Bank Act* was too late to help the war effort but the money stock tripled during the war, prices rose 80 percent, and the gold premium on the dollar rose to 200 percent (Fig. 5.1). At the end of the war, a House resolution stating "the necessity for a contraction of the currency with a view to as early a resumption of specie payment at the business interests of the country would permit," passed by a vote of 144–6. The Secretary of the Treasury, Hugh McCulloch, determined to bring the country back to the "specie basis … at the earliest date practicable" (Unger 1959, p. 41).

When the Treasury accordingly contracted the money stock, however, "the resolution soon proved not to reflect the real sentiment of the peo-

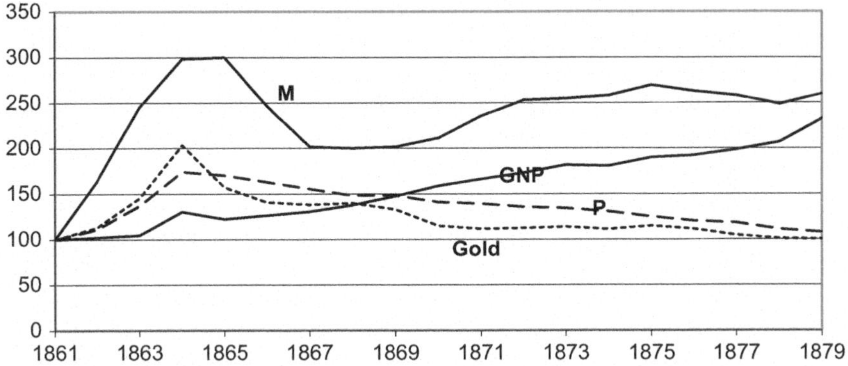

Fig. 5.1 Money, Dollar value of gold, price level, and real GDP, 1861 = 100. (Sources: Gold value (Mitchell, *History of Greenbacks*, Table 1), Money (Friedman and Schwartz, *Monetary History*, Table A1), P and GNP (Balke and Gordon, *American Business Cycles*, App. B))

ple" (Dewey 1922, p. 335). Debtors did not want deflation, creditors did not want their borrowers ruined, and an avalanche of complaints to Congress induced it to slow and then, in 1868, halt the retirement. The retirement of the greenbacks remained an active political issue for the next decade, and was never carried through, but the dollar reached its prewar gold value in January 1879 (Unger 1959; 1964, p. 41). Resumption was accomplished not by reducing the currency (which actually rose) but by the growth of the economy into the currency. In terms of the *quantity equation* MV = PY, P was restored to its prewar value by a growth in Y rather than by the initially planned reduction in M.

The slow American resumption of 1864–79, twice as long as the U.S. and U.K. resumptions after the Napoleonic Wars and World War I, was criticized on moral and economic grounds. Yet the post-Civil War resumption was the least damaging of the group—deflation was slower and smoother, and prosperity reigned. The determinations of the expert, politically distant central banks rode roughshod over the electorate in a way that the politically more sensitive Congress was unwilling to do. Deflations on the heels of inflations are painful. Many plans are disappointed. The "embarrassment" of "the great host[s] of debtors … and … creditors" [voters], Congressman James G. Blaine (1886, ii, p. 328) said, ought as much as possible be avoided.

The Resumption Act of 1875 was criticized as unlikely to achieve its desired effect. The Act directed the Treasury to redeem greenbacks at the rate of 80 percent of increases in national bank notes, with the proviso that greenbacks, which had risen to $382,000,000, not be reduced below $300,000,000, and set a date, January 1, 1879, for resumption at the prewar dollar value of gold.

Its leading advocate, Senator Sherman, refused to speculate on details of the Act's enforcement, but said the difficulties envisioned "may never arise…. But if there is any doubt …, I leave every Senator to construe the law for himself," and trust that those in charge will make the necessary decisions (*CR*, December 22, 1874). In the event, although the 80 percent greenback/bank-note rule sounded inflationary, it was actually contractionary because greenbacks were high-powered money, and, helped by a surge of agricultural exports to make up for poor harvests in Europe, the gold value of the dollar was resumed on schedule

The Treasury, overseen by the House of Representatives, had continued to stabilize the currency. When George Boutwell (1869–73), President Grant's first secretary of the Treasury, was criticized for reissuing $5,000,000 of retired greenbacks in 1872, he replied that relief from panics had never been attained even in England "without the personal intervention of men possessing power." His use of the greenback reserve was

> … in its effect … substantially what is done by the Government of Great Britain through the Bank of England. The Secretary furnished temporary relief … by adding to the circulation of the country, diminishing its value … and changing the relations of debtor and creditor…. Clothed with authority by law, … the Secretary of the Treasury could not sit silent and inactive while ruin was blasting the prospects of many and creating the most serious apprehensions in all parts of the country. It was a great responsibility; but it is a responsibility which must be taken by men who are clothed with the authority (*CR*, January 22, 1874).

Speaking for the Morrison resolution (see below) which directed the Treasury's cash management, Kentucky Senator James Beck reminded his colleagues that whereas the laws creating the other executive departments enjoined their heads to advise and act under the direction of the president, the secretary of the Treasury was required to "report … to either branch of the Legislature … and generally to perform all such services relative to the finances as he shall be directed to perform…. We with the Secretary of the Treasury manage the purse; the president and the other secretaries control the sword" (*CR*, January 29, 1886).

Congressmen complained of the large sums in Treasury vaults, and the Appropriation Act of 1881 gave the Treasury discretion to redeem government debt. Balances remained high, however, and rose at first during the democratic Cleveland administration (1885–89), which desired a "prudent" reserve (Timberlake 1993, p. 154). However, Secretary Charles Fairchild (1887–89), who "always considered the needs of banks," used a Civil War loophole in the law (to allow loan proceeds to be deposited in such specie-paying banks as the secretary might select) to expand Treasury bank deposits from $13 million to $54 million during recession. On the other hand, President Benjamin Harrison's (1889–93) Secretary William Windom (1889–91), "a strict observer of the letter of the Law of 1846, ... believed that the policy of depositing public money in banks was wholly unjustifiable," and cut the Treasury's bank deposits to $21 million; but also said after relieving the stringency of 1890 that the Treasury's practice "to furnish relief" has, "when possible, in all commercial crises from 1846 to the present time ... been its uniform policy" (Taus 1943, p. 82; Kinley 1910, p. 205).

Those wanting an increase in money got Congress's approval of the Morrison resolution (July 1886) which directed the Treasury to apply "its surplus or balance ... over $100,000,000 ... to the payment of the interest-bearing indebtedness of the United States" at a maximum rate of $10,000,000 a month. (Morrison, a democrat, was chairman of the House Committee on Ways and Means).

Some thought the Treasury's help came at the expense of market discipline. *The Commercial and Financial Chronicle* noted:

> The time was when our banks provided beforehand for the fall trade and so trimmed their sales through the summer months to avert a storm by preparing themselves for the crop demand. Of late years they have looked to the Treasury wholly and have gone through the summer trenching on their reserves regardless of any increased drain sure to come later on. (December 6, 1890; Taus 1943, p. 88)

In 1886, Ohio's A.J. Warner quoted Lord Overstone, author of the monetary rule in the Bank (of England) Charter Act of 1844: "In adopting a paper circulation we must unavoidably depend for a maintenance of its due value upon the adoption of a strict and judicious rule for the regulation of its amount. "Senator Beck argued that it was a responsibility of Congress to direct the secretary to relieve him of temptation and political embarrassment. Maine's Nelson Dingley, on the other hand, thought Congress should avoid "a question which exclusively pertains to administration." The compromise between rules and discretion took the form of a minimum balance at the Treasury with debt purchases subject to conditions (*CR*, July 13, 1886, pp. 6884, 6887; July 14, p. 6397; July 29, p. 7675; August 4, p. 7998).

Monetary policy during the last decades of the nineteenth century was dominated by the *politics of silver*. The United States was officially on a bimetallic (gold and silver) monetary standard, but because the market price of silver had been higher than the mint price, the silver dollar had not been in circulation since 1836, and was officially discontinued in 1873. However, the price of silver began to fall in 1872, due to the western silver strikes, reinforced by a shift in demand from silver to gold as several countries shifted from silver- to gold-based currencies. The price of silver fell from $1.33 an ounce in 1870 to 94¢ in 1888 and 53¢ in 1910, meaning a fall in the gold/silver ratio from 15.5/1 to 39/1 (about 75/1 in 2017), given the price of gold fixed at $20.67 (Friedman and Schwartz 1963, pp. 113–14).

A fall in gold production combined with the increased demand for gold produced a one-third fall in the price level between 1873 and 1896. A similar price decline in Great Britain was called "the Great Depression" (Saul 1969). Opponents of deflation along with silver producers wanted to restore silver to the money stock, that is, return to bimetallism. They hoped the increased demand would raise the price of silver, but their proposals (given an increased political weight by the admission of six western states to the Union between 1886 and 1890) also called for government purchases at above-market prices.

Their sound-money opponents saw the dependence of foreign investment on a stable dollar, meaning the continuation of the gold standard which the United States shared with leading trading nations, and might be disrupted by the introduction of volatile silver. In a compromise reached during the recession of 1890–91, the Sherman Silver Purchase Act provided for the government's purchase of 4.5 million ounces of silver "at no more than" $1.18 an ounce, with Treasury notes issued for the purchase. This arbitrage opportunity (see above) led to gold drains from the Treasury, paid for with silver money, and a run on American gold by foreigners fearful of the country's commitment to the gold value of the dollar. Under the pressure of these withdrawals, Congress repealed the Silver Purchase Act during a special session called by President Grover Cleveland in 1893. Ohio Senator Sherman defended the Act and his change of position:

> Sir, 'give the devil his due.' The law of 1890 may have many faults, but I stand by it yet, and I will defend it, not as a permanent public policy, not as a measure that I take any pride in, because I yielded to the necessity of granting relief, but I do say that … without it, in 1891 and 1892, we would have met difficulties that would have staggered us.… The immediate result of the measure was to increase our currency, and thus relieve our people from the panic then imminent, similar to that which we now suffer. The very men who now denounce from Wall Street this compromise were shouting 'Hallelujah!' for their escape by it from free coinage. (Miller 1913, xiv, p. 398)

Legislators again showed a combination of economic understanding and sensitivity to their constituents lacking the next century.

However, the silver movement, led by William Jennings Bryan, who in the keynote address at the 1896 Democratic convention promised that "mankind shall not be crucified upon a cross of gold," still threatened, and the gold standard was not assured. The government sold bonds to bolster its gold reserves, which, however, were themselves withdrawn from the Treasury. Only with Bryan's defeat in the presidential election of 1896 and the rise in world gold production was the convertibility of the dollar assured, enabling Congress to shift formally from bimetallism to gold in the Gold Standard Act of 1900.

U.S. monetary policy from the last years of the nineteenth century, as in other leading trading nations, most conducted by central banks, aimed at stability under the gold standard. Both Houses of Congress were controlled by the Republican Party from 1895 to 1911. Presidents were Republican throughout the period, except Cleveland (1893–97), who was also a sound-money man. That this was the nation's preference was indicated by national elections. After closely contested contests in the five presidential elections between 1876 and 1892, when the ratios of Democratic to Republican votes were 1.06, 0.99, 0.99, 1.02, and 1.07, the former's adoption of Bryan and easy money in contradiction to their Jefferson-Jackson heritage brought four consecutive landslide losses with Democrat/Republican ratios 0.91, 0.88, 0.67, and 0.84 from 1896 to 1908.

There was considerable stability among the makers of monetary policy during the Independent Treasury. For example, Rhode Island Senator Nelson Aldrich (father of Mrs. John D. Rockefeller, Jr., and grandfather of

Chase National Bank Chairman Winthrop Aldrich) was a member of the Senate Finance Committee from 1881 to 1911, chairman from 1899. John Sherman served on the committee from 1861 to 1897 (chairman 1864–65, 1868–77) except four years (1877–81) during which he was Secretary of the Treasury. This was quite a political feat in a swing state in which issues were strongly contested. *Bartlett's Familiar Quotations* credits him with the classic line:

> I have come home to look after my fences. (Speech to his neighbors, Mansfield, Ohio (reference to his farm).)

Significant parts of pre-Federal Reserve monetary policies can be told in the experiences of these two politicians. In Sherman's case, we begin with the experiences of his father, Charles Sherman (1788–1829), who moved from Connecticut to Ohio in 1810, practiced law, and became an Ohio supreme court justice in 1823. In 1813, he was appointed collector of federal Internal Revenue [taxes on spirits, salt, sugar, carriages, and auction sales, and a stamp duty of 1 percent on bank notes] for the Third District of Ohio, for which he employed a deputy collector in each of the district's six counties, all of whom were required to post bond, as was Sherman as chief collector. "At this period the only money in Ohio was local bank paper money. No silver or gold coins could be had, and the purchasing power of notes varied with the success or defeat of our armies in the field," John Sherman wrote in his autobiography. "No difficulty seems to have occurred until July 1817, when the government, without previous notice, refused to take the paper then in circulation in Ohio, but demanded notes of the Bank of the United States, or its branches, one of which was located at Chillicothe. This left upon the hands of [Sherman's] deputies a large amount of money that soon became utterly worthless. The system of local banking failed and the loss fell upon the holders of notes, and, largely, upon the collectors of internal revenue and their deputies." Sherman never recovered from this financial blow, as he "applied the proceeds of all his property, and a large part of his earnings, to make good, as far as he could, the defalcations of his deputies" (Sherman 1895, i, pp. 18–20).

Charles Sherman died in 1829, leaving his wife with eleven children, including John, age six, and William Tecumseh, age nine. Several of the children were taken in by relatives or friends, William by Thomas Ewing, future U.S. senator, Secretary of the Treasury, and first Secretary of the Interior, whose daughter married "Cum." The younger children mainly stayed at home until they left for work, John as a junior surveyor at age fourteen. He studied law at an older brother's practice in Mansfield, Ohio, prospered, and in 1847, helped buy a house in Mansfield for his mother and unmarried sisters.

Sherman had taken the middle way during the post-Civil War greenback debate, "sitting on the fence" between those who wanted to resume "as soon as practicable" and those opposed to deflation. Nor did he take a firm position on the Bland-Allison (silver purchase) bill of 1878 (stimulated by the Panic of 1873 and a sluggish economy), passed by Congress over the president's veto. "In view of the strong public sentiment in favor of the free coinage of the silver dollar," he wrote, "I thought it better to make no objections to the passage of the bill" (Sherman 1895, p. 623). We have seen that he also arranged a compromise easy-money bill in 1890, and joined in its repeal in 1893.

David Kinley's history of the Independent Treasury referred to "a decade of vacillating policy after resumption." Secretaries paid lip service to the law regarding Treasury specie in good times but supplied reserves to the money market during periods of stringency. These actions "raised a good deal of criticism and protest," with secretaries on the defensive. "Under the administration of Secretary Gage, however, the volume of [bank] deposits increased pretty rapidly, and we have the first clear evidence of the adoption by the Treasury Department of the policy of accumulating a volume of deposits determined by the state of the money market." The machinery used to relieve stringencies had become a continuous regulator of the money market (Kinley 1910, pp. 117–22).

The years 1897–1909 have been called the heyday of the Treasury's monetary policy, when the effects of its operations on bank reserves and the money stock resembled a central bank's. Friedman and Schwartz suggested that the Treasury's "central-banking activities ... were being converted from emergency measures to a fairly regular and predictable operating function" (Friedman and Schwartz 1963, p. 149). Secretaries were dedicated to the gold standard as the key to sound money, and as much monetary stability as could be achieved under that standard, which they knew was not automatic. Unlike most developed nations, the United States had not established a formal central bank for these purposes, but a stable political majority had molded existing institutions to accomplish their ends. The time was auspicious. The federal budget was close to balance, usually in surplus, and the gold strikes toward the end of the century brought gold reserves and rising prices.

Secretary Lyman Gage (1897–1902), in his *Treasury Report* for 1899, said that "Stability [of the] currency should be safely guarded, [but] *flex-*

ibility – the power of needful expansion – must also be provided." Secretary Leslie Shaw (1902–1907) got around the requirement that customs receipts be kept in the Treasury by declaring banks to be Treasury offices. When his actions were condemned as autocratic and primarily for the benefit of "a ring of powerful Wall Street speculators," he answered during a speech to the American Bankers' Association: "It has been the fixed policy of the Treasury Department for more than half a century to anticipate monetary stringencies, and so far as possible prevent panics" (Timberlake 1993, p. 192). George Cortelyou (1907–1909) was active in supplying funds to the banking system during the panic of 1907. Secretary Franklin MacVeagh (1909–1913) stated in his last annual report:

> Taking large sums of actual money out of the ordinary financial use and locking it up as a dead mass in the vaults of the Treasury is a proceeding as unscientific and unreasoned as any other part of our unreasoned and unscientific banking and currency system (U.S. Treasury 1912, p. 3).

These officials regularly advocated monetary reforms that would include an agency directed to the stabilization of bank reserves, but in the meantime used the Treasury to that end as much as they were able; which was significant because their actions received at least the tacit support of Congress, which, as in other times, was unable to agree on legislation. But because the Independent Treasury law "has been repealed piecemeal, … step by step the separation of the Treasury and the banks has been done away with by [practice and] special legislation… [F]ormal repeal of the law now would be largely perfunctory" (Kinley 1910, p. 207).

Creating the Federal Reserve

> Financial textbook writers of Europe have characterized our American system as "barbarous," and eminent bankers of this country who, from time to time, have appeared before the Banking and Currency Committee of the House have not hesitated to confess that this bitter criticism is merited. Five times within the last 30 years financial catastrophe has overtaken the country under this system; … The System literally has no reserve force. The currency based upon the Nation's debt is absolutely unresponsive to the Nation's business needs. The lack of cooperation and coordination among the more than 7300 national banks produces a curtailment of facilities at all periods of exceptional demand for credit. (Carter Class introducing the Federal Reserve bill in the House of Representatives, Sept. 1913.)

Origins: The Problem and Proposed Solutions A financial panic (or "catastrophe" as Glass called it) is a rush for cash. Business, particularly inventory and securities management by production, retail, and financial firms, requires cash today and its assurance tomorrow. The frequent interruptions of cash flow in the United States had several causes which together resulted in an "inelastic currency." Currency consisted primarily of bank notes backed by U.S. bonds. The inelastic quantity of the latter prevented currency from meeting the needs of business expansion cyclically or seasonally.[4] Regarding the latter, the typically increasing demands for currency during busy fourth quarters depleted banks' reserves when their resources should have been rising to meet credit demands. This had been recognized, as we saw, by the U.S. Treasury.

The large number of commercial banks—about 27,000 in 1913, compared with 11,000 in 1896—was also a problem. Shifts in reserves from money centers to the interior, as happened during harvests, led to crises in the former. The "National Banking System was not really a system at all," Robert West (1979, p. 29) wrote, "but rather a loose body of independent banks responsible only to themselves and … for themselves."

Obvious potential responses to the problem included (1) branch banking and (2) a central bank ready to be lender of last resort, as had operated successfully in some other countries. However, both were political anathema in the United States. The thousands of small banks with local monopolies stood in the way of permissive branching laws until the bank difficulties of the 1980s, and central banking, which suggested control from New York, was resisted by rural and even Main Street America. Reformers at the end of the nineteenth century had to take the banking structure as given. "We also made a careful study of the branch banking system of Canada," Glass told the House,

> and while we found that it had admirably served its purpose in that country we came to the conclusion that it would not be possible to apply it to the American system without vital alterations which would run athwart the banking principles and the business habits to which the American people have been so long accustomed. (*CR*, September 10, 1913)

[4]The availability of eligible U.S. bonds did not in fact limit national bank notes, which were never more than 30 percent of the amount permitted. James (1976) attributed this to the greater profitability of bank loans, which were more often extended in the process of deposit creation than bonds.

An 1894 proposal known as the Baltimore Plan because it was presented at a conference of the American Bankers' Association in that city was to back bank deposits by total bank assets instead of by U.S. bonds as provided by the National Bank Act. Secretary William Richardson (1873–74) had indicated that "There is a prevailing sentiment that more elasticity should be given to the volume of the currency, so that the amount in circulation might increase and diminish according to the necessities of the business of the country." The Baltimore presentation was part of New York bankers' practice of operating in the background to avoid the animosity felt toward "Wall Street" (U.S. Treasury 1893; West 1977, p. 43).

The Indianapolis Monetary Commission's plan of 1900 would have linked banks' currency issues to their capital (West 1977, pp. 42–45; Wicker 2005, pp. 24–32). Neither the Baltimore nor the Indianapolis plan made significant political headway, nor did proposed legislation to expand the powers of the Treasury or clearinghouses.

An American central bank would have to wait for a significant political shift and a structure peculiar to the country of its birth. Prominent intellectual and political contributors to the eventual central bank included banker Paul Warburg, Senator Nelson Aldrich, Virginia Congressman Carter Glass, his advisor, Washington and Lee Professor Parker Willis, and President Woodrow Wilson.

Warburg took an early conceptual step toward an American central bank, and Aldrich brought it into the realm of the politically possible, which Glass and Wilson completed. Warburg has been called "the single most powerful force in shaping the direction of American banking reform" (West 1977, p. 56). A member of the ancient Hamburg family banking firm, he married Nina Loeb in 1895, emigrated to the United States and became a Kuhn, Loeb partner in 1902, and an American citizen in 1911. He believed the American banking system was inferior to the European because it lacked the centralization of reserves that could be distributed as needed on the basis of commercial paper (bills of exchange; see the plate). European money markets were based on commercial paper created in the process of exchange and for which there was a secondary market. *Real* bills were created in the process of financing purchases of real goods, such as inventories, which might be resold to a central bank for reserves.

For example, the buyer of \$98 worth of goods might issue the seller a bill promising payment of \$100 in 3 months' time. The discount rate is

$$[(100 - 98)/100]\ 12/3 = 8\ \%\ \text{per annum}$$

A good bill (promissory note) is negotiable and might be sold (rediscounted) many times before its maturity, including to the central bank.

Warburg's plan for "A Modified Central Bank" (1907), or "A United Reserve Bank" (1910), envisioned a central bank in Washington and twenty operating zones spread throughout the country, a regional concept shared with Victor Morawetz (1909, 1911). Their ideas made an impression in Washington, most importantly with Senate Finance Committee Chairman, Nelson Aldrich, who developed the Aldrich Bill of 1908 after the panic of 1907.

Aldrich's bill proposed a system of currency associations voluntarily organized by banks which in times of crisis might issue emergency currency backed by private and government bonds deposited by the banks. This was opposed by western banks whose principal assets were different and who claimed the Aldrich Bill was merely a scheme to aid the "Money Trust." The Aldrich-Vreeland Act of 1908 was a compromise in which emergency currency issued by currency associations was based on both commercial paper and government bonds.[5] It was a temporary measure, scheduled to expire in 1914, until a permanent arrangement could be agreed. Even the temporary act passed narrowly along party lines. It came into play once, when it provided currency during the financial crisis on the outbreak of World War I.

The Aldrich-Vreeland Act also provided for a National Monetary Commission to study money and banking problems and propose solutions. Chaired by Senator Aldrich, it commissioned several studies of foreign and historical banking systems. These studies appeared too late to influence legislation because Democrats, who won the House in the elections of 1910, as well as the Senate and the presidency in 1912, opposed any bill coming from Aldrich and the "money trust."

Historian Gregory Kolko wrote that "banking reform at the beginning of 1912 seemed a dead issue, of interest only to a few bankers and … seriously divided" citizens groups. Bankers continued their efforts, however, and found an ally in Carter Glass of the House Banking and Currency Committee. Glass with Willis' help developed a Federal Reserve System of regional banks patterned after Aldrich's currency associations, and obtained the support of president-elect Wilson as an early step of his New

[5] Edward Vreeland was a Republican Congressman from western New York, Chairman of the House Banking and Currency Committee 1911–13, and vice-chairman of the National Monetary Commission.

Freedom. An important bankers' condition, as George Reynolds, Chicago banker and president of the ABA, testified before Glass's committee, was the avoidance of a true central bank (such as the Bank of England which competed with other banks), although the Committee could count on the ABA's support for an "organization with branches located in various sections of the country dealing only with banks and the government" (Kolko 1963, pp. 217, 226; U.S. House 1913; Glass 1927, p. 86).

Most important for monetary policy, each of the twelve regional banks, from Boston to San Francisco, had the power to create U.S. currency in the process of lending to banks (discounting bills of exchange) and buying U.S. securities. The Fed thus controlled the monetary base and could guarantee that there would be no more currency shortages as long as they could be backed by at least 35 percent gold. The banks got what they most wanted from the Act: a ready supply of low-cost reserves without government-backed competition.

Because the public resisted an institution centered in New York, both the Aldrich and Glass plans provided for decentralized control, a "politically clever" way to secure a central bank, Professor Harold Reed (1922, p. 18) wrote. To Glass's chagrin, Wilson made a political Federal Reserve Board a condition of his support. It would have seven members: the Secretary of the Treasury the Comptroller of the Currency ex officio, and five members appointed by the president for ten-year terms on a rotating basis: initially being a Boston lawyer (Charles Hamlin), a Harvard educated college professor (Adolph Miller) (both members of the Wilson administration), an investment banker (Paul Warburg), a railroad executive (Frederic Delano), and an Alabama commercial banker (W.P.G. Harding).

Bankers retained the lion's share of the System's operations. The district banks, in whose hands monetary policy largely rested in the form of the discount window, were governed mainly by bankers, whose relations with the "supervisory" Federal Reserve Board were unclear. The System possessed enormous powers to create money, although its enunciated objectives were limited to an elastic currency and the maintenance of the gold standard, in neither of which it succeeded during the next two decades.

Membership in the Federal Reserve System was required of national banks, but made voluntary for state banks to avoid their opposition. Legal restrictions on bank participation in international finance which had been imposed by the Comptroller's rigid interpretation of the National Bank Act were lifted to make good Aldrich's (1909) promise "to make the United States the financial center of the world." The Federal Reserve Act was overwhelmingly accepted by both Houses (Table 5.1), and "the New York bankers got all they wanted, with the single exception of [complete] banker control" (Wicker 2005, p. 94) although they got a lot even of that.

Congress had created a new institution with enormous powers over money and credit, but little direction (except to allay currency panics, which might have been achieved by means of the Treasury, clearing houses, or Aldrich-Vreeland), and uncertain lines of authority between the district banks and the Board.

Wyoming Congressman Frank Mondell wondered during the debate over the Act how the proposed powers would be exercised: Advocates of the new institution argued that it was a means by which "the people, through their Government, [exercise] their right to control the issue of currency and supervise the business of banking. The gentlemen may as well save themselves that kind of effort, for they will fool nobody whose opinion is worthwhile. [Supervision] so far as is necessary for the benefit and protection of all the people" is generally accepted. However, "the people pretty clearly understand nowadays that control through a Government bureau, by political appointees, is not synonymous with control by the people and for the people. Neither do people of ordinary intelligence confuse regulation and management. We regulate the railroads, we do not manage them. We regulate the packing of meats, we do not appoint the men who run the business." Speaker Champ Clark had promised that presidents would only appoint men "of ability, character, and patriotism on the Federal reserve board, and then keep close watch on them to the end that all the people may be treated impartially and that our prosperity may increase." But Mondell wanted a self-regulating system under the law. The "Speaker unwittingly suggests the strongest argument against the proposed plan," Mondell said, "when he [takes] the view that it is wise or necessary to add to the tremendous tremendous power of the presidential office a further 'stupendous trust' which he can only hope to properly fulfill by keeping a 'close watch' on his appointees" (*CR*, September 10, 1913).

Some Fed supporters saw it as a means "to fix the rate of interest," preferably at a low level, so that "the business men of the country can … know reasonably in advance what money will cost them in their enterprises," according to Robert Owen of Oklahoma, manager of the bill in the Senate. He later advised the Federal Reserve as it raised interest rates during the postwar inflation that it should set rates by the criterion used by commercial banks, which were "justified in charging six and seven per cent because they pay two and three per cent for deposits…. If the Reserve

Banks [which print money] would be content with the same margin of profit,... they would be charging a rate of between three and four percent" (Harding 1925, pp. 195–200).

One's attitude to the Fed, House Majority Leader Oscar Underwood said, depended on "faith in the President's Board, the whole question being whether the Board was angel or devil." So the president controlled the Board, Texas Democrat Oscar Callaway exclaimed, and the Board in combination with the banks controlled the currency, but "Where," he asked, "will the people come in? We are told to ... have faith, simple faith.... Faith, faith, faith; faith in man, fallible man, swept by all the passions, prejudices, and ambitions, mental misgivings, shortsightedness, and misconceptions of man." The country has experienced discretionary government, and "Who usually gets a hearing, the man on the ground or the trusting man" (*CR*, September 13, 1913)?

Be Careful What You Wish for. Federal Reserve Monetary Policy and Prices Before Martin

An appropriate measure of the new institution's performance would seem to be the stability of prices. Its enormous failure during the Great Depression of 1929–1933 dominates the Fed's early history, but the years before that time do not lack interest or importance. First consider the years *1914–22,* when prices shown in Fig. 5.2 were dominated by the war. Constraints and guides for the Fed, legal and intellectual, were discarded as the Fed came under the direction of the Treasury for the purpose of financing the war effort. Government deficits were large and Fed credit expanded from $523 million to $3390 million between 1917 and 1920, as its lending continued to rise even after the November 1918 armistice. Prices more than doubled between 1914 and 1920, with inflation sometimes exceeding 20 percent per annum, while the Fed's discount (lending) rate rose only from 3½ percent to 4 percent. In the words of the Federal Reserve Board's chief economic advisor,

> [T]he Federal reserve banks were guided in their rate policy chiefly by the necessity for supporting the Treasury. The level of discount rates was kept low and preferential rates were granted on loans secured by Government obligations ... and the discount rate was thus not used as a means of credit control – but as a method of helping the Government to raise the funds necessary for the prosecution of the war. It was not until the summer of

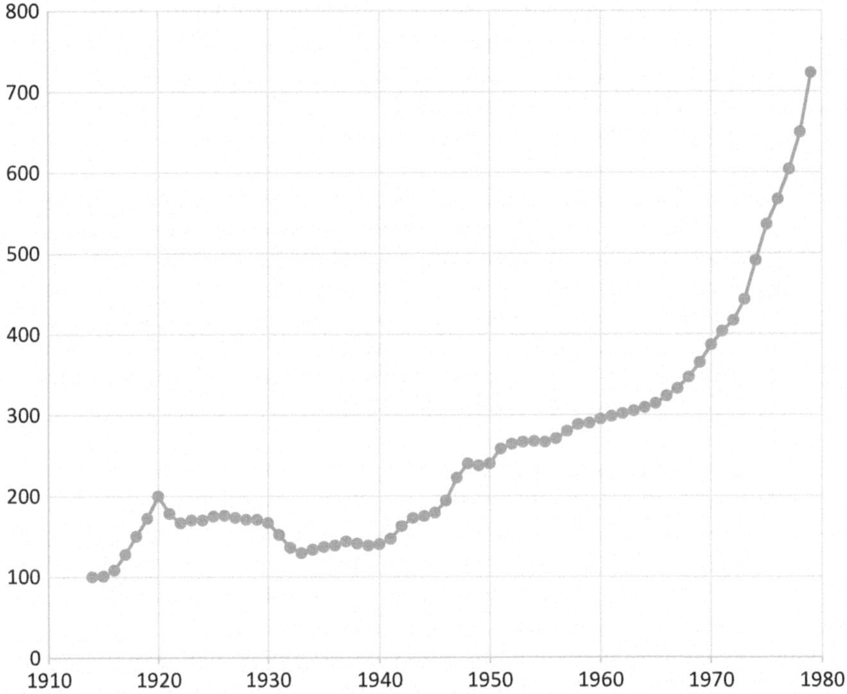

Fig. 5.2 Consumer price index, 1914–79. (Source: Based on data from Historical Statistics of the United States)

> 1919 that the use of the discount rate as a means of credit control received serious consideration. (E.A. Goldenweiser, *Federal Reserve System in Operation*, p. 40.)

Even after the war, to be repeated after World War II, the Fed was directed by the administration not to raise rates because, said the Assistant Secretary of the Treasury, the government was "honor bound" to avoid the infliction of capital losses on the patriotic citizens who had financed the war effort (Leffingwell 1921). Glass, who had become Secretary of the Treasury, threatened to ask the president to remove the New York Fed's Benjamin Strong because of his objections (Wicker 1966, pp. 37–38).

When the Treasury finally gave its okay, the Fed raised its rate vigorously—from 4 percent to 4¾ percent in November 1919, to 6 percent in

January 1920, and 7 percent in June—which was maintained until March 1921, almost throughout the sharp 1920–21 recession. The price level fell substantially, but still only about a third of the way back to its 1914 level. A congressional inquiry later concluded that the Fed's tight money was a consequence of the Treasury's earlier easy-money pressures.

> The commission is of the opinion that the … discount policy of the Federal Reserve … should not have yielded to the apprehension of the Treasury Department. [H]ad discount rates been raised by the Federal Reserve banks promptly and progressively beginning with the spring of 1919, much of the inflation, expansion, speculation, and extravagance which characterized the following 12 months or more might have been greatly retarded, if not wholly prevented. (*Credit*, Report of the Joint Commission of Agricultural Inquiry, 67th Cong., part II, p. 44, Oct. 1921.)

This was easy for congressmen to say after the event even though Strong reminded the commission that at the time "there was a very strong outcry in Congress for the protection of the interests of [bond] holders" (U.S. Congress 1921, p. 503). The unfortunate consequences of its submission to the Treasury after World War I no doubt supported the Fed's disastrous independence during the Great Depression.

Fed policies were further complicated by differences between the Banks and the Board. District Bank presidents were more inclined than members of the Board to rely on interest rates to regulate credit. Possibly because they were more distant from markets than Bank presidents, or because they were more influenced by the atmosphere (the outcry) of Washington, the Board preferred discussion—moral suasion—to changes in interest rates. The greater commitment of Bank presidents to price stability, involving less submission to the needs of government finance, has continued (Wood 2005, pp. 348–49).

Led by the New York Fed's Benjamin Strong, the Fed developed a policy that was almost entirely addressed to the New York and Chicago money markets. The "Strong Rule" stated that the best guide to changes in Fed credit was "the amount of borrowing (from the Fed) by member banks in principal centers, and particularly in New York and Chicago. Our experience has shown that when New York City banks are borrowing in the neighborhood of $100 million or more," and money rates exceed the discount rate, the latter needs to be raised to pull back loans. Low interest rates and bank borrowings from the Fed, on the other hand, imply that monetary policy is sufficiently liberal. Applying this model to the Great Depression allowed the Fed to believe that additional bank reserves and money were unnecessary (Wicker 1969; Friedman and Schwartz 1963, PP. 375–80).

The stability of money and prices was greater during 1922–29 than any other period of similar length in American history. Friedman and Schwartz (1963, Ch. 6), called it the "High Tide of the Federal Reserve." What the Fed did not take into account was the gold standard and its requirement that prices fall back to the level existing before the 1914–19 inflation.

Nearly all countries had suspended the gold standard as they financed their war efforts by inflationary increases in money, and after the war conducted deflationary monetary policies to restore their prewar exchange rates. Gold imports to pay for goods or safekeeping had relieved the United States of the necessity of devaluation during the war, but all postwar central banks had to perform in a fragile, deflationary environment (Mazumder and Wood 2013).

The United States had gone from debtor country for most of its history to the world's largest creditor after the war, and when it raised interest rates during 1928–29 (the New York Fed's discount rate was raised from 3½ percent in January 1928 to 6 percent in August 1929) to combat the rise in stock prices, the international flow of funds was reversed, and a worldwide deflation was underway. The fall in prices, especially of real estate, forced bank failures, frightened depositors' withdrew currency, and money and credit plunged as the Fed failed to replace bank reserves. It raised interest rates to protect its gold reserve when Great Britain suspended the gold convertibility of the pound in September 1931. The institution that had been created to stabilize the currency presided over its fall by more than a quarter in three and one-half years.

The U.S. House of Representatives conducted several hearings into the crisis, primarily designed to persuade the Federal Reserve to expand the money stock. Over fifty bills to increase money and prices were introduced in the 72nd Congress (1931–33), although none became law and the Fed was not persuaded. It conducted some open-market purchases in early 1932, when Congress was in session, but those were soon stopped and anyway had been offset by reduced Fed discounting.

Franklin Roosevelt's administration which came to office on March 4, 1933, took control of the Fed and monetary policy. The gold value of the dollar was reduced—the cost in dollars per ounce rising from $20.67 to $35—which led to increases in gold money and prices during the 1930s, except 1937–38, when the Fed helped bring on a recession by doubling bank reserve requirements.

Then came World War II, which, as during World War I, the Fed was expected to finance. The administration ordered the Fed to peg government securities at low rates (0.375 percent for Treasury bills and 2 percent for bonds). Even so, reported prices rose only a sixth during the war (4 percent per year) because of rationing, price controls, and black markets. Prices rose by a third the next three years, after controls were lifted, and we see in Fig. 5.2 that they had more than tripled by the 1970s.

The Fed pressed the Treasury to allow it to regain control of monetary policy by letting interest rates fluctuate, with little success. Their conflict continued even longer than after World War I, and intensified with the inflation that followed the outbreak of the Korean War in June 1950, and is reviewed in the next chapter.

References

Aldrich, Nelson. 1909. Speech on *The Work of the National Monetary Commission*, Economic Club of New York, Nov. 29; Senate Doc. 406, 61st Cong., 2nd sess.

Bagehot, Walter. 1873. *Lombard Street*. London: Henry King. (Reprinted with Introduction by Harley Withers, E.P. Dutton, 1920).

Balke, Nathan S., and Robert J. Gordon. 1986. Appendix B: Historical Data. In *The American Business Cycle*, ed. Gordon. Chicago: University of Chicago Press.

Baring, Francis. 1797. *Observations on the Establishment of the Bank of England and on the Paper Circulation of the Country*. Minerva Press. (Reprinted with *Further Observations*, Augustus M. Kelley, 1967).

Barro, Robert J. 1979. Money and the Price Level under the Gold Standard. *Economic Journal* 89: 13–33.

Blaine, James G. 1886. *Twenty Years in Congress*. Norwich: Henry Bill.

Calomiris, Charles W., and Stephen H. Haber. 2014. *Fragile by Design: The Political Origins of Banking Crises and Scarce Credit*. Princeton: Princeton University Press.

Clarke, M.St. Clair, and D.A. Hall, eds. 1832. *Documentary History of the Bank of the United States*. Gales and Seaton. (Rep. New York: Augustus Kelley 1967).

Davis, Joseph, and Marc D. Weidenmier. 2016. *America's First Great Moderation*, NBER WP 21856, January.

Dewey, Davis R. 1922. *Financial History of the U.S.* 8th ed. New York: Longmans, Green and Co.

Eichengreen, Barry. 1992. *Golden Fetters. The Gold Standard and the Great Depression*. New York: Oxford University Press.

Fair, Ray C. 1978. The Effect of Economic Events on Votes for President. *The Review of Economics and Statistics* 90:159.

Federal Reserve Board. 1943. *Banking and Monetary Statistics, 1914-41.* Washington, DC: Federal Reserve Board.

Friedman, Milton, and Anna J. Schwartz. 1963. *A Monetary History of the United States, 1867–1960.* Princeton: Princeton University Press.

Gibbs, George. 1846. *Memoirs of the Washington and Adams Administrations, Edited from the Papers of Oliver Wolcott, Secretary of the Treasury.* New York: William Van Norden.

Glass, Carter. 1927. *An Adventure in Constructive Finance.* Garden City: Doubleday, Page.

Goldenweiser, E.A. 1925. *Federal Reserve System in Operation.* New York: McGraw-Hill.

Gouge, William M. 1833. *A Short History of Paper Money and Banking in the U.S.* Philadelphia: Grigg & Elliott. (Rep. New York: A.M. Kelley, 1968).

Hammond, W. Bray. 1957. *Banks and Politics in America from the Revolution to Civil War.* Princeton: Princeton University Press.

Harding, W.P.G. 1925. *The Formative Period of the Federal Reserve System.* Boston: Houghton Mifflin.

Highfield, Richard A., Maureen O'Hara, and John H. Wood. 1991. Public Ends, Private Means. Central Banking and the Profit Motive, 1823–1832. *Journal of Monetary Economics*, October.

Historical Statistics of the U.S. 2006. Ed. Susan Carter. Online: Cambridge University Press.

Holdsworth, John T. 1910. *The First Bank of the United States.* National Monetary Commission. Washington, DC: Government Printing Office.

James, John A. 1976. *The Conundrum of the Low Issue of National Bank Notes.* Vol. 84, 359. Journal of Political Economy.

Kaufman, George G. 1991. Lender of last resort: A contemporary perspective. *Journal of Financial Services Research* 5: 95–110.

Kinley, David. 1910. *The Independent Treasury of the United States and its Relation to the Banks of the Country.* National Monetary Commission, Senate Doc. No. 587, 61st Cong., 2nd Sess. Government Printing Office.

Kolko, Gabriel. 1963. *The Triumph of Conservatism.* New York: Free Press.

Krooss, Herman E., ed. 1969. *Documentary History of Banking and Currency in the U.S.* New York: McGraw-Hill.

Leffingwell, Russell C. 1921. The Discount Policy of the Federal Reserve Banks: Discussion. *American Economic Review*, March.

Lincoln, Abraham. 1907. *Life and Works,* ed. Marion Miller. New York: Current Literature Publishing Co.

Marshall, John. 1807. *The Life of George Washington.* Philadelphia: C.P.Wayne.

Mazumder, Sandeep, and John H. Wood. 2013. The Great Deflation of 1929–33: It (Almost) Had to Happen. *Economic History Review* 66: 156–177.

Miller, Marion M., ed. 1913. *Great Debates in American History.* Current Literature.

Mitchell, Wesley C. 1903. *A History of the Greenbacks.* Chicago: University of Chicago Press.

Morawetz, Victor. 1909. *The Banking and Currency Problem in the United States.* New York: North American Review Publishing Company.

———. 1911. The Banking and Currency Problem in the United States, Proceedings of the Academy of Political Science, *The Reform of the Currency.*

Nettels, Curtin P. 1962. *The Emergence of a National Economy, 1775–1815.* New York: Holt, Rinehart and Winston.

Reed, Harold L. 1922. *The Development of Federal Reserve Policy.* Boston: Houghton Mifflin.

Saul, S.B. 1969. *The Myth of the Great Depression, 1873–1896.* New York: Macmillan.

Saunders, Anthony, and Marcia M. Cornett. 2012. *Financial Markets and Institutions.* New York: McGraw-Hill Irwin.

Schumpeter, Joseph A. 1912. *The Theory of Economic Development.* German: Published in English by Harvard University Press, 1934.

Selgin, George, and Lawrence H. White. 1999. A Fiscal Theory of government's Role in Money. *Economic Inquiry* 37: 154.

Sherman, John. 1895. *Recollections of Forty Years in the House, Senate and Cabinet.* Chicago: Werner.

Sylla, Richard, Robert E. Wright, and David J. Cowan. 2009. Alexander Hamilton, Central Banker: Crisis Management During the U.S. Financial Panic of 1792. *Economic History Review.*

Taus, Esther R. 1943. *Central Banking Functions of the U.S. Treasury, 1789–1941.* New York: Columbia University Press.

Temin, Peter. 1969. *The Jacksonian Economy.* New York: Norton.

Thoreau, Henry. 1849. Civil Disobedience. In *Aesthetic Papers*, ed. Elizabeth Peabody. New York: G.P. Putnam.

Timberlake, Richard H. 1993. *Monetary Policy in the United States. An Intellectual and Institutional History.* Chicago: University of Chicago Press.

U.S. Congress. 1921. *Credit*, Report of the Joint Commission of Agricultural Inquiry, 67th Cong., 1st sess., part II, p. 44, Oct.

U.S. House of Representatives. 1913. *Congressional Record.* September.

Unger, Irwin. 1959. Business Men and Specie Resumption. *Political Science Quarterly* 74: 46–70.

———. 1964. *The Greenback Era.* Princeton: Princeton University Press.

Van Fenstermaker, J. 1965. *The Development of American Commercial Banking, 1782–1837.* Kent: Bureau of Economic and Business Research, Kent State University.

Walters, Jr., Raymond. 1945. The Origins of the Second Bank of the United States. *Journal of Political Economy.*

Walters, Raymond, Jr. 1957. *Albert Gallatin: Jeffersonian Financier and Diplomat.* New York: Macmillan.

Warburg, Paul. 1907. A Plan for a Modified Central Bank, in *Essays on Banking Reform in the United States.* Proceedings of the Academy of Political Science, Vol. IV, No. 4. (Summarized in Warburg, 1930, pp. 21–24)

———. 1910. *A United Reserve Bank of the United States,* Presented March 23, 1910, to Finance Forum of the YMCA of the City of New York; published in Proceedings of the Academy of Political Science in the City of New York, Vol. 1, No. 2 (reprinted in Warburg 1930).

———. 1930. *The Federal Reserve System: Its Origin and Growth.* New York: Macmillan.

West, Robert C. 1977. *Banking Reform and the Federal Reserve, 1863–1923.* Ithaca: Cornell University Press.

Wicker, Elmus. 1966. *Federal Reserve Monetary Policy, 1917–33.* New York: Random House.

———. 1969. Brunner and Meltzer on Federal Reserve Monetary Policy during the Great Depression. *Canadian Journal of Economics* 2: 318.

———. 2005. *The Great Debate on Banking Reform.* Columbus: Ohio State University Press.

Wood, John H. 1970. Two Notes on the Uniqueness of Commercial Banks. *Journal of Finance* 25: 99.

———. 2006. Independent Central Banks: New and Old. *The Cato Journal* 26: 593–605.

———. 1975. *Commercial Bank Loan and Investment Behaviour.* New York: Wiley.

———. 2005. *A History of Central Banking in Great Britain and the United States.* Cambridge: Cambridge University Press.

———. 2015. *Central Banking in a Democracy.* New York: Routledge.

CHAPTER 6

Chairman of the Fed

Martin rose rapidly through the army ranks to become a colonel, liaison between the Army and Congress for the lend-lease program (by which the United States supplied materials to its World War II allies), and supervisor of the program for the Soviet Union. One of his tasks was to persuade members of Congress that despite their ingratitude and misuse of funds to dominate Eastern Europe, assistance to the Soviets was in America's interests. After the war, Martin became chairman of the government's Export-Import Bank that extended credit to nations for postwar reconstruction and development. It was another job filled with political controversy as he pushed for economically sound loans for genuine development programs, often in conflict with the State and other departments that wanted funds for other purposes, such as support of Chiang Kai-shek in the Chinese civil war. The Bank was in the Treasury Department, and Martin established a relationship with Secretary John Snyder, a Democrat, St. Louis banker, and friend of President Truman. He became assistant secretary of the Treasury for International Affairs in January 1949 (Bremner 2004, Ch. 4–5).

This chapter describes the Fed's battle to end the government bond support program (the "peg"), the advent of the new fiat monetary standard with enhanced responsibilities of the central bank, a summary of the models of monetary policy available to the Fed in the 1950s, Martin's policy model as revealed by his speeches and other statements, his application of that model as chairman of the Federal Reserve Board and Open Market Committee, and his defenses of Fed policies to Congress. It is a

J. H. Wood, *Who Governs?*, Palgrave Studies in American Economic History, https://doi.org/10.1007/978-3-030-33083-5_6

story of the relations between the head of the agency charged with the execution of Congress's monetary powers and other groups—the public, banks, economists, the president, and Congress itself—and their diverse views of appropriate monetary policies. The Fed's control of monetary policy varied between weak and strong, but the institution has never been independent.

The End of the Peg[1]

In April 1942, the Fed publicly committed itself to an interest rate of 3/8 percent on (three-month) Treasury bills, and a ceiling of 2½ percent on long-term (10 years and over) U.S. bonds. T bill rates were allowed to rise slightly after the war—reaching 1 percent in 1950—but the Treasury insisted on keeping the 2½ percent ceiling on long terms. Fed requests for the independence to fight inflation by raising rates took on a greater urgency with the outbreak of the Korean War in June 1950. The Fed was tired of subordinating price stability to the Treasury's fiscal needs. Its patriotic duty to submit had been lessened by the end of the world war and was incompletely rejuvenated by the Korean War.

"I don't understand why the bankers want to upset the credit of the nation in the midst of a terrible national emergency," President Truman wrote Russell Leffingwell, chairman of J.P. Morgan. As assistant secretary of the Treasury in 1920, Leffingwell had favored the Treasury's control of interest rates. At J.P. Morgan after World War II, he was not so sure. Secretary Snyder believed that New York Fed president Allan "Sproul and New York bankers and brokers were trying to recapture the primacy in fiscal and monetary affairs that had been lost to Washington during the New Deal" (Donovan 1982, pp. 328–29).

Fed leaders wanted stable prices and accepted a competitive economy. Truman and Snyder, on the other hand, saw limited benefits to free markets and never a rate of interest that was too low. It is common to associate easy money with populism, presumably in an attempt to justify it

[1]This section is based on Hetzel and Leach (2001), Eccles (1951, pp. 398–499), Wood (2005, pp. 226–38).

North Korean forces invaded South Korea in June 1950, and had advanced nearly to the tip of the peninsula, when aided by a brilliant landing at Inchon, Allied forces regained ground and by October were approaching North Korea's border with China, when Chinese forces poured across the border and by January 1951, had pushed the Allies back to the North-South border (38th parallel).

intellectually, or at least socially, although the name was associated with sound money in the early nineteenth century, and today justifies large or small government according to the user's tastes (Wood 2005, pp. 128–30; Mudde and Kaltwasser 2017).

Harry Truman worked hard all his life without financial success. He was pressed to forego college to help his father on the family farm when the latter's financial speculations failed. Truman's venture in a clothing store in Kansas City after World War I failed, not helped by fluctuating postwar prices (see below). He subscribed to the view common in the corridors of power that emergencies demand controls. Or perhaps they just provide excuses to suppress free markets.

In January 1951, Truman called Fed Chairman Thomas McCabe at home to urge him to "stick rigidly to the pegged rates on the longest bonds," and followed up with a letter directing that

> the Federal Reserve should make it perfectly plain ... to the New York Bankers that the peg is stabilized.... I hope the Board will ... not allow the bottom to drop from under our securities. If that happens that is exactly what Mr. Stalin wants (FOMC Minutes, 1/31/51).

Truman thus stood on its head the dictum attributed to Lenin that "the best way to destroy the capitalist system is to debauch the currency" (Keynes 1919, p. 148).

The Fed's security purchases—the principal source of Fed credit—are decided by the Federal Open Market Committee (FOMC), which is thus the principal maker of monetary policy. It consists of the seven (when at full strength) members of the Board of Governors (the chair of the Board serving as chair of the FOMC), the president of the New York Fed serving as vice-chairman, and four of the remaining Fed presidents on a rotating basis.

The Fed's resistance to Executive control was bolstered by the president's political weakness arising from the unpopularity of the Korean conflict, as well as concern in Congress about inflation. A report of the Subcommittee on *Monetary Credit and Fiscal Policies*, chaired by Illinois Senator Paul Douglas, a former distinguished economist at the University of Chicago, stated:

> As a long run matter, we favor interest rates as low as they can be without inducing inflation, for low interest rates stimulate investment. But we believe that the advantages of avoiding inflation are so great and that a restrictive monetary policy can contribute so much to this end that the freedom of the

> Federal Reserve to restrict credit and raise interest rates for general stabilization purposes should be restored even if the cost should be a significant increase in service charges on the Federal debt and a greater inconvenience to the Treasury in its sale of securities for new financing and refunding purposes.

Long-time Fed critic, Texas Congressman Wright Patman, expressed the opposite position during an exchange with Board member Marriner Eccles testifying before the Joint Economic Committee in relation to the Economic Report (Jan. 25, 1951):

Patman: Don't you think there is some obligation of the Federal Reserve System to protect the public against excessive interest rates?

Eccles: I think there is a greater obligation to the American public to protect them against the deterioration of the dollar.

Patman: Who is master, the Federal Reserve or the Treasury? You know, the Treasury came here first.

Eccles: How do you reconcile the Treasury's position of saying they want the interest rate low, with the Federal Reserve standing ready to peg the market, and at the same time expect to stop inflation?

Patman: Will the Federal Reserve System support the Secretary of the Treasury in that effort [to retain the 2½ percent rate] or will it refuse? ... You are sabotaging the Treasury. I think it ought to be stopped.

In addition to the control of interest rates by Executive Order in September 1950, the president brought back World War II's wage and price controls, including the Office of Price Stabilization and the Wage Stabilization Board. The regulations were complicated, filled with exceptions, and ineffective. Consumer and wholesale prices rose 9 and 15 percent, respectively, during the twelve months after June 1950, and wages were not far behind. Corporate profits were high and labor advocates complained that the regulations discriminated against wages. The United Steelworkers called a strike for higher wages, and instead of proclaiming a cooling-off period under the Republican-passed Taft-Hartley (Labor-Management Relations) Act, Truman declared a government seizure of the steel industry in April 1952, which in June, the U.S. Supreme Court ruled was beyond his authority. The administration also adopted credit controls.

Governor Eccles played a key part in the dispute. He had been appointed to head the Federal Reserve Board in 1934 and was the driving force behind the Banking Act of 1935, and its intention to centralize the Fed's power in the Board. His guide to monetary policy in the 1930s and 1940s was subordination to the president. Their relationship, Herbert Stein wrote, "seemed to include freedom for Mr. Eccles to argue and advise on all kinds of matters and ultimate authority for the president on everything." That loyalty was undermined in 1948, when without explanation Eccles was not reappointed to the Board chairmanship—possibly because Fed decisions had provoked the enmity of some of the president's financial contributors. Nevertheless, Eccles, whose term as governor extended to 1958, consented to Truman's request to remain on the Board (Stein 1969, p. 42; Eccles 1951, pp. 434–56).

Returning to the Treasury-Fed dispute, the Treasury feared that market concerns over possibly rising interest rates instilled a fear of capital losses that would threaten future refundings and wanted a public commitment from the Fed. Sproul and McCabe met with Snyder on January 3, 1951, and McCabe met with Snyder and Truman at the White House on January 17, during which the record was replayed: the Treasury demanded a commitment to the peg by the Fed, which replied with concerns about inflation. Nevertheless, the next day Snyder announced that he had received the desired commitment from McCabe.

The New York Times called this "the first occasion in history on which the head of Exchequer of a great nation had either the effrontery or the ineptitude, or both, to deliver a public address in which he has so far usurped the function of the central bank as to tell the country what kind of monetary policy it was going to be subjected to." In fact, central banks have traditionally operated within narrow limits set by their governments. The Treasury had been in control of monetary policy since 1933, as well as during and after World War I. The Bank of England's Bank Rate was the chancellor's decision between 1931 and 1997, as during several earlier periods, and many central banks have been even more decidedly under their governments' thumbs. Nevertheless, the *Times* article represented support for the Fed's position.

McCabe told the Federal Open Market Committee (FOMC, 1/31/51) that he was shocked by the inaccuracy of Snyder's account of their position, and Senator Douglas questioned its authenticity in congressional hearings. On January 29, "in an open challenge to the Treasury," the Fed raised the bond yield. Although it remained under 2½ percent, the action prompted Snyder to ask the president, for the first time in history, to call a meeting at the White House with the entire FOMC on January 31.

The FOMC worked on a joint statement for the meeting. Governor James Vardaman, Jr., said they should be guided by their commander-in-chief, to which Sproul objected that this "would make the Federal Reserve a bureau of the Treasury and, in light of the responsibilities placed in the System by the Congress, would be both impossible and improper." Work on a statement was dropped (Hetzel and Leach 2001).

A Missouri businessman and banker, Vardaman had been an early supporter of Senator Truman. He served in the Navy during World War II, became the president's naval aide in 1945, and was appointed to the Federal Reserve Board in 1946. He was thought to be the source of leaks of Fed meetings (including erroneous reports of disagreements) to the administration.[2]

At the White House meeting, Truman said, "The present emergency is the greatest this country has ever faced, including the two World Wars and all the preceding wars.... If the people lose confidence in government securities, all we hope to gain from our military mobilization, and war if need be, might be jeopardized." McCabe responded by explaining the responsibility of the Fed "to promote stability in the economy by regulating the volume, cost, and availability of money, keeping in mind at all times the best interests of the whole economy."

Nevertheless, the next morning the White House issued a statement that "The Federal Reserve Board has pledged its support to President Truman to maintain the stability of Government securities as long as the emergency lasts." The Treasury made a similar announcement, and the president sent McCabe a letter to the same effect, which was released to the press. Members of the Fed were reluctant to confront the president regarding his false statements, and decided that McCabe should meet with him privately. However, McCabe had gone home to Philadelphia for the weekend.

Eccles, who did not share his colleagues' reluctance to make the depth of the dispute public, told reporters that the administration's releases were false. He arranged to have the FOMC's memorandum of its meeting with the president, which included a denial of the commitment, reported in the papers the next day.

[2] Vardaman denied these charges but later resigned when confronted with evidence of leaks in 1958. (Hamby 1995, pp. 236, 263, 303; Meltzer 2003, pp. 706–707 and 2009, p. 185).

The memorandum was headline news and an embarrassment to Truman. However, the FOMC still had to be concerned with its relations with the administration, which had not admitted defeat, and never would. Snyder defended his previous "understanding" of their January meetings, and Truman told a press conference that "it was his understanding that a majority of the Reserve Board members sided with him on the interest rate question between the Board and the Treasury."

Furthermore, the Fed was let down by a group of congressmen (members of the Committee on Banking and Currency), who advised it to yield to the Treasury for the present. At this point, February 10, Snyder took his doctor's advice to schedule cataract surgery the next day, and asked McCabe to do nothing the two weeks he expected to be in the hospital. Snyder also asked three Democratic members of the Committee to make the same request, with which they cooperated. Further pressure on the Fed came from the refusal of support by the Federal Advisory Council (twelve bankers with the responsibility of advising the Fed), whom Eccles accused of a lack of "courage and realistic leadership." These positions indicated the reluctance of segments of society to resist presidential claims of crisis powers.

Nevertheless, the Fed took action which "forced resolution of the dispute. It informed the Treasury that as of February 19, it 'was no longer willing to maintain the existing situation in the Government security market'. [U]nless there was someone at the Treasury who could work out a prompt and definitive agreement with us … we would have to take unilateral action." The Treasury, on its part, faced large debt issues on the immediate horizon and decided it needed a resolution of the dispute to secure the public's confidence.

It is at this point that Martin took a decisive role. Although Assistant Secretary for International Affairs, he was also involved in other Treasury activities and was drawn into its talks with the Fed regarding the peg. While Snyder was in the hospital for a cataract operation, the Treasury's team was led by Martin, who notified the Fed that he desired negotiations based on the FOMC's February 7 letter to Truman, which included the following:

> We favor the lowest rate of interest on government securities that will cause true investors to buy and hold these securities. Today's inflation … is due to mounting civilian expenditures largely financed directly or indirectly by sale of Government securities to the Federal Reserve…. The inevitable result is more and more money and cheaper and cheaper dollars.

The letter followed from the belief, most often expressed within the FOMC by Sproul, that "the central bank controls inflation through the monetary control made possible by allowing market determination of the interest rate." He said the next month:

> [T]he Committee did not in its operations drive securities to any price or yield.... [M]arket forces had been the determining factor, and only in resisting the creation of reserves had the committee been a party to an increase in interest rates. That ... was the result of market forces, and not the action of the Committee. (FOMC, 3/1/51)

These statements reflected the classical economics view later expressed by Martin in the FOMC and his public speeches.

Martin established staff connections between the Treasury and the Fed, and on March 1, was able to present the resulting compromise to the FOMC stated at the top of the chapter. The Fed announced the Accord on March 4, although the administration's agreement was grudging and in the future, as in the past, accompanied by continuing requests for support. The administration also demanded the resignation of McCabe, with whom they were irritated, and his succession by Martin, one of their own, they thought.

Martin later recalled Truman's efforts to preserve the bond supports:

> The president called me in and said he wanted to make me chairman of the Fed. He told me a story. He said that when he was in the Army in World War I he had bought Liberty Bonds, and when he got back to Kansas City the bonds were down to 82. "You wouldn't let that happen again, would you Bill?" he asked.

Martin could give no guarantee and the interview ended.

> Later he called me back and said it just made him sick to think of the bonds going down. He said: "You will do the very best you can to see that doesn't happen, won't you?" I said I would do my best but they might go down anyway. So I got the job. (Lindley Clark, *Wall Street Journal*, March 4, 1978)

Years later, Martin encountered Truman on the street in New York City. Truman stared at him, said one word, "traitor," and passed on. Yet Martin's acceptance speech had included the statement:

> Unless inflation is controlled, it could prove to be an even more serious threat to the vitality of our country than the more spectacular aggressions of enemies outside our borders. I pledge myself to support all reasonable measures to preserve the purchasing power of the dollar. (*Federal Reserve Bulletin*, April 1951, p. 377)

Truman had ironically wanted a repeat of the monetary policy (controls) that had damaged his business after World War I. He sold farm interests for funds to invest in a haberdashery in Kansas City with army buddy Eddie Jacobson. The store opened at the beginning of the Christmas shopping season at the end of 1919. Business was good initially, but declined and in September 1922, closed deeply in debt.

Unfortunately, they had started a month before the beginning of the severe recession lasting from January 1920 to July 1921. They bought their initial inventory during the postwar inflation financed, under pressure from the Treasury, by the Fed's low rates. The Fed was allowed to begin fighting inflation by raising rates in January 1920, and the consumer price index fell more than 40 percent during the twelve months following May 1920. Fortunately, the end of the peg in 1951, unlike 1919, was not followed by deflation and recession.

Congress's monetary agent had a different view of its job than the executive or much of Congress. Future politicians would pay lip service to stable prices, but they continued to be more interested in the Fed as a means of monetizing the federal debt and evading the scrutiny of taxpayers. Although the Accord has been celebrated, especially by the Fed, as a victory in its struggle for independence, that victory was limited, as demonstrated by continued inflation.

In 1951, inflation in conjunction with the president's weakness enabled the Fed to have its way. The situation was similar to 1979, when President Jimmy Carter, beset by stagflation and doubtful of renomination, assured Fed Chairman Paul Volcker of his acquiesce to restrictive monetary policy. Presidents Johnson and Nixon, discussed below, were different stories.

The New Monetary Standard

Central banking was different after World War II. The end of the peg was an historic occasion. For the first time, central banks had complete control of money and prices, which hitherto had been governed by market forces in commodity systems, most recently the gold standard. Earlier fiat systems, such as Civil War greenbacks, had been temporary accommodations of (mainly wartime) government financial requirements. The ends of the restrictions of the gold standard in the 1930s, and the Treasury's directions in 1951, severed the technical limits to the Fed's capacities to create money. Gold reserve ratios on Fed deposits and currency remained on the books until the 1960s, but their eliminations before they could bind was a foregone conclusion. Gold reserve requirements were in fact ended in the 1960s (Krooss 1969, pp. 3081, 3170).

The 1944 Bretton-Woods treaty arranged an international gold exchange standard, overseen by the International Monetary Fund and often referenced in arguments for stable prices. But its internal inconsistencies were too many to succeed. It was a fixed exchange rate system, but rates could be relaxed for "good reason" that were in fact usually the result of inflation which was supposed to be discouraged by fixed rates and were therefore ineffective. Inflationary Keynesian policies in fact took precedence over fixed exchange rates, the supply of gold reserves fell as its cost of production rose, and the arrangement collapsed in 1971.

The new fiat-money system demanded answers to the questions of what Federal Reserve credit (and therefore money) should be, and what form it should take. The Fed's answers had to depend on its objectives and its model, that is, on its views of how the world worked, including the effects of its credit on the economic system. Nor was that all. A variety of interests had to be considered. The Fed was supposed to be independent—usually meaning independent of the government's wish for cheap finance—and the Accord was a step in that direction. However, even in the best of times, agencies must consider their political survival, which in the Fed's case means good relations with the banking industry, Congress, the Executive, and other politically important interests.

The new situation also required decisions about matters formerly made by markets. The deflation from the 1870s to the 1890s, followed by rising prices to 1913, were due to changes in the gold industry. The function of the central bank under the gold standard was merely to insure the short-term finance necessary to smooth the financial markets and facilitate the gold value of the currency. After the 1930s, however, the monetary base shifted from market-determined gold to politically determined currency and bank reserves supplied by the Federal Reserve.

The gold anchor had been lost (or pulled up), but the new freedom possessed potential merits. The gold standard had been criticized by its contemporaries—including the prominent economists David Ricardo (1816), Alfred Marshall (1887), Knut Wicksell (1898), and Irving Fisher

(1911)—for the instability of the price level caused by the variable cost of gold. (They didn't know how lucky they were.) Martin and the Fed wanted to replace the constant dollar value of gold as a central bank objective by a stable index of prices in general.

This left the choice of monetary policy framework open, that is, the assumed relations between the Fed's actions and its objectives. The next section considers several well-known theories or models, followed by Martin's.

Models of Monetary Policy

The Classical model's primary component is informed rational decision-makers who produce and consume in light of market-clearing prices. The competitive Classical system is efficient in the sense that the prices to which producers and consumers respond equate utilities and costs. Goods are produced at prices which consumers are willing to pay. Interferences with this system (such as encouraging rice production in the desert by free water or aggregate demand by officially depressed interest rates) cause inefficiencies. An increase in profitable projects causes interest rates to rise as investors compete for funds. Interest rates limit borrowing and spending to their most valued activities. The proper role of government is to stay out of the way or at most encourage the system by assisting the enforcement of contracts.

The Classical model was at least partly an invention of John Maynard Keynes, who claimed that it prevailed among his forebears and contemporaries, and underlay their *laissez faire* approach to economic policy. His *General Theory of Employment, Interest and Money*, written during the Great Depression and published in 1936, was an attack on existing policy views and the Classical model, which he argued was limited to a special case different from "the economic society in which we actually live, with the result that its teaching is misleading and disastrous if we attempt to apply it to the facts of experience" (Keynes 1936, p. 3). The clearing of labor markets at real wages equal to the marginal products of labor along with the absence of prolonged unemployment were, Keynes wrote, the most dangerous assertions of the Classical model.

Keynes sought to develop a general theory by introducing uncertainty and the recognition of nominal (money) prices and wages in place of the classical concentration on real values. The unwillingness to take wage cuts even during deflations and the failure of investment in the face of uncertainty—both violations of classical market-clearing—implied a stimulus role for government, in particular, the promotion of demand during depression by increased government spending and reduced taxes.

Keynes's alleged followers did not develop his model but advocated his activist policy prescriptions which they have sought to apply to all phases of the business cycle. The role of monetary policy in this view is to support that spending.

For several years after World War II, they ignored inflation except for blaming it on nonmonetary cost-push forces arising from the monopoly powers of unions and business corporations (Ackley 1959, 1961, pp. 439–59). Recognizing the influence of money on prices would have raised doubts about the validity of their policy model. They also ignored expectations and monetary credibility that had been important parts of Keynes's discussions except during deep depressions when the economy was stuck—and might be stuck for long periods. The damages of Keynesian models arise from their general applications of policies appropriate to deep depression.

The inadequacy of fiscal policy in theory and practice forced its abandonment and the shift to monetary policy. Fiscal policy would probably have been too cumbersome for countercyclical policy even if it had been tried, but it was never tried as Congressional decisions continued to be based on political considerations. Although Congress recognized the possibility of fiscal policy in the Employment Act of 1946, it made no institutional provisions for a timely fiscal policy. In the 1960s Keynesians (a better term might be "interventionists") turned for their primary tool to monetary policy, which could in principle be more timely. They noticed the frequent inverse relation between inflation and unemployment (the Phillips Curve) and hoped to take advantage of it (Phillips 1958; Samuelson and Solow 1960; Wood 2009, Ch. 4).

Monetarism emphasizes the importance of money and monetary policy within the framework of a classical model. A well-known policy prescription of monetarism is Milton Friedman's (1959, pp. 88–92) constant growth of money, which seeks to prevent erratic money and monetary policy from disrupting the economy.

They eschewed rules, but central bankers before World War II behaved in line with the Classical model in the sense that they supported an efficient and self-equilibrating economy by supporting the payments system. Indeed, we have seen that the primary stated objective of the Federal Reserve Act of 1913 was an "elastic currency."

The New Classicals, bringers of the Rational Expectations Revolution that affected economic thinking from the 1960s, was well-named because they represented a return to the Classical system of rational decisions, market clearings, and consideration of the future. Inflationary expectations and the credibility of monetary policy resumed their importance.

Martin was criticized by both the leading groups of macroeconomists: Monetarists for not committing to a money rule (they particularly disliked Martin's policy of "leaning against the wind") and the Keynesians for not being sufficiently responsive to events. Robert Hetzel (2008, p. 312) credited Martin with creating "the modern Fed with the inauguration of lean-against-the-wind monetary policy in the 1953 recession." Moreover he anticipated mainstream economists by behaving as later suggested by the New Classicals who took expectations and credibility into account and saw no advantages to inflation.

Martin's Model

> Our detailed study of the Federal Reserve's procedures reveals that their knowledge of the monetary process is woefully inadequate, unverified, and incapable of bearing the heavy burden that is placed upon it.... The Federal Reserve does not have a rational foundation for policymaking. Two features of the Federal Reserve System seem to account for their failure to analyze and test their conception of the monetary process. First, their analysis and their approach to monetary policy is dominated by extremely short-run week-to-week, day-to-day, or hour-to-hour events in the money and credit markets. Second, their viewpoint is frequently that of a banker rather than that of a regulating authority for the monetary system and the economy. (Allan Meltzer, U.S. Congress, 1964, p. 932)

What's wrong with that? Central bankers have traditionally been drawn from the ranks of the banking and trading communities, and over time made responsible for the short-term continuity and stability of payments, to provide, in the language of the Federal Reserve Act, an "elastic currency." By the time Meltzer wrote, however, central banks were thought by many, perhaps most, to be responsible for a wide range of macroeconomic variables. The Fed along with other government agencies was expected to the Employment Act of 1946 "to promote maximum employment, production, and purchasing power." It was also expected, particularly by economists, to possess, like their own, an explicit (preferably mathematical) policy framework relating instruments and their expected effects. According to James Tobin (1977), Yale professor, Nobel Laureate, and former member of the Council of Economic Advisors (CEA)[3]

[3] The three-member Council of Economic Advisers in the Executive Office of the President is charged by the Employment Act of 1946 with "offering the President objective economic advice on the formulation of both domestic and international economic policy."

> Models are highly imperfect, but they are indispensable. The model used for policymaking need not be any of the well-known forecasting models. It should represent the policymakers' beliefs about the way the world works, and it should be explicit. Any policymaker or advisor who thinks he is not using a model is kidding both himself and us. He would be well-advised to make explicit both his objectives for the economy and the model that expresses his view of the links of the economic variables of ultimate social concern to his policy instruments.

It is argued here that in fact Martin had a model in all Tobin's senses. Tobin's criticisms were valid only if to be explicit means using economists' language. Martin did not use equations or diagrams, but it would be hard to be more explicit about the effects (or lack thereof) of money and the determinants and effects of interest rates. The real complaints of Meltzer and Tobin turn out to be their differences from Martin's model and his conservative views of the powers of monetary policy. Tobin's (Keynesian) criticism was of Martin's beliefs that inflation was due to excessive money and did not promote output. Meltzer's criticism was that the Fed did not follow a Monetarist rule for money growth. Monetarists were unhappy with the volatility of money, Keynesians with the lack of it. Both assumed more power on the part of the Fed than Martin believed existed. Let's look at Martin's model as reflected in his statements, their applications to monetary policy, and his congressional testimony.

A Classical Model "In thinking back through" meetings at the Treasury and other official organizations concerned with financial "controls during … and immediately after the war, the thing that struck me forcibly," Chairman Martin (1960) told the stockholders of the Federal Reserve Bank of Boston, was "the fact that people … said at one time or another, there is one thing you must not permit to happen and that is to let interest rates fluctuate. In the councils of government, … nobody thought it would be possible to unpeg the government securities market [which had been controlled by the Fed for a decade] without having disaster in the United States."

However, Martin said, "The forces you have in a strong, growing, dynamic economy are too big for government controls unless you want to sacrifice all your freedoms." Freely fluctuating interest rates are essential for growth, and their control threatens totalitarianism. "That is something that seems to be very difficult for a lot of people to comprehend."

This speech to Boston bankers was part of Martin's campaign to persuade Congress and others that free markets—with flexible prices and interest rates—were essential to strong and efficient growth. He was surrounded by adversaries. The New (Keynesian) economists were devoted to the stimulation of aggregate demand and politicians failed to understand why the Fed (a government agency, after all, which should be devoted to the public's welfare) did not keep interest rates low for the benefit of their constituents. These groups denied, implicitly or explicitly, that their policies led to inflation, which they blamed on cost-push even though increases in prices or wages cannot be maintained without the means to pay for them.

They denied the obvious. The price level is the inverse of the purchasing power of money, whose value depends on its supply, increased by government deficits financed by money creation, Martin often pointed out. Proposed cures that did not take this into account, which did not attack the problem directly, were ineffective. "I attended a great many meetings where people would say, raise reserve requirements." Or use "selective controls." Nothing worked.

"Now there is a fiction," he said, "that the Federal Reserve can control interest rates completely. I happen to be one of those who still believe that the credit and money basis of this country is formed at the grass roots. [T]he composite judgments which come up through groups in various towns and hamlets throughout this great country have more to do with [its] credit basis … than … the Treasury and the Federal Reserve put together, although damaging effects may be felt if we in the Federal Reserve miscast our policy at a given time."

You come "back to the fact, with all due respect to those who say it is outmoded, to the law of supply and demand, which is still in operation. You may be able to dam it up for various periods. You may be able to change the nature of the supply and alter the composition of the demand" for a while. "But the market forces are still at work and at certain points they get too big for government."

"I watched it carefully in the exchange control of the Bank of England immediately after the war," when a condition of an American loan was the preservation of the gold convertibility of the pound at the overvalued rate of $4.03. This was followed, as surely "as night follows the day," in the words of the Bank's deputy governor, by a run on the pound and its devaluation to $2.80. "[W]hen the patriotism of the people began to wane, … as one official of the Bank of England said to me, the fish got too big for the net and went through it so rapidly that it was perfectly obvious there was absolutely no way to control it. This is essentially what we faced when we unpegged the government securities market. The alternative to doing this was unbridled inflation. And despite the threats of dire disaster, very modest adjustments in interest rates made it possible to reestablish market forces in such a way as to get this situation temporarily, at least, under control" (Dow 1964, pp. 23, 151, 162).

Although interest rates rose after the end of the peg (short and long rates from 1.40 percent and 2.46 percent, respectively, in March 1951 to 1.73 percent and 2.70 percent in December), and annual inflation fell from 8.8 percent to 1.4 percent, the economic expansion continued. Martin had thought that "we came through that period with some understanding of what was involved" in interest rate policy, but he had "been discouraged in recent years" by advocacy of interest ceilings which suggest "that by and large the community ... does not understand interest rates, despite all we have gone through, and still has a belief [that] somebody, the Federal Reserve or somebody else, can produce with mirrors or magic a fixed interest rate and maintain it" (Dow 1964, pp. 23, 151, 162).

Martin's monetary policy founded on free markets was classical in its theory. In 1898, the Swedish economist Knut Wicksell proposed the following interest rule for banks:

> So long as prices remain unaltered the banks' rate of interest is to remain unaltered. If prices rise, the rate of interest is to be raised; and if prices fall, the rate of interest is to be lowered; and the rate of interest is henceforth to be maintained at its new level until a further movement of prices calls for a further change in one direction or the other. (Knut Wicksell, *Interest and Prices*, p. 189)

"A rise in prices is the result," Wicksell wrote, of credit offered by monetary institutions on abnormally favorable terms. "A tightening of credit has, of course, the opposite effect." If the rate of interest is 2 percent, for example, but the return expected on investments is 1 percent, interest is too high for price stability. Money is tight even though the rate of interest may be "low" by historical standards (Wicksell 1898, pp. xiv–xv). Famous evidence of a failure to understand this relation was the Fed's monetary during the Great Depression.

The Fed's frequent announcements (on which it frequently reneged) during 2016–17 that it would soon start raising interest rates, as should be happening during an expansion, even though inflation was below its target level, showed the lesson had not been learned. "Janet Yellen, the Federal Reserve chairwoman said … the Fed plans to keep raising its … interest rate despite the mysterious weakness of inflation" (*The New York Times*, September 26, 2017).

Let "me make clear, as I always do to congressional committees," Martin said, "I do not favor high interest rates. I would like to see as low interest rates as it is possible to have without having inflationary pressures, but I know of no other way" than by interest high enough to bring stable prices. Congressmen shook their heads in disbelief when Martin told them the Fed could not control interest rates, because they did not consider the Wicksell/Martin qualification.

The Phillips Curve? Policy activists believed easy money would be worth the costs of inflation because of its beneficial effects on output, giving the policy trade-off between inflation and output called the Phillips Curve. Because it fails to account for expectations, however, the Phillips Curve crashed as a practical matter in the 1970s, as well as theoretically in the rational expectations revolution. Martin anticipated this failure, or, we should say, followed the classics in rejecting the trade-off. John Stuart Mill, for example, had denied the claims of inflationists in his *Principles of Political Economy* (1848, p. 550). "It is unnecessary to advert to any other of the objections to this plan [growth through the stimulation of inflation] than that of its total impracticality. It calculates on finding the whole world persisting for ever in the belief that more pieces of paper are more riches, and never discovering that, with all their paper, they cannot buy more of anything than they could before."

Similarly, Martin told the Joint Economic Committee in 1965:

> If labor had reason to fear a persistent substantial rise in the cost of living, it would have felt compelled to seek compensatory increases in wages; and if management had had reason to expect a general increase in the price level, it would not have felt compelled to resist such demands. In that case, wages would certainly have risen faster than productivity; prices would have been raised in consequence; and the feared inflationary spiral would have become actuality.

"One of the tragedies of the last ten years … is that the Federal Reserve has been asked to do more than it should, when we tended to rely too much on monetary policy to do things monetary policy simply could not achieve and was never designed to achieve," which on their good days the Volcker (1979–87) and Greenspan (1987–2006) Feds appreciated. "Monetary policy basically is a single tool and you can only implement one goal consistently," Greenspan said. Volcker said that "price stability … is to be treasured and enshrined as the prime policy priority … inextricably part of a broader concern about the basic stability of the financial and economic system" (Capie 1993, pp. 258, 343).

It can be argued that he was more sophisticated in his economics, though not expressed in mathematics, than his critics or indeed the economics mainstream, although this view of Martin is not general. A prominent economist wrote that "academic thinking about monetary economics … has altered drastically since [the early 1970s] and so has the practice of monetary policy.… The former has passed through the rational expectations and real-business-cycle revolution into today's 'new neoclassical synthesis'," leading the latter "into an era of low inflation that emphasizes the concepts of central bank independence, transparency, and accountability." Fluctuations in inflation since World War II, a team of leading economists patronizingly wrote, resulted from the applications of "a crude but fundamentally sensible model of how the economy worked in the 1950s to more formal but faulty models in the 1960s and 1970s to a model that was both sensible and sophisticated in the 1980s and 1990s" (McCallum 2002; Romer and Romer 2002a). The latter authors in the same year acknowledged that the good economic performance of the 1950s was at least partly due to the sophistication of monetary policy, particularly the Fed's conviction that money caused inflation that brought no lasting increase in output.

Deficit Finance The only serious explanation of the persistent inflation since 1950 is to be found in the Fed as financier of federal deficits. Before the Fed, deficits were limited to wartime (when spending exploded) and depression (when revenue collapsed). The discipline of the gold standard had given way to expanded government spending financed by inflation ("a thief in the night," Martin called it) rather than taxes. Lip service was paid to balanced budgets for a while, and central bankers were supposed to be guardians of their currencies. The Fed with some independence was in a position to refuse to be an agent of inflation, but only in the short run because the legislature was in a position to have its way.

Deficits cannot be blamed on Keynesianism stabilization because the implied budget surpluses in good times offset the deficits in bad times, although it has been argued that the removal of the onus from deficits in principle might have opened the door to the acceptance of deficits in general (Buchanan and Wagner 1977, p. 3). With or without Keynes, the removal of the gold constraint made it politically safer to ease than to tighten, resulting in the long-term inflationary bias that we have seen. Martin resisted, but he was eventually outnumbered even in the Fed. He dragged his heels against the inflationists as much as he could without threatening the consensus within the Fed or the existence of the organization.

His Boston speech touched on these problems. "I say that you have to have a tendency to [balance] over a period of years in your budget or you are not going to be able to pay your bills. If when times are relatively good, you don't provide anything in the way of a surplus, when times are bad and you are forced to adopt some deficit financing, you are in a pretty bad general position."

The failure to take this advice had led to what some called the "wage-price spiral," as if inflation could be explained without reference to money. "Certainly the central bank has no control" over wages, which result from productivity and collective bargaining, Martin said. On the other hand, easy money made the spiral possible. "In 1956 I had the privilege of talking to a few people in both labor and management. Both sides felt confident that they could pass on to the consumer whatever agreement they came up with."

Keynesians and Monetarists v. Martin The fine-tuning and rule-based policies of the Keynesians and the monetarists lacked rigorous underpinnings. The former ignored time, money, and expectations, blaming inflation on cost-push, and suffered repeated forecasting and policy errors. Monetarist's money-growth rule had no impact on Martin's monetary policy for good reasons. Friedman and Schwartz's 1963 *Monetary History of the United States* did good service when it reminded the economics profession that money and prices went together. A rule limiting money growth would probably limit inflation. However, while rules and other precise monetary constraints have their uses, they have sometimes had harmful consequences, as evidenced by the British crises of 1847, 1857, and 1866, as bank gold reserves approached their limits, as well as the Fed's concern for its gold reserve ratios during the Great Depression and American commercial banks' concerns for their required reserves during the country's many bank panics (Redish 2001; Hawtrey 1938, pp. 20, 25, 81; Wood 2005, pp. 96–207). Friedrich Hayek quoted Walter Bagehot's observation that "In a sensitive state of the English money market the near approach to the legal limit of reserve would be a sure incentive to panic" (Hayek 1990, p. 81; Bagehot 1873, p. 314).

Perhaps the best case for a flexible but restrained monetary policy remains that of banker Henry Thornton (1802, pp. 239, 258), who wrote during the fiat-money inflation following the wartime suspension of gold convertibility in 1797. He pointed out that "the encrease of industry will by no means keep pace with the augmentation of paper," and inflation with its attendant evils, including the inevitable reaction, will be the consequence. It was incumbent upon the central bank, therefore,

> To limit the total amount of paper issued, and to resort for this purpose, whenever the temptation to borrow is strong, to some effectual principle restriction; in no case however, materially to diminish the sum in circulation, but to let it vibrate only within certain limits; to afford a slow and cautious extension of it, as the general trade of the kingdom enlarges itself; to allow of some special, though temporary, encrease in the event of any extraordinary alarm or difficulty, as the best means of preventing a great demand at home for guineas; and to lean on the side of diminution in the case of gold going abroad, and of the general exchanges continuing long unfavourable; this seems to be the true policy of the directors of an institution circumstanced like that of the Bank of England. To suffer either the solicitations of merchants or the wishes of Government to determine the measure of the bank issues, is unquestionably to adopt a very false principle of conduct. (Thornton, *Paper Credit*, p. 259)

This is like "leaning against the wind," and is not bound by rigid rules. The financial system must have, and be confident of having, sufficient means of payment. "It has been shewn already," Thornton wrote, "that in order to effect the vast and accustomed payments daily made in London, payments which are most of them promised beforehand, a circulating sum in bank notes nearly equal to whatever may have been its customary amount is necessary.... The amount of the bank notes in the hands of each banker, of course, fluctuates considerably; but the amount in the hands of all probably varies very little; and this amount cannot be much diminished consistently with their ideas of what is necessary to the punctuality of their payments and to the complete security of their house." The quantity of notes is small, and cannot be made smaller without threatening "a general insolvency in London, of which the effect would be the suspension of confidence, the derangement of commerce, and the stagnation of manufactures throughout the country."

Conditions are likely to be made worse by the hoarding of gold, and although the introduction of substitutes for the Bank's notes might be attempted, their credit would be inferior to the Bank's and have little effect. Rising interest rates and falling prices might attract foreign gold, but after the damage had been done.

> The idea which some persons have entertained of its being at all times a paramount duty of the Bank of England to diminish its notes in some sort of regular proportion to that diminution which it experiences in its gold is, then, an idea which is merely theoretic. (Thornton, *Paper Credit*, pp. 113–16)

Friedrich Hayek carried Thornton's view into his criticism of "Friedman's proposal of a legal limit on the rate at which a monopolistic issuer of money was to be allowed to increase the quantity of money in circulation.... I would not like to see," Hayek (1990, p. 81) wrote, "what would happen if under such a provision it ever became known that the amount of cash in circulation was approaching the upper limit and that therefore a need for liquidity could not be met."

It is interesting that textbooks and quantity theorists, who see money as a macroeconomic determinant of the price level, have paid little attention to the money market. Martin, on the other hand, followed Thornton (and anticipated Hayek) in the conviction that monetary policy should in the first instance maintain the continuity of payments.

Bills Only

This concern for the money markets influenced Martin's approach to the composition of the Fed's security purchases. His first decade there was the period of "bills only." His belief in the efficiency of free markets had strong implications for the conduct of monetary policy. A regrettable but unavoidable problem with modern monetary policy was the necessity of official intervention, which should be conducted in such a way as to disrupt markets as little as possible. The purpose of the Federal Reserve, Martin said in remarks on "The transition to free markets" before the Economic Club of Detroit in 1953, is "to see that, so far as its policies are a controlling factor [Martin never conceded that the Fed completely controlled money], the supply of money is neither so large as to induce destructive inflationary forces nor so small as to stifle our great and growing economy.... Under our Governmental institutions and our economic system, the maximum benefits for all of us flow from utilizing private property, free competitive enterprise, and the private motive in accordance with the dictates of the market place – something that was almost forgotten for a period of years.... The process of returning to acceptance and use of the market place is slow, painful, and hard.... It is not achieved because people necessarily like it; it is achieved because alternative ways don't work."

One of the problems with the 1951 restoration of competitive securities markets was uncertainty regarding the actions of the Fed. Psychology is important in financial markets, and for that reason Martin wanted transparency in the interests of predictability and credibility. It has been our purpose, therefore, "to develop methods of operation which ... give those who participate in the market a familiarity with how the Federal Reserve may intervene, when it may intervene, and for what purpose it may intervene."

Martin wanted interest rates to reflect their real values as determined by saving and investment, so that, "Since the unpegging, we have endeavored to confine open market transactions to the effectuation of credit policy, that is, to maintain a volume of member bank reserves consistent with the needs of a growing and stable economy." The regulation of money requires Fed participation in the money markets, but we should have as little effect on free-market prices, and therefore efficiency, as possible. So "we have tried to confine our operations to short-term securities, ... largely T bills, ... which are the closest substitutes for cash, [and] least affected by open-market [see below] operations."

The Fed had even backed away from assisting Treasury refunding (despite the assurance given in the Accord) because "we found ... that when the Federal Reserve, with its huge portfolio and its virtually unlimited resources, intervened in the market during Treasury refundings, many investors ... tended to step to the sidelines and to let the market form around the System's bids."

> Private investors, whose funds the Government seeks to attract, may now fairly appraise a new Government securities offering through market processes. They may invest in the new issue with confidence that the market price reflects not just an arbitrary decision by the Treasury and the FOMC but instead the composite evaluation of its worth by thousands of investors in the light of their judgments as to the current and prospective demand and supply of credit.

There would still be uncertainty about what the Fed might do to "maintain orderly conditions," or "correct disorderly conditions," but Martin believed the best approach came from a hands-off attitude that fluctuations tend to be self-correcting in well-organized markets. "Of the movements that are not self-correcting, most reflect basic changes in the credit outlook that should be permitted to occur. Only very rarely is there likely to be a disorderly situation that would require Federal Reserve intervention for reasons other than credit policy."

The "bills only" policy was unpopular with interventionists, who believed it was the Fed's job to enforce the "sizeable price changes" necessary to "achieving credit policy objectives." Another Keynesian described Martin's position that money and credit are (or should be allowed to be) determined at some "mythical" grass roots as "cajoling oratory" (Ahearn 1963, pp. 65–69; Weintraub 1955; Wood 2005, p. 254).

Martin's Monetary Policy. The FOMC[4]

This section recounts Martin's applications of his model during FOMC meetings, that is, to the making of monetary policy. His term may be separated into four main periods: Bills only, 1951–60 (although we begin with the opening of Ike's term in 1953); Operation twist, 1961–65; LBJ's pressures on the Fed, 1965–68 (two wars at once); and fighting inflation under Nixon, 1969–70. All these periods illustrate, Martin's preferred strategy of *leaning against the wind* as well as his resistances to inflation, and often, in the process, his colleagues on the FOMC. The business cycle in Table 6.1, and interest rates, stock price, and inflation in Figs. 6.1 and 6.2 provide a background to these discussions.

Bills Only Under President Eisenhower Our discussion is based on the FOMC's minutes, dated and related to the business cycle, beginning in January 1953, before the cyclical peak in July. The rising stock prices and long-term interest rates in Fig. 6.1 suggest a period of growth, although parts of the increases were due to inflation. The Committee's procedure under the courteous chairman was a go-round in which every member stated his views of the economy and his preferred policy, with Martin's summary consensus at the end. If there *was* a consensus, one might question, but Martin usually managed to find one. His common summary—"Well we are not far apart"—was a stretch at times, an advisor recalled, but was normally accepted by the Committee (Axilrod 2009, p. 20; Kettl 1973, pp. 85–86).

[4]The following accounts of Martin's participation in the FOMC used Meltzer's *History* as well as FOMC transcripts on the Federal Reserve Board's website.

Table 6.1 Business cycles, 1948–75

Business cycle reference dates	
Peak	*Trough*
November 1948	October 1949
July 1953	May 1954
August 1957	April 1958
April 1960	February 1961
December 1969	November 1970
November 1973	March 1975

Source: National Bureau of Economic Research

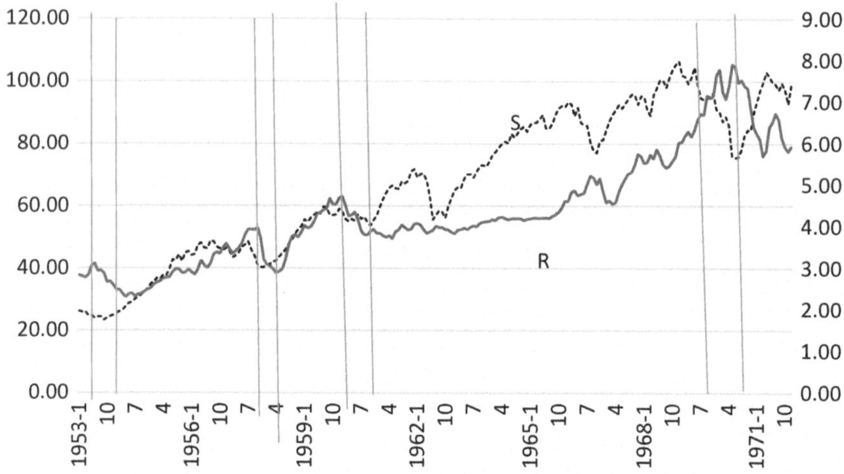

Fig. 6.1 S&P 500 and long-term U.S. interest rate, 1953–71 (rectangles indicate recessions). (Source: Based on data from Shiller 2015)

Arguments over whether Martin was a strong leader (Meltzer 2009, p. 571) have no simple answer. On the one hand, as normally somewhat more anti-inflationary than the Committee as a whole, he was sometimes able to tilt policy in that direction. On the other hand, his desire for consensus pulled him into more inflation than he wanted. According to the FOMC minutes:

January 9, 1953 Toward the end of the 1949–53 expansion, which included the 1950–51 Korean War inflation, the Committee decided to increase the discount rate (the Fed's lending rate to banks) – which should have been done some time before, Martin said. They received easy-money pressure from Congress and the Executive when twenty congressmen introduced a resolution that would have required the Fed to support government securities at par, and CEA Chairman Arthur Burns advocated credit controls (Meltzer 2009, pp. 102–104).

September 24, 1953 The cyclical peak had been reached in July, but the FOMC, although possessing considerable easy sentiment, wanted to avoid the inflation of the preceding expansion, which with expectations of its continuation, is hard to stop. Martin's task was made easier, Christina Romer and David Romer (2002b) wrote, by the "fundamental abhorrence of inflation by virtually all members of the FOMC.... The discussion was often so fervent and the predictions so dire that it is hard to believe that inflation was actually very low." Martin's (and the Committee's) performance during this period went unappreciated until after it was lost in the 1970s, when the costs of inflation were experienced, Martin's reputation rose, and his policies were duplicated, as seen in Fig. 6.2.

On this occasion, Martin straddled the policy range by agreeing with his understanding of the Committee's views that transactions for the System account should be with a view to avoiding deflationary tendencies without encouraging a renewal of inflationary developments. "This was the first recession under a Republican president since 1929," and although the Eisenhower administration had stressed fiscal prudence and worried about the size of government, it was sensitive to critics' claims "that it lacked con-

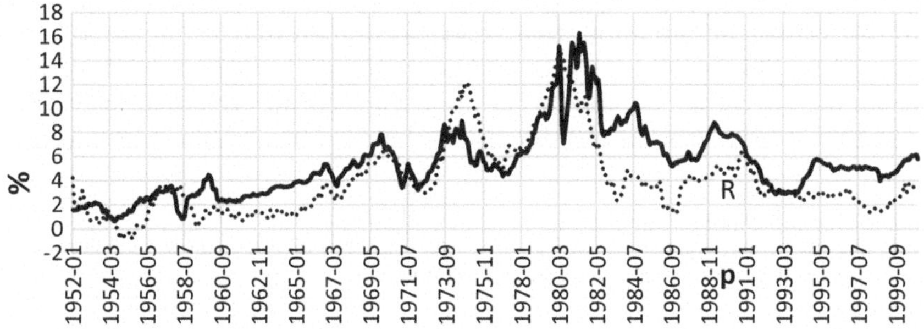

Fig. 6.2 Money market (3-month T bill) rate (R) and 12-month moving average CPI inflation (p), 1952–2010. (Source: Based on data from Fred, Federal Reserve Bank of St. Louis)

cern about rising unemployment," Alan Meltzer wrote. For many years, Republicans found themselves running against memories of Hoover and the Great Depression. Eisenhower "recalled the Republican party's commitment to use the full resources of the federal government to prevent another 1929." The administration had a stand-by public works program (which was not used), and lowered tax rates in 1954 in line with its campaign promise to reduce wartime rates (Meltzer 2009, p. 107).

During the succeeding expansion, Martin expressed concern in the Executive Committee (11/9/54) about a speculative boom. "[T]here were indications of an exuberance of spirit among intelligent businessmen with respect to 1955 business prospects that seemed to him dangerous." "Most other members did not share his concern. They were wrong," Meltzer wrote, and the economy picked up steam (Meltzer 2009, p. 112).[5]

December 7, 1954 With GNP rising at a 5 percent annual rate, Martin proposed to "re-examine the active part of the phrase 'active ease'." Sproul agreed but Board Vice Chairman Canby Balderston opposed any announcement of a change on the grounds that it would confuse the public. Martin felt strongly that the phrase should be removed. His concern was inflation. "[H]e did not believe that inflation provided jobs for people on a sustained basis, although it might temporarily promote jobs." "Active" was removed but "ease" was retained.

March 22, 1955 Martin "felt that in general the policy the Committee had been following had come as close as possible to satisfying the various views presented at this meeting." His own view would lean a little on the side of less ease, his general feeling being one of a little more confidence in the economic situation than had been indicated by some of the Committee. He invited it to reexamine the first sentence of the directive, which included the decision "to arrange for securities transactions with a view to fostering growth and stability in the economy by maintaining con-

[5] For more than twenty years after its formal establishment in 1935, the FOMC selected from among its members an executive committee of five, which met more frequently and oversaw open-market operations within the broad framework of policy laid down by the full committee." At the June 1955 meeting Martin's proposal to terminate the Executive Committee was agreed unanimously, including by the New York bank even though the measure might be interpreted as reducing New York's influence. In fact, most or all FOMC members, as well as Bank presidents not currently on the Committee, had attended Executive Committee meetings (Youngdahl 1960; Meltzer 2009, pp. 70–71).

ditions in the money market that would encourage recovery." However, despite the expansion being nine months old, none of the other members indicated a desire for revision.

May 10, 1955 Finally, the business recovery being "an accomplished fact," Martin and the Committee supported Sproul's motion to alter the directive by changing "encourage recovery," which had been added in January 1955, to "fostering growth and stability in the economy by maintaining conditions in the money market that would avoid the development of unsustainable expansion"—i.e., lean against the wind.

August 2, 1955 To the argument that inflation was potentially a problem but not yet dangerous, Martin replied, "I think personally that all the danger signals … are now flashing red. Inflation is a thief in the night and if we don't act promptly and decisively we will always be behind. All of us know that it sometimes takes a long time for seeds to germinate, but then they flower … with explosive force."

Martin's model, unlike Keynesian models of the day, was dynamic.

August 23, 1955 The staff opened the meeting with a report that "The economic situation continues to be one of … strong credit demands with accompanying upward pressures on interest rates." Martin suggested a continuation of the policy of restraint decided at the last meeting. "I think the wage cost push is still with us and the psychology that that creates is still with us…. I would emphasize a point that I think we exaggerated at … the last meeting. We used the terms 'theatrical' and 'dramatic' in connection with the [small] discount rate increase…. What I was trying to say at the last meeting was that the action should be decisive and clear."

> I want to comment on the philosophy of restraint. Behind the wage cost push is a sort of general conviction, one that has been growing for a number of years, that inflation, if not desirable, is something that it is not politically feasible to hold down. There are those in Wall Street who assume it will not be politically feasible to restrain inflation, that the economy has an inflationary bias, and that they might as well resign themselves and relax and enjoy it. I want to present my own thinking on that point. I have been in the Government now for ten years and I am fully aware of Government pressures. There are margins of error in all these things, but it is perfectly clear to me that it is politically feasible and practicable, if judgment is sufficiently

> wise, to restrain a situation before it develops. It is much more difficult in my judgment to restrain a condition after it has developed. I believe we should approach the problem of credit policy with that philosophy. In other words, it is possible to restrain a person before he does something, and while he may not like to be restrained he will forgive you for it later, but if he goes ahead and does something and then you act to pull him back your action becomes a form of punishment for what he has done that is not feasible in a democracy.

October 25, 1955 Martin believed the Committee had been dilatory in approaching the build-up in the spring and summer of the year. If the System had acted more dramatically earlier it would have been in a better position at this time. However, he agreed with Sproul that, even if this were true, that was not a reason at this later juncture to put more burden on monetary policy than it could bear.

After nearly stable prices between October 1952 and October 1955 (a 0.6 percent total rise in the CPI in three years), the CPI rose 6 percent between 1955 and 1957, before falling to under 2 percent annually the next eight years.

November 16, 1955 Governor J.L. Robertson emphasized "that there are inflationary pressures present which should be checked *now.*"

January 24, 1956 After the round-table, Martin stated that the "Committee should be extremely careful in determining policy not to let it be weighted by apprehensions as to what the political implications of our decisions may be, … or because it might be interpreted by the public in terms of politics. We should be objective about economic developments and about determining our policy for the good of the economy.

Also, I have the strong feeling that none of us can gauge the economy very accurately. When we deal in fine degrees, we are falling into the error that Mr. Sproul has pointed out many times of giving a little credence to the idea that monetary policy can do more than it can, and we can turn on this faucet or turn off the faucet and can achieve a precise objective."

Our concern should be stability. "If I were doing it over again, I would say that perhaps we followed a policy of active ease a little too long and we let ourselves get into a position of a strait jacket, of letting the [inflationary?] 'even keel' become the status quo rather than of having the flexibility we desire in monetary policy." Meltzer (2009, p. 136) maintained that "Martin's desire to build a consensus slowed" Fed responses. We see in Fig. 6.2 that interest rates failed to keep up with inflation several times in the 1950s, although this was less true when Martin and the Committee got tougher in the 1960s. Central banks have long been known for the exacerbations of economic fluctuations caused by their slow responses (Hawtrey 1938, pp. 213–14; Wood 2005, pp. 333–36).

March 6, 1956 Martin believed that the members of the Committee were in fairly close agreement on the existing economic situation and the credit policy called for. All wanted no change in policy, although about half leaned towards more restraint, if they had to choose one or the other, and 1 or 2 towards ease.

March 27, 1956 Martin believed the Committee "has had a tendency ... to permit its directive to remain unchanged too long and not to recognize shifts in the economy." Specifically, it seemed to him that the Directive, "which now required that operations take account of deflationary forces [during a vigorous expansion], was not in keeping with the majority sentiment."

The expansion had picked up steam and Sproul discussed the wage-cost spiral and the Phillips Curve. A "difficult problem [is] the possibility of our running into a cost-price spiral growing out of increased wages and other costs which producers attempt to pass on to consumers. This might encounter consumer resistance which would have a dampening effect on production and employment, or what seems more likely in the present state of the economy it might generate an inflationary spiral. We haven't yet had to run head-on into the philosophy of the Employment Act of 1946 to that extent and it wouldn't be easy, so maybe we had better hope that some degree of economic responsibility on the part of management and labor will avoid presenting the problem in serious form."

There was discussion of the political costs to the Fed of restraining inflation (Sproul and Vardaman) and acknowledgment that the Fed was not in complete control. Still, several members stated, the Fed should do all it could to restrain inflation.

The Fed raised the discount rate seven times during the 1954–57 expansion, from 1½ to 3½ percent, much to the annoyance of the administration and Congress. The *Joint Economic Committee* held hearings on the rise in 1956, and Arthur Burns and Secretary of the Treasury George Humphrey testified in opposition to the Fed's actions. At Eisenhower's urging, Humphrey told Martin that he should resign instead of opposing the president. Martin replied that he would resign if his leadership was opposed by the president, and informed the Board of his possible resignation. However, after a conversation with Martin, who promised to ease credit if the economy slowed, Eisenhower gave him his confidence. Ike decided against "overruling of the financial experts with a purely political judgment," and in two press conferences expressed confidence in the Fed, and added: "I personally believe that if money gets ... too tight, they will move in the other direction" (Meltzer 2009, p. 135). Martin was shortly reappointed to a new fourteen-year term as a governor and a four-year term as chairman.

May 23, 1956 The Committee favored restoring the Directive's reference to deflation, although Martin warned that "The committee should make clear the direction in which it is going."

June 26, 1956 Hayes (New York) said the System should supply sufficient reserves to take care of the credit expansion that was expected, but "lean back a little." Martin agreed. The System would be criticized, but plant and equipment should not be financed out of bank loans. Tight monetary policy would not hinder the economy. The Directive's statement to take account of deflation should not be deleted.

September 25, 1956 There was a discussion of money market conditions in light of the coming Treasury financings. Some members worried about a panic in the government securities market. If we are going to make errors in this case, Martin conceded, they should be on the side of ease.

January 8, 1957 Nevertheless, he said a few months later, "The consensus seemed to be that operations should be directed towards recapturing the restraint that existed early in December."

May 7, 1957 Martin said that "Inflation is the most serious problem confronting the countries of the western world today." However, "Monetary policy could [should?] not be used to restore a price level that had been lost through inflation processes."

The August 1957–April 1958 recession was the shortest but sharpest downturn since the end of the war. The FOMC remained concerned about inflation and was slow to ease.

September 10, 1957 Fed critics in recent Senate hearings had argued that raising interest rates caused inflation through their effects on costs.[6] Advisor Winfield Riefler dismissed those ideas in the meeting, and no one on the committee disagreed. They agreed that money and prices were positively related, and focused their attention on the proper measures of that relation. The best indication of monetary tightness in their view was net borrowed reserves (bank borrowing from the Fed less bank excess reserves) or its negative, free reserves. There were no precise money or interest-rate targets, and there was also criticism in and outside the FOMC of what many thought were vague and unhelpful directives using such undefined and perhaps undefinable terms as "tone" and "feel," especially with the arrival of Keynesian-leaning members in the 1960s. Nevertheless, the directive did not change significantly until Congress required money and interest targets in the 1970s (Brunner and Meltzer 1964; Wood 2009, pp. 137–39).

The economy had turned downward—the cyclical peak was later designated as August—but the directive continued to emphasize the problem of inflation until December 17, when it included:

> ... cushioning adjustments and mitigating recessionary tendencies in the economy.

The FOMC was quicker to react to the 1958 expansion than it had been to the 1957 downturn.

July 8, 1958 Although the recovery was only two months old, Martin favored an increase of one-half percent in the discount rate, but not before the next meeting. It was raised from 1¾ to 2 percent in September, and in steps to 4 percent in September 1959 (the highest rate since early 1930).

August 19, 1958 Martin said monetary policy cannot do "much when budget decisions, debt management, and fiscal policy are all in the picture with monetary and credit policy. The System didn't create the recent

[6] During hearings of the Senate Finance Committee, 85th Cong., 1st sess., June–August 1957. For a critique of this theory, see Horwich (1966). Hetzel and Leach (2001) suggest that the Fed's economists, led by Riefler at the Board (advising McCabe and Martin) and John Williams at the New York Bank (and Harvard), recognized that "the most important policy problem after the war was inflation rather than depression," and "recognized the importance of monetary and its relation to inflation some 20 years before the economics profession began to debate seriously that possibility."

recession." In his opinion, "the discount rate should have been raised much earlier in 1957, but we deferred to the Treasury. The 5 million unemployed are due to the dominance of inflation the last few years. Monetary policy did its best to restrain but there were severe budget flip-flops, especially in defense."

Which the Fed had to monetize, it seems to be implied.

> The System has to stand up to inflation psychosis and psychology. It had let the money supply run away with it. Commentators and the public say the System starts a recession when they raise the discount rate. "There is a distinct bias toward easy money, for when the System moves down everyone applauds.... [T]he other direction ... runs into more resistance."
>
> Inflation might temporarily reduce unemployment. But if inflation should get up a head of steam, unemployment might rise to 10 or 15 million.
>
> Senator Proxmire's opinion that there were "other means of controlling inflation" (meaning direct controls) was a prevalent attitude.
>
> The System had not faced up to the problem, whether it be called inflation psychosis or inflation psychology.

September 30, 1958 Martin was disappointed at the recent irregular discount rate increases (even if caused by the lack of uniformity of scheduled directors' meetings). It was his opinion that if conditions call for an upward adjustment, it should be by ½ percent [across the board] "so that there would be no misunderstanding of System policy."

December 16, 1958 Martin was as "anxious to get the unemployed back to work [as anyone], but a balanced recovery would not come about if price pressures were ignored ... or through easy money."

August 8, 1959 Martin noted that a bill authorizing the president to eliminate the interest rate ceiling on Treasury bonds had been tentatively approved by the House Ways and Means Committee, and then reversed. It remained a matter of concern to him that little progress had been made in explaining the role of interest rates in the economy.

The cyclical Peak came in April but:

April 12, 1960 Martin felt that any overt action on the part of the System in either direction would be unfortunate at this time.

July 6, 1960 Martin: All that was called for at present was to mark time, although errors "could be more on the side of ease than under other circumstances." The discount rate had been lowered in June and would be lowered again in August.

September 13, 1960 Martin said it was hard to know the effects of money, but he did not think money and credit policy could do the whole job [of recovery]. He did not want to repeat the easy money period of 1958, when the Fed went too far.

The Eisenhower administration increased spending, including the extension of unemployment compensation, but it did not propose a reduction in taxes or put pressure on the Fed, to the chagrin of Republican presidential candidate Richard Nixon.

October 25, 1960 The staff report referred to outside suggestions that the Fed should narrow the interest spread to encourage investment by buying long-term securities, but doubted that such artificial action would work [because it lacked permanence?] There would be a loss of confidence if it were recognized that yields were artificially influenced by the Fed. Martin agreed although Hayes and others thought long-term yields were too high for the prevailing stage of the business cycle.

November 22, 1960 We are on a modified gold standard, Martin said. We should not force money into the market when it was the competitive pricing of goods and services that was really the problem of the world at the moment. People rant against the gold standard when they find the rules of the game are a little hard.

Martin showed a sophisticated understanding of the gold standard, including its implication that money was demand-determined.

> The System had played its part well in the current recession by providing the maximum stimulus it could to any economy that was bound to decline when it reached that particular stage.
>
> He noted Hayes' views on the possibility of dealings in long-term securities, "but we should be careful. We don't want to get back to pegged interest rates."

President Kennedy and Operation Twist In January 1961, the 43-year-old Democrat succeeded the 70-year-old Republican, and it was expected that the new interventionist economics would take the place of the traditional. Those trained in Keynesian economics were succeeding the Old Guard. Although the economy had surpassed immediate postwar expectations, when a return of the Great Depression had been feared, during the 1960 election Democrats called attention to the underperformance of the economy under the Republicans, including three recessions (1953–54, 1957–58, and 1960–61), and a 2.5 percent per annum rate of growth. Unemployment was near a postwar high of 7 percent when Kennedy took office. The Democratic platform had promised to "put an end to the present high-interest, tight-money policy and to double the growth rate to 5 percent, increase social security payments, raise the minimum wage to $1.25 per hour, and increase housing starts to two million a year using government loans if needed."

On the other hand, the president had inherited a smattering of balanced-budget and sound-money views which he sought to join with his growth objectives. "I know everyone [his liberal advisors] thinks I worry about this [gold and the dollar problem] too much," Kennedy said to a confidant "one day as we pored over what seemed like the millionth report on the subject. But if there's ever a run on the bank, and I have to devalue the dollar or bring home our troops, as the British did, I'm the one who will take the heat. Besides it's a club that DeGaulle and all the others hang over my head. Any time there's a crisis or a quarrel, they can cash in all their dollars, and where are we?" Kennedy "had some evidence to back his suspicions that the gloomy rumors which triggered the gold withdrawals of 1960 had been deliberately spread by American bankers to embarrass him politically," advisor and biographer Ted Sorenson (1965, p. 408) wrote, "and he did not want to be vulnerable to the same tactic in 1964." On the other hand, Kennedy "refused to believe that he had to choose between a weaker economy at home or a weaker dollar abroad." And the Fed's cooperation was questionable.

Martin's replacement was considered, but the chairman designate of the CEA, University of Minnesota Professor Walter Heller, found him "cooperative, open-minded and cordial" in their discussions of prospective monetary policy. Martin even agreed to regular luncheons with the Council as well as meetings with the president, the chairman of the Council, and the Secretary of the Treasury, called the Quadriad (Hargrove and Morley 1984, p. 190). Furthermore, his retention lent credibility to the administration's fiscal and monetary soundness, the new Secretary of the Treasury, Republican financier Douglas Dillon, suggested.[7]

Martin might have thought the meetings would enable him to persuade the administration to the Fed's views, but they turned out to be forums for the former's harpings on the necessity of easy money. The administration's idea of cooperation was the Fed's submission to the financing of its fiscal programs. For example, the new administration's plan to achieve the potentially conflicting goals of growth and a strong dollar assigned Operation Twist to the Fed, which in the process was forced to abandon bills only. The Fed would twist the yield curve by buying long-term securities, putting downward pressure on long-term rates of interest to promote growth and selling short-terms to put upward pressure on short-term rates to attract short-term foreign investment. The plan was consistent with the stability of money and prices because long-term open-market purchases would be offset by the sales of short-terms.

Dillon warned of "limitations to what can be accomplished," and Martin tried to weaken the plan's commitment, but agreed to abandon "bills only" in favor of "operation nudge" (which became "operation twist"), while asking for the avoidance of "any public implication that they are taking these new steps as a result of outside pressure." Kennedy ignored the request and announced the policy in his first economic message on February 2. Martin had agreed although the FOMC had yet to consider the issue (Meltzer 2009, p. 317).

February 7, 1961 Martin's half-hearted effort to persuade the Committee, to change its operating procedure in the absence of new ideas or events, met considerable skepticism. He was doubtful of the outcome but he was not sure it wouldn't work, and in light of the criticisms of the Fed's rigidity, he believed it was necessary to show that it was open-minded and willing to experiment "to enable the System to escape from the charge of doctrinaire commitment to a laissez faire, free private market position."

[7]Presidents appoint Fed chairmen from among Board members for four-year terms not coterminous with president's terms, which meant that Martin's term as chairman would end in February 1963. Presidents have sought to make chairmen's terms coincident with their own without success. Martin had offered to resign when Eisenhower became president in 1953, but was asked to remain. In 1961, however, since Martin and the Fed's monetary policy had been made campaign issues, he felt that as a matter of principle he should not offer his resignation (Meltzer 2009, p. 269).

Several Committee members regretted that they were shifting from a much-studied and successful method to one whose basis was unclear, but with one exception they went along (all the Bank presidents joined him) in the spirit of being willing to try an experiment. The New York contingent had always want to operate across the full range of the securities market, but Governor Robertson probably expressed the feelings of several members when he said "that in deviating from its established policies the FOMC was asserting, without reason or conviction, that it made a critically incorrect judgment eight years ago and had pursued incorrect operating procedures since, and that critics of present methods … were relying on the simplest theories of determination of market interest rates and making allegations of postulates having little if any basis in empirical fact."

Robertson argued that "the Committee was running serious risk of undermining domestic and foreign confidence in the System's integrity and judgment, and the reliability of the new administration's assertions of an intent to maintain the stability of the dollar," that is, substituting insubstantial tricks for genuine well-understood stable-price policies. He also thought that such a radical reversal of policy should be accompanied by its announcement and reasons for it. However, the Committee accepted Martin's advice to do neither, possibly because there was little that could be said.

In the event, Operation Twist's critics need not have worried. FOMC members often wondered what the policy was, whether it was being followed, and whether it was effective. Martin referred to "groping" for a policy and also doubted its effectiveness. He told Heller that the FOMC was pursuing the policy against most of its members' better judgment, and that he and the Committee had lost any conviction that it could succeed (Meltzer 2009, pp. 319–321).

> *June 6, 1961.* Yet in striving for the appearances of unity and cooperation, Martin, ever the diplomat, urged that "Those in the System should not go around saying the operation was a failure [even though] the so-called nudging effect was getting to be a matter of flying into the wind. One could make a good case for getting out entirely but that could not be done at present in light of the public discussion."

In the end, Operation Twist had no apparent effect (the greater rise in short than in long rates during 1961–64 was normal for expansions), partly because it was not seriously tried. The Fed's efforts varied from "half-hearted" to "timid," in Heller's view, and the Treasury acted contrary to declared policy by issuing more long than short debt, normal policy when interest rates are expected to rise. "As a result, the maturity of the debt lengthened appreciably, instead of shortened as the policy would require," Chicago economist Harry Johnson (1963) noted.

Martin's performance as a team player was suspect. It can be argued that he managed to keep the majority's support of Operation Twist, weak though it was, by an execution that was almost imperceptible. Heller recalled that

> ... we'd have a meeting with Kennedy ... and before the meeting Bill would be out there buying those long-term securities, but afterwards his buying would flag... Jim Tobin would keep track of this and he'd say, "Walter, you'd better arrange another meeting ... because Martin isn't buying enough long-term bonds." So I'd call a meeting and sure enough the purchases would rise again, and Martin would be able to tell Kennedy, "We're doing everything we can". (Hargrove and Morley 1984, p. 191)

It was in any case impossible according to the prevalent theory of the term structure of interest rates, according to which market arbitrage equates long rates with averages of current and expected short rates. The theory was validated when the Treasury tried to peg long rates at 2 percent and bills at 0.375 percent during World War II, and the public refused to buy the latter. A policy to raise short rates permanently without raising long rates is impossible.

A similar fate awaited the plan's goal of manipulating spreads between national interest rates in the presence of fixed exchange rates. All such attempts were sure to be defeated by arbitrage—which Martin understood but the Keynesian market skeptics did not.

Two Wars at Once Politics and monetary and fiscal policies were increasingly dominated by the Vietnam War and the War on Poverty as the 1960s wore on. Government outlays doubled during the decade, rising 60 percent in real terms, most after the middle of the decade. Lyndon Johnson, who had succeeded Kennedy as president in November 1963, recoiled from choosing between military and social programs. "I was determined to be a leader of war and a leader of peace. I refused to let my critics push me into choosing one or the other. I wanted both." Believing Congress would reduce spending for social programs if he proposed a tax increase,

Johnson tried to hide the true rise in defense spending from the public, Congress, and the Fed, whose holdings of the Federal debt more than doubled, which must have told it something (Meltzer 2009, pp. 269–70).

"For both strategic and political reasons, ... this escalation was kept a closely held secret. Along with numerous other government offices, the Federal Reserve was given no information on [the military] buildup.... Martin learned about the 1965 increase independently.... President Johnson apparently believed policy coordination should go one way only" (Meltzer 2009, p. 270; Stockwell 1989, p. 37). Martin might have hoped the regular meetings would give the Fed more of a say in overall policy, but the effect was the other way, particularly because the administration's frequent promises of fiscal responsibility (as part of its pleas for monetary ease) were not kept.

Opposing the president is always difficult, even for an agency responsible to Congress. The period of low inflation immediately after the Fed escaped its dominance by the Treasury in the Accord had raised its reputation as monetary manager and gave it a degree of political cover. Inflation was unpopular and politicians had to take it into account in their statements and programs. On the other hand, the real and immediate popularity of more spending and lower taxes were threats to price stability, assisted by the Keynesian leanings of some of the Board's new members.

There had been no academic economists on the Federal Reserve Board since Adolph Miller (1914–36), until Professor Sherman Maisel (1965–72) of the University of California was appointed by President Johnson. George Mitchell (1961–76), Illinois Democrat and economic advisor to Adlai Stevenson, and Dewey Daane (1963–74), Harvard Ph.D. and deputy under-secretary of the Treasury (1960–63), had been appointed by Kennedy, and Johnson later appointed the Harvard Ph.D. and assistant Secretary of Commerce Andrew Brimmer (1966–74) and Texas businessman William Sherrill (1967–71). Not all were Keynesians but the Fed had become less conservative.

In 1958, Martin, born in 1906, was the youngest member of the Board and one of two who had not been born in the nineteenth century. In 1971, at the end of his time at the Fed, Martin was second oldest and surrounded by liberals, most of whom had studied economics after the publication of Keynes' *General Theory*. So, it is not surprising, given the Johnson administration's pushes for more spending on the controversial

War on Poverty and the increasingly unpopular Vietnam War, that the Federal Reserve was expected to provide a good part of the finance.

Differences between views of the purposes of central banks had widened since the 1930s. Historically (notwithstanding the Fed's failure during the Great Depression), its purpose (at least in theory) had been to support the payments system. After World War II, however, money for economists was a direct means of influencing output and employment. This turned out to mean, in the view of government economists, a constant fear of low or slowing growth and persistent pressures for increased money. They were always able, by means of a perpetually insufficient "Potential GNP," to ask for more government spending and lower taxes, supported by easy money.[8]

This emphasis on money as a macroeconomic tool defied history on economic and democratic grounds. Alexander Hamilton (1790) had recommended the private ownership of the Bank of the United States to avoid political exploitation:

> The stamping of paper is an operation so much easier than the laying of taxes, that a government in the practice of paper emissions would rarely fail, in any ... emergency [perhaps not necessarily an emergency] to indulge itself too far in the employment of that resource, to avoid, as much as possible, one less auspicious to present popularity.

As we saw in Chap. 5, although frequently violated, limits on lending to governments without the express consent of legislatures have commonly been written into bank charters.

Not wishing to be bound by such Constitutional niceties, in July 1965, President Johnson, doubtful of the public's support when he announced that more American troops would be sent to Vietnam, did not reveal the size of his plans. The then chairman of the CEA remembered that "There was a period of a couple of months – six weeks maybe – in the summer in which there was, I think, a deliberate effort not to let anybody know what was going on. But the people in Defense knew it, and the people in Budget and the Council did not know it" (Hargrove and Morley 1984, p. 249).

[8] For example, *Economic Report of the President*, 1964, pp. 36–39. Except for two quarters in 1955, there was a continuous deficiency (gap) between potential and actual GNP from mid-1953 through 1963.

Whatever they knew, they promised not to tell the Fed. Budget Director Charles Schultze memoed the president: "I have instructed my staff not to discuss the budgetary outlook with the Fed. Quite apart from security considerations I am afraid that the budgetary outlook would be used as an excuse to tighten up on monetary policy" (Meltzer 2009, p. 449). Johnson later said the reason for secrecy was to prevent the Soviet Union and China from increasing their support to North Vietnam (Johnson 1971, p. 149; Meltzer 2009, p. 149). Word got around, however, including to Martin, who had connections in Congress and the Defense Department. He confronted the president several times, and warned that interest rates might have to rise. In fact, they were already rising with inflation.

One might wonder how Johnson thought his projects would be financed if neither by taxes nor by investors attracted by high returns. The answer had to be money printed by the central bank. The relations between monetary and fiscal policy changed radically in the 1960s. Previously, increased spending had been associated with increased taxes (although not equally), especially in wartime. Since the 1960s, however, particularly during the administrations of Johnson, Reagan, and the younger Bush, increased spending has been accompanied by reduced taxation.

The proportion of the FOMC opposed to tightening, and even favoring more ease, grew during the early 1960s as Martin urged a policy of "firmness," or "steady in the boat," as he continued to be able to observe that "the members do not seem to be very far apart this morning" (FOMC, 3/6/62). Even so, he felt called upon to issue some admonishments:

May 29, 1962 Martin thought the System had gone as far as it should with a policy of easy money, which had outlived its usefulness. The result had been a "backwash of speculation that had been going on all around the country.... The System could not just go along thinking that easy money would produce an exuberant economy."

June 19, 1962 "It was time for members [who thought there was too much ease] to stand up and be counted."

July 10, 1962 "Monetary policy has done what it could to help the recovery and had about played itself out. It was easy to think we can achieve certain things just by easing money or something."

Notwithstanding Martin's fears, inflation during the early 1960s was a fairly steady 1 percent, a better performance, in fact, than the 1950s, especially considering the long expansion following the cyclical trough of February 1961. However, the 1965 increase in government spending inspired a Martin speech on June 1 that "shocked both the administration and the financial community." He saw "the threat of another Great Depression.... We find disquieting similarities between our present prosperity and the fabulous twenties."

CEA Chairman Gardner Ackley (1964–68, a cost-push devotee) told LBJ that Martin was unaware of the enormous progress of economics and economic policy the previous thirty years. Ackley shared the view of Walter Heller, his predecessor at the Council, that non-Keynesian policies reflected the "paralyzing grip of economic myth and false fears." "It is hard to know what Bill was really driving at in his speech," Ackley (1971, pp. 5–6; Kettl 1973, p. 103; Heller 1966, p. 1) memoed the president. He believed inflation was "deeply imbedded in the economic structures of modern western societies," and described his job as "President Johnson's principal agent in attempting to hold down wages and prices by 'jawboning'."

Board member Maisel was encouraged by what turned out to be empty Treasury and Council offers "to coordinate monetary and fiscal policies." Ackley and the secretary of the Treasury "told me" that the administration was considering fiscal restraint, and promised that "if fiscal policy were not tightened, they would urge President Johnson to call for a tighter monetary policy in his State of the Union message" (Maisel 1973, pp. 74–75). Nothing of the kind was done, and Martin continued to warn the president of the need to restrain spending, preferably by increased taxes, or if not by tighter monetary policy. Martin explained the FOMC's failure to act as follows:

October 12, 1965 As Chairman, Martin had the responsibility of maintaining System relations within the Government, and he had recently given the President a paper expressing his personal views [that tightening might have to occur]. The President had not taken a rigid position on the matter—he had not suggested that the Committee should abdicate its responsibility for formulating monetary policy—but thought it would be unwise to change monetary policy now. With a divided Committee and in the face of strong Administration opposition, he did not believe it would be appropriate for him to lend his support to those who favored a change in policy now.

So, what were they to do? The Federal Reserve Act had assigned the Fed responsibilities for an elastic currency, its gold value, and bank supervision, but its primary objective soon became the monetization of the federal debt (during World War I and again during World War II). The gold standard was abandoned in 1933 and the Executive took control of the Fed without the benefit of legislation. The Fed regained substantial but uncertain control in 1951, although the Employment Act of 1946 declared it to be "the continuing policy and responsibility of the Federal Government to coordinate and utilize all its plans, functions, and resources … to promote maximum employment, production and purchasing power."

Whether the law implies an independent Fed focused on price stability or a monetary-and-fiscal policy coordinated by the executive depends on one's macroeconomic model: the classical neutrality of money, with costly inflation, according to Martin, or the interventionist Keynesianism of the Employment Act? The Fed might take its cues from Congress, whose creature it is, although that body has many spokespersons and interpretations of its wishes.

Federal deficits might also be interpreted as evasions of democracy, that is, spending more than the taxes voted by Congress, the elected representatives of the people (Wood 2009, pp. 69–71; Keech 1995, pp. 160–61). So the Fed's occasional resistance to presidents may have been due less to differences in economics than defenses of the *Constitution*, particularly Article I, Section 7.1, which provided that "All Bills for raising Revenue shall originate in the House of Representatives." Taking this power seriously means that Section 8.2, which gives Congress the power "To borrow Money on the credit of the United States," implies that borrowing is in anticipation of taxes. In any case, Federal Reserve purchases of government debt, although implied by congressional decisions, are not directly considered or voted on by Congress. Legislators benefit politically from spending without paying the election costs of taxes.

As 1965 approached its end, having given up on the administration's promises and unimpressed with its studies which concluded that there was nothing to worry about, Martin stiffened. "He was finally ready," in Meltzer's words, "to accept the challenge." He knew the government's spending plans had continued to grow. When on October 6, Martin told Johnson that a rate increase was necessary, the latter said: "I'm scheduled to go into the hospital tomorrow for a gall bladder operation. You wouldn't raise the discount rate while I'm in the hospital, would you?" Martin replied: "No, Mr. President, we'll wait until you get out of the hospital." On December 3, after considerable lobbying by Martin and Hayes, the Board voted 4–3 to recommend increases in discount rates, and the Reserve Banks raised their rates from 4 to 4.5 percent (Meltzer 2009, p. 453). Martin warned of the risk to the System's independence if it acted against the president's wishes, but said: "There is a question whether the Federal Reserve is to be run by the administration in office."

The Board also raised the maximum rate payable on bank time deposits, which threatened to fall below market rates and cause deposit drains. The Banking Act of 1933 included Regulation Q, which prohibited interest on demand deposits and directed the Fed to fix ceilings on time deposits. The maximum rate payable on savings deposits was 2½ percent from 1935 through 1956, when the Fed began to raise it in line with market rates (Federal Reserve Board 1976, p. 673; Wood 2005, p. 32).

At the same time, the Fed accommodated to market interest rates. The twelve (generally equal) Federal Reserve Bank discount rates are decided (recommended) by their Boards of Directors subject to the approval of the Federal Reserve Board, which at full strength is the majority of the FOMC. New York President Hayes led off November's round-table discussion:

November 23, 1965 Most of the directors of the New York Bank have felt for some time that an increase in the discount rate is overdue. Indeed, on a number of occasions some of them have urged that the Bank take the initiative in this area. I am now prepared to recommend that they vote a ½ percent discount rate increase within the next week or so.

Most of the rest of the FOMC were on the fence, and Martin gave them a pep talk. "The time for decision had arrived, and he wanted the record to reflect his opinion that it was not possible to run away continually from making a decision. [I]t was necessary to make fundamental judgments, [which] was easy for him ... because he believed the country was in a period of creeping inflation already... [H]e thought the economy was going too fast at the moment. This was where one came up against the basic problem – to which he did not know the answer – relating to the economics of full employment. Here there were different schools of thought. Personally he felt that at some point, if the economy went too fast, the possibility of achieving sustainable full employment would be destroyed. And he thought the situation was about at that point now." Not for the first time, Martin anticipated the stagflation of the next decade.

After the December 3rd rate increase, Johnson summoned Martin to his ranch in Texas where he was recovering from his operation. "You've got me in a position where you can run a rapier into me and you've done it," the president said. "[Y]ou went ahead and did something that I disapproved of … and can affect my entire term.… You took advantage of me and I just want you to know that's a despicable thing to do" (Bremner 2004, p. 209).

The Fed continued its pressure into 1966, and short-term market rates began to exceed maximum rates on bank deposits. Deposits fell, banks restricted credit, and on September 13, 1966, Hayes told the FOMC "that the financial community was experiencing growing and genuine fear of a financial panic." However, the Committee stayed with the directive of "firm but orderly conditions." Martin was "impressed by its high degree of agreement on policy."

October 4, 1966 The Directive continued "firm but orderly conditions in the money market; provided, however, that operations shall be modified in the light of unusual liquidity pressures or of any significant deviation of bank credit from current expectations."

What happened, however, was monetary expansion. The president got his way, after all. Money and prices accelerated, inflation rose from 1.3 per percent per annum during 1960–65 to 4.7 percent in 1968 and 6.2 percent in 1969. The Fed financed half the deficits. Martin said later that the Fed's ease had partly stemmed from the disappointed hope that the temporary income-tax surcharge pried from Congress would suppress demand (more on this below). In Meltzer's words, "Martin had shown courage and determination by refusing to back down under intense pressure from the president. Then he retreated" (Meltzer 2009, p. 493).

In July 1966, the Board disapproved several Reserve Bank requests for rate increases. Governor Daane explained his position: "Every economic ground said to increase the rate; his reluctance was because such an action would be harmful to relationships with the administration" (Meltzer 2009, p. 505). Martin later explained his reluctance to take action against inflation:

October 24, 1967 Martin admitted that large deficits in the budget are generating "inexorable forces that might prove more important than any decisions the committee would take."

On the other hand, he resisted the president's pressures to ease. Unable to obtain a permanent tax increase, LBJ asked in his State of the Union message of January 1967, for a temporary income-tax surcharge. The reluctant Congress finally gave him a bill to sign in July 1968, which imposed a one-year 10-percent surcharge (later extended for a year at 5 percent). In addition to providing revenue for the Vietnam War, the tax was expected (hoped) to slow inflation-driven private spending and allow the easing of interest rates—which the administration's economists expected, or hoped, the Fed to accommodate.

August 17, 1968 Economic slowdowns were forecast by the administration's economists as well as the Fed's staff and some of the governors. Martin was having none of this. In his judgment the present inflationary difficulties were largely traceable to the long delay in introducing fiscal restraint and to the fact that monetary policy had moved toward restraint too slowly. He now thought that the discount rate should have been raised to the current 5½ percent level considerably earlier than it had been. He remarked that business was good and he was not as pessimistic as the staff about the economic outlook.

September 10, 1968 The Board's Director of Research and Statistics, Daniel Brill, admitted that his and the administration's self-supporting forecasts had been mistaken. A "study" by the Treasury, Budget Bureau, CEA, and Brill and his staff, who were generally in favor of ease and at odds with Martin, had recommended no tightening in monetary policy at least until the publication of the federal budget in January, given that "a step-up in Federal spending [was] unlikely," even though Martin knew the opposite was true (Bremner 2004, p. 206). Economists later pointed out that the small effect of the income tax surcharge on spending was not surprising in light of the permanent income hypothesis, according to which as income earners spread tax changes over their lifetime earnings (Eisner 1969). Martin repeated his previous month's skepticism, and in December, a month after Nixon's election, the Fed tightened.

Fighting Inflation Under Nixon

January 14, 1969 Martin reported that he had told the new president that inflation was the primary economic problem facing the nation, and the administration would have to deal with it effectively from the beginning if it were not to get out of control. He told the Committee that it would be better to risk overstaying, rather than understaying, a policy of restraint.

In 1966, the Fed had caved in, which they blamed partly on their expectation/hope that the administration would keep its promises of fiscal restraint. This time, Martin promised, they would stay the course.

Richard Nixon did not trust Martin, whom he blamed for his defeat in the 1960 presidential election. The economy had peaked in April 1960 and bottomed in February 1961. In his book *Six Crises*, Nixon described his friend Arthur Burns's advice in March 1960 that monetary policy should be eased to avoid an "economic dip just before the elections." However, neither Eisenhower nor Martin could be persuaded to change course.

Nixon offered Martin, whose term as chairman extended to February 1970, the job of Secretary of the Treasury in order to open the Fed chairmanship to Burns, but Martin said he would serve out his term at the Fed (Bremner 2004, pp. 260–61).

The president and his Council of Economic advisors hoped to reduce inflation with a minimal increase in unemployment. Council Chairman Paul McCracken referred to their plan as "gradualism." A little bit of monetary tightening would slowly lower inflation toward price stability, which, when achieved, would promote the return to full employment. This fine-tuning exercise in small, smooth, temporary movements along static, well-behaved curves did not take account of spenders' expectations, Martin believed. The failure of the income-tax surcharge to slow spending had been a recent case of the futility of temporary measures. He was not a gradualist. The market needed to be shocked.

July 15, 1969 The go-around discussion revealed sentiment for shading monetary policy in both directions depending on the effects of the current policy of restraint. His personal view was that policy should not be loosened because he did not favor fine-tuning to the degree to which some apparently were inclined. He did not agree with those who argued that it was necessary only for the System to pull the right levers to do an effective job of stabilization. Shading towards ease would be a mistake because of the risk that it would be interpreted as a more significant move toward ease than desired. Inflationary psychology remained the main economic problem. It would be a mistake to take any action that might reinforce inflationary expectations just at the time they might be weakening. The System had been overly hasty in moving toward ease in the summer of 1968, after the credit crunch and in response to the administration's promise of fiscal restraint.

Accordingly, the Committee voted unanimously for a directive which included: "System open market operations ... shall be conducted with a view to maintaining the currently prevailing firm conditions." Martin informed Congress and the public of the Fed's determination. "There is no gadgetry in monetary mechanisms ... that will save us from our sins," he told a group of bankers. Expectations of inflation were deeply embedded, and their elimination would require "a good deal of pain and suffering." The Fed had indicated, "perhaps unwisely," after the 1966 credit crunch that "we don't want a recurrence." However, "if you don't take some risk in policy you never get any result." Martin strongly implied that the Fed would not back down again even in the event of increased unemployment (U.S. Congress 1969, pp. 648–651, 668–69; Matusow 1998, p. 25; Bremner 2004, p. 253).

Martin and Congress

Martin and the Fed were under almost constant attack by congressional critics for their allegedly tight money policies. The advocacy of easy money seems always in the modern world to be thought politically advantageous. Chairman Wright Patman of the House Committee on Banking and Currency, complained during 1964 hearings into "The Federal Reserve after Fifty Years" that

> From the spring of 1951 [when Martin came on board] until now [1964] our great and essentially healthy ... economy has three times been throttled by the ... Federal Reserve.... I will let the facts speak for themselves. The recession of 1953–54 began in July 1953. Interest rates began to rise early in 1953. The growth of the money supply fell steadily beginning in January 1953.

Rising interest rates had also preceded the 1957–58 and 1960–61 recessions. "No one but Mr. Martin knows," Professor Tobin had written, "how much slack the Federal Reserve is willing to force upon the economy in the effort to stop inflation." Patman asked 23 professors, "How much independence the Fed should have?" They unanimously replied, "None." Four, including Milton Friedman, favored monetary rules, and the rest recommended the subordination of monetary policy to the president. Stanford's John Gurley said Fed independence "is like having two managers for the same baseball team, each manager independent of the other." It was unthinkable, even "ludicrous," that monetary policy did not conform to the program of elected officials. Bankers, on the other hand, who expressed satisfaction with the structure and policies of the Fed, were rebuked by Patman as a "special interest … with an ax to grind" (U.S. House 1964, p. 1884; Tobin 1958).

It is hard to take these tight-money complaints seriously in light of the significant inflation of the 1950s. Yet Senator William Proxmire of the Joint Economic Committee was able to recite the stated preferences of several distinguished economists for lower interest rates. Martin responded by pointing out that easy money produced the opposite of the congressmen's wishes. "It is my conviction, Senator … that generally speaking we follow a too easy monetary policy." He had said two years earlier:

> I do want to point out that in eight years of experience in the Federal Reserve System, I am convinced that our bias, if anything, has been on the side of too much money rather than too little. (U.S. Congress 1960, p. 185)

Martin denied the accusation of a "mystical attachment to high interest rates and deflation" at the Fed.

> I say respectfully that a mystical attachment to low interest rates can be just as misguided and harmful as mystical attachment to high interest rates.

In any case, "we want the right interest rates."

> We want the right interest rates to come out of a balance between the supply and demand for funds … so that the flow of funds is as appropriately adjusted as it can be in a free market economy to the needs and requirements of the economy. That should be our goal. I hope that all of us will stop shilly-shallying about this matter of interest rates because it is only a price attached to credit

Proxmire refused to be drawn into a discussion of the role of interest rates and accused Martin himself of generalities and questionable definitions so that trying to understand you "is like nailing a custard pie to the wall." "And frankly, Mr. Martin, without specific goals, criteria guidelines, it is impossible to exercise any congressional oversight over you, and I think you know it" (U.S. Congress 1962, pp. 611–12, 625–33).

The Senate Banking and Currency Committee held hearings in 1958 in connection with the Committee's Report on *Federal Reserve policy and economic stability*. The Report was critical of slow Fed responses to developments, particularly leading up to the contractions of 1953–54 and 1957–58 and during the expansion of 1955–56, adding to inflationary pressures in the latter case and to declines in the other cases.

Martin and other Fed witnesses conceded that the Fed had been too slow on occasion, mainly due to data difficulties: including the slow arrival and interpretation of information and the normal human hesitancy to act, as well as an excessive reliance on the power of small changes in interest rates. The Report quoted an exchange between Senator Edward Martin, Republican from Pennsylvania, and the Fed chairman during a Finance Committee hearing in 1957:

Senator Martin: "When did this current inflation begin?"

Chairman Martin: We began to get worried in 1955, but let me go back just a little. Our initial approach to the 1953 inventory recession began well, but by the end of 1953 and the early part of 1954, I personally think that we were overdoing it a bit. We were using the phrase "active ease."

One thing you find out about this is that while your weapons may be more effective in inducing restraint than in galvanizing the economy, nevertheless it is more difficult to get people to recognize the need for action when it comes to restraint. We got a little bit enthusiastic about increasing money in 1954, when we lowered the discount rate from 2 to 1¾ to 1½ in February and April.

It took us from April 1954 to April 1955, – "a whole year" – to move back to 1¾ "because the constant discussion in the System was, 'Well, better not take a step, you had better not do anything to slow things down. You see, everybody likes expansion."

Senator Martin: Do you feel you acted soon enough?

Chairman Martin: No.

The Finance Committee Report was a composite of the standard criticisms of the Fed. However, a response by the Federal Reserve Board's staff, largely consistent with Martin's views, was allowed at the end of the document.

The Fed Staff responded to the Report's criticisms by pointing to the mildness of postwar recessions compared with prewar. The Report had also ignored the problem of inflation, which was "the most persistently grave threat to economic stability during the postwar period…. It … ignores the growing tendency on the part of business management in this period to anticipate future construction needs in an effort to avoid expected future increases in construction costs, and the effects of these anticipatory decisions on construction costs and surplus plant capacity. As a result the paper gives inadequate recognition to the effect of the developing inflationary psychosis on the prices of fixed-interest securities, and on the level of long-term interest rates."

The price level rose 15 percent during the 1950s, large by the standards of the day, and doubled during the quarter century after the war. Someone buying a twenty-five-year $1000 bond at the end of the war received half that in real terms on maturity.

The Committee Report also "appears to favor a sledgehammer approach of sharper and more active [countercyclical] actions on the basis of forecasts presumed to be accurate." Martin in his testimony had indicated that the Fed had been too quick to expand although too slow to apply restraint—the opposite of Keynesian criticisms.

The Report concluded with a criticism of the Fed's lack of transparency. When the chairman of the Banking and Currency Committee questioned why on occasion the Fed had not explained its actions, Martin replied that "Our actions should speak louder than our words. [I]t is by action rather than by announcement and statement that we get our results."

Congressional criticism of bills only as too restrictive increased in 1960. Twenty-one senators sent a letter to the Fed urging four reforms: (1) tighten regulation of securities dealers, including margin requirements for their customers; (2) end bills only; (3) permit money to grow at the rate of output growth; (4) increase money by means of open-market operations rather than lowering reserve requirements (Meltzer 2009, p. 206). Regarding the last, after reserve requirements were raised during the 1930s and 1940s, they began a downward trend in the 1950s that continued for decades, largely concessions to bank lobbying. Congress would have preferred to retain the tax implicit in the high bank reserve demands for government currency, but had yielded to the political influence of banks (Lown and Wood 2003).

At the June 1961 FOMC meeting, Martin and Hayes relayed messages from members of the Joint Economic Committee which reminded Martin of the president's statement that "the full financial influence of government must be exerted in the direction of credit ease and money growth while the economy is growing." Henry Reuss, democrat from Wisconsin, asked Hayes to pass on to the FOMC the message that it should adopt the suggestion of the majority of the JEC that the Federal Reserve "abandon its inflexible portfolio policy and, at least, weigh the desirability of its portfolio alignment," and if it didn't, tell the JEC why it had not done so.

A representative Martin exchange with Congress was his 1957 testimony before the Senate Finance Committee, which he was to repeat for the 1964 Patman hearings (U.S. House 1964, pp. 2002–2003):

Senator Russell Long:	Would you elaborate upon … the degree to which the Federal Reserve Board [he equated the Federal Reserve System with the Board] exercises its judgment … with regard to the direction of our economic and fiscal policies?
Martin:	Well, we feel ourselves bound by the Employment Act and by the Federal Reserve Act. And in the field of money and credit, we consider ourselves to be, regardless of what the decisions of the administration may be – we consult with them but we feel that we have the authority, if we think that in our field, money and credit policies, that we should act differently than they, we feel perfectly at liberty to do so.
Long:	In other words, you feel that you have freedom in promoting what you believe to be the full employment policy of the law?
Martin:	That is right.
Long:	To adopt policies that may not be the policy of the administration itself?
Martin:	That is right.
Long:	And you feel that there is the right within the Board to adopt a policy that may be completely at variance with the attitude and the direction of the policy of the administration?
Martin:	Well, I wouldn't say that – we will discuss it at considerable length.
Long:	You have the right to disagree with them?

Martin: Exactly.
Long: And you believe that the Federal Reserve Board, if it does disagree, has the right to pursue a policy that is completely contrary to the policy that the administration proceeds to follow, … you feel that under the law you have that right?
Martin: Under the law we feel it is our prerogative; yes, sir.

Strong words, stronger than the Fed's actions.

Summary and Conclusion

Martin was not an academic economist, and he avoided their language. However, he demonstrated a knowledge of economic relationships at least as sophisticated as theirs', and applied that knowledge to monetary policy in light of expectations, credibility, arbitrage, and the workings of markets.

The legislation of 1913 (the Federal Reserve Act), 1933 (effectively ending the gold standard), and 1946 (the Employment Act) influenced the workings of the monetary system, which were offset to some extent by Martin's conservative leanings. But he was playing a losing game. It has been said, as biographers are wont to do, that Martin had a lasting effect on the Fed, but inflation continued. Nor did the Accord provide independence. The Fed's goals continued to take a backseat to political demands, particularly the desires of administrations and Congresses for the monetization of their spending.

Martin felt a failure. Inflation had risen on his watch, he lamented (Bremner 2004, pp. 6, 207). On the other hand, it is hard to see how he could have done any better given the forces arrayed against him—presidents, Congresses, and economists—and the weakness of the support given him by those who ought to have preferred stable prices, particularly finance and the public. Figure 6.2 presents the main evidence supporting the rise in Martin's reputation, with the experiences of the 1970s and 1990s demonstrating the superiority of his low-inflation policies.

References

Ackley, Gardner. 1959. Administered Prices and the Inflationary Process. *American Economic Review*, May.

———. 1961. *Macroeconomic Theory.* New York: Macmillan.

———. 1971. *Stemming World Inflation.* Paris: Atlantic Institute.

Ahearn, Daniel S. 1963. *Federal Reserve Policy Reappraised, 1951–59*. New York: Columbia University Press.

Axilrod, Stephen H. 2009. *Inside the Fed*. Cambridge, MA: MIT Press.

Bagehot, Walter. 1873. *Lombard Street*. Henry King. (Reprinted with Introduction by Harley Withers, E.P. Dutton, 1920).

Bremner, Robert P. 2004. *Chairman of the Fed. William McChesney Martin, Jr. and the Creation of the Modern American Financial System*. New Haven: Yale University Press.

Brunner, Karl, and Allan H. Meltzer. 1964. *Some General Features of the Federal Reserve's Approach to Policy: A Staff Analysis*. Subcommittee on Domestic Finance, HR Committee on Banking and Currency, 88th Cong., 2nd Sess.

Buchanan, James M., and Richard E. Wagner. 1977. *Democracy in Deficit: The Political Legacy of Lord Keynes*. New York: Academic Press.

Capie, Forrest H., ed. 1993. *The Future of Central Banking*. Cambridge: Cambridge University Press.

Donovan, Robert J. 1982. *Tumultuous Years: The Presidency of Harry S. Truman, 1949–53*. New York: W.W. Norton & Co..

Dow, J.C.R. 1964. *The Management of the British Economy, 1945–60*. Cambridge: Cambridge University Press.

Eccles, Mariner S. 1951. *Beckoning Frontiers*. New York: Knopf.

Eisner, Robert. 1969. Fiscal and Monetary Policy Reconsidered. *American Economic Review*, December.

Federal Reserve Board. 1976. *Banking and Monetary Statistics, 1941–70*. Washington, DC.

Fisher, Irving. 1911. *The Purchasing Power of Money*. New York: Macmillan.

Friedman, Milton. 1959. *A Program for Monetary Stability*. Fordham University Press.

Friedman, Milton, and Anna J. Schwartz. 1963. *A Monetary History of the United States, 1867–1960*. Princeton: Princeton University Press.

Hamby, Alonzo L. 1995. *Man of the People. A Life of Harry S. Truman*. New York: Oxford University Press.

Hamilton, Alexander. 1790. *Report on a National Bank*. Treasury Department to the House of Representatives, December 13.

Hargrove, Edwin C., and Samuel A. Morley. 1984. *The President and the Council of Economic Advisors: Interviews with CEA Chairmen*. Boulder: Westview Press.

Hawtrey, R.G. 1938. *A Century of Bank Rate*. London: Longmans, Green & Co..

Hayek, F.A. 1990. *Denationalisation of Money*. 3rd ed. Institute of Economic Affairs.

Heller, Walter W. 1966. *New Dimensions of Political Economy*. Cambridge, MA: Harvard University Press.

Hetzel, Robert L. 2008. *The Monetary Policy of the Federal Reserve. A History*. Cambridge: Cambridge University Press.

Hetzel, Robert L., and Ralph F. Leach. 2001. The Treasury-Fed Accord: A New Narrative Account. Federal Reserve Bank of Richmond *Economic Quarterly* 87 (1): 37–55.

Horwich, George. 1966. Tight Money, Monetary Restraint and the Price Level. *Journal of Finance* 66 (1): 15–33.

Johnson, Harry G. 1963. An Overview of Price Levels, Employment, and the U.S. Balance of Payments. *Journal of Business* 36: 279.

Johnson, Lyndon B. 1971. *The Vantage Point.* New York: Holt, Rinehart and Winston.

Keech, William R. 1995. *Economic Politics. The Costs of Democracy.* Cambridge: Cambridge University Press.

Kettl, Donald F. 1973. *Leadership at the Fed.* New Haven: Yale University Press.

Keynes, J.M. 1919. *The Economic Consequences of the Peace.* London: Macmillan.

———. 1936. *The General Theory of Employment, Interest and Money.* London: Macmillan.

Krooss, Herman E., ed. 1969. *Documentary History of Banking and Currency in the U.S.* New York: McGraw-Hill.

Lown, Cara S., and John H. Wood. 2003. The Determination of Commercial Bank Reserve Requirements. *Review of Financial Economics* 12 (1): 83–98.

Maisel, Sherman J. 1973. *Managing the Dollar.* New York: Norton.

Marshall, Alfred. 1887. Remedies for Fluctuations of General Prices. *Contemporary Review*, March.

Martin, William McChesney, Jr. 1953. The Transition to Free Markets. Speech to the Economic Club of Detroit. (Federal Reserve Bank of St. Louis. Federal Reserve Archival System for Economic Research (FRASER)).

———. 1960. Thirty-Sixth Annual Stockholders Meeting, Federal Reserve Bank of Boston. Speech. (Federal Reserve Bank of St. Louis. Federal Reserve Archival System for Economic Research (FRASER)).

Matusow, Allen J. 1998. *Nixon's Economy.* Lawrence: University Press of Kansas.

McCallum, Bennett T. 2002. Recent Developments in Monetary Policy Analysis: The Roles of Theory and Evidence. Federal Reserve Bank of Richmond *Economic Quarterly* 88 (1): 67–96.

Meltzer, Allan H. 2003, 2009. *A History of the Federal Reserve*, I, II. Chicago: University of Chicago Press.

Mudde, Cas, and Cristòbal R. Kaltwasser. 2017. *Populism. A Short Introduction.* New York: Oxford University Press.

Phillips, A.W. 1958. The Relation between Unemployment and the Rate of Change of Money Wages in the United Kingdom, 1861–1957. *Economica* 25: 283.

Redish, Angela. 2001. *Lender of Last Resort Policies.* ms. University of British Columbia.

Ricardo, David. 1816. *Proposals for an Economical and Secure Currency.* 2nd ed. London: John Murray.

Romer, Christine D., and David H. Romer. 2002a. The Evolution of Economic Understanding and Postwar Stabilization Policy. *Stabilization Policy*, Federal Reserve Bank of Kansas City.

———. 2002b. A Rehabilitation of Monetary Policy in the 1950s. *American Economic Review*, May.

Samuelson, Paul A., and Robert Solow. 1960. Analytical Aspect of Anti-Inflation Policy. *American Economic Review*, May.

Shiller, Robert. 2015. *Irrational Exuberance*. Princeton: Princeton University Press.

Sorenson, Theodore C. 1965. *Kennedy*. New York: Harper & Row.

Stein, Herbert. 1969. *The Fiscal Revolution in America*. Chicago: University of Chicago Press.

Stockwell, Eleanor, ed. 1989. *Working at the Board, 1920–70*. Board of Governors of the Federal Reserve System.

Thornton, Henry. 1802. *An Enquiry into the Nature and Effects of the Paper Credit of Great Britain*. (Rep. with Evidence, Notes, Speeches, and Introduction by F. A Hayek. London: George Allen and Unwin, 1939)

Tobin, James. 1958. Defense, Dollars, and Doctrine. *Yale Review*, March.

———. 1977. Macroeconomic Models and Policy. In *Frontiers of Quantitative Economics*, ed. M. Intrilligator. North Holland.

U.S. Congress. 1960. Joint Economic Committee. *Hearings. Review of Annual Report of the Federal Reserve System for the Year 1960*. 87th Cong., 1st Sess.

———. 1962. Joint Economic Committee. *Hearings. State of the Economy and Policies for Full Employment*. 87th Cong., 2nd Sess.

———. 1969. Joint Economic Committee. *Hearings*, 91st Cong., 1st Sess.

U.S. House of Representatives. 1960. Joint Economic Committee. *Hearings on the Economic Report of the President*, 86th Cong., 2nd Sess.

———. 1962. Joint Economic Committee. *Hearings*, 87th Cong., 2nd Sess.

———. 1964. Subcommittee on Banking and Currency. *Hearings, The Federal Reserve after Fifty Years*, 88th Cong., 2nd Sess.

U.S. Senate 1957. Finance Committee. *Hearings*, 85th Cong., 1st Sess.

Weintraub, Sidney. 1955. Monetary Policy: A Comment. *Review of Economics and Statistics*, May.

Wicksell, Knut. 1898. *Interest and Prices*. Trans. R.F. Kahn, 1936. Royal Economic Society. Scribners.

Wood, John H. 2005. *A History of Central Banking in Great Britain and the United States*. Cambridge: Cambridge University Press.

———. 2009. *A History of Macroeconomic Policy in the United States*. New York: Routledge.

Youngdahl, C. Richard. 1960. Open-market operations. In *The Federal Reserve System*, ed. H.V. Prochnow. New York: Harper & Brothers.

CHAPTER 7

So Who Governs?

The previous chapters examined two sets of financial legislation and the resulting bureaucracies—the securities acts of the New Deal and the Federal Reserve Act—to better understand their origins, intentions, applications, and effectiveness. Financial regulations have typically targeted perceived market misbehavior and deficiencies such as fraud, speculation, cartels, volatility, and/or illiquidity, which have been blamed for crises and other economic misfortunes.

Bureaucracies are formal organizations that perform functions beyond, so it is said, the capacities of individuals, as well as, it is implied, those of markets. They operate by rules which constrain groups under their direction. They have often been criticized for their red tape and insensitive, undemocratic behavior. Nevertheless, they grew substantially during the twentieth century and are still growing because, it is argued, not only are they budget maximizers, efficiency in an increasingly complex society requires the informed decisions of ever-growing committees of experts. The benefits of bureaucracies are commonly expressed in terms of trade-offs between efficiency and democracy (Meier 1997; Lowi et al. 2018, Ch. 8; Kiewiet and McCubbins 1991; Niskanen 1971).

General theories of government bureaucracies contend that bureaucrats have goals of their own, such as size and power, which they are often able to achieve because of their superior knowledge relative to their congressional masters. Contrary to initial hopes, however, American bureaucracies have not taken politics or legal conflicts out of government,

J. H. Wood, *Who Governs?*, Palgrave Studies in American Economic History, https://doi.org/10.1007/978-3-030-33083-5_7

although as we saw in Chap. 3 above, courts have tended to defer to their supposed expertise.

We also learned in the above chapters that some of the impediments to bureaucratic behavior have been overlooked, including resilient markets reflecting private interests that may be as much regulating as regulated, as well as changes in the political environment. To be effective, a law or regulation which seeks to alter an industry's behavior must overcome the potentially persistent interests underlying that behavior. For example, the offending risky and conflict-of-interest practices of the New York Stock Exchange in 1934—such as joint brokers and dealers, short selling, and specialists—have survived the Securities and Exchange Commission, and the monetization of federal deficits have continued under the Federal Reserve, as indicated by the fourteen-fold increase in the price level since 1913.

The effectiveness of a law or regulation depends on the validities of legislators' identifications of problems, their causes, and their potential corrections, as well as the expertise of its assigned bureaucracy. If the collapse of security values during the Great Depression was due to fraudulent sales made possible by the lack of accurate investor information during the previous prosperity, a law requiring the dissemination of useful information under the oversight of the SEC might be appropriate.

Indeed, such agencies as the SEC, with considerable discretion in enforcement, are considered by their supporters as essential to effective laws because of the necessity of revised definitions and enforcement procedures under changing conditions, including new financial practices, institutions, and instruments. Laws are outlines, according to this argument, with the details of interpretation and enforcement filled in and updated by the relevant bureaucracies.

Less has been written about bureaucracies' effects on laws as administered, which are often, including the cases studied here, influenced more by current (which determine budgets) than founding legislatures. Their supporters (such as Frankfurter and Landis in Ch. 2–3) have seen bureaucracies as ways of replacing the popular/political debates of Congress by the technical decisions of expert bureaucracies. In fact, in the United States, at least, there have been more places for politicking.

For example, the effects of laws directed at trading practices affecting the profits of financial institutions may be influenced by their applications (bureaucratic enforcements) as much as by their original compositions (by Congress). Bureaucracies depend on changing Congresses for support, not only for funds but for legislation affecting their missions. With respect to the *Securities Exchange Act of 1934*, for example, a cautious (because the Executive did not wish to retard the economic recovery and Wall Street soon regained its political influence) SEC sought to induce the NYSE to adopt trading changes voluntarily. When the Exchange resisted, the SEC was reluctant to press, partly because government priorities had turned elsewhere, and partly because of an imperfect understanding of the markets in question, that is, the lack of expertise. Specialists, floor traders, short sales, and broker/dealer combinations looked like elements of a casino to William Douglas, unnecessary, he felt, because he apparently believed that markets made themselves—perhaps like the unassisted intersections of textbook supply and demand curves.

The encouragement of war production meant minimal interference with industry's finance, and the SEC was moved out of Washington to make space for more important agencies. It continued to decline during succeeding administrations, and even in the 1960s President Johnson advised the SEC and other non-defense agencies to avoid causing political problems that might interfere with support for more important programs.

The SEC's primary goal seems to have been its own security, even up to the 1960s, when after the moribund Truman and Eisenhower years it began, albeit under pressure, seriously to address the securities industry's shortcomings. It still relied on voluntary regulation by stock exchanges, and the NYSE was claimed to be "the envy of the world." SEC Chairman, Manuel Cohen began his term in 1964 by saying that "Neither the Commission nor the industry can allow a disagreement [about an exchange rule] to lead to a breakdown in the lines of communication or to a failure of cooperation in other tasks." Dick Whitney would have felt at home.

Nevertheless, the Exchange's fixed commissions, refusal of institutional membership to institutions (so they could not avoid brokerage fees), and refusal of permission for members to trade on other exchanges brought suits for damages by private parties, and the Department of Justice pointed out that the securities acts had not eliminated the relevance of the antitrust laws. Congress itself had come under the pressure of investor constituents. All were influenced by the developing intellectual leanings toward competition.

The NYSE moved slowly, and did not endorse competitive commissions until after the Justice Department's Antitrust Division held hearings in which leading academic economists testified that neither the industry nor the public would be harmed by competition, and filed a brief in 1969. "Where was the SEC all those years?" MIT Professor Paul Samuelson asked during his discussion of the SEC's "very small progress" toward effective competition in the securities industry. "[It] should long ago have acted to promote equitable and efficient competition and to control private monopoly."

Copying a strategy of the NYSE during the 1930s, the SEC had used its time and energies for studies instead of action. It had become, or remained, like the ICC before it, a protector of firms at the expense of individuals. Princeton Professor William Baumol testified that "For the regulator, it is the most difficult thing in the world to take the responsibility for some firm going out of existence; and so, as soon as it threatens to do something for the consumer, which means somebody gets hurt, that is when the regulator is tempted to say, 'Stop. It is becoming destructive'." One legal writer sympathetic to the SEC saw the demise of investment banks "under its regulatory care" as evidence of failure, although he also regretted that Congress and the agency were more concerned about investors' frivolous lawsuits than in protecting them (Seligman 2003, pp. 352–58, 383, 403–14; U.S. Senate 1972, p. 142; Poser 2009).

FDR's First Hundred Days are a famous example of major political accomplishments, which, however, should mean more than the passage of laws. Many laws were passed but the securities acts have not proved to be very good examples of accomplishment. None of the NYSE's trading practices alleged to have caused problems for investors were significantly altered even after the Exchange's governance was rearranged for what turned out to be cosmetic purposes. The crisis-driven regulations of short sales, which had predated the securities acts, continued. The reports required by the Securities Act of 1933 to raise the transparency of securities issues was of dubious value because they failed to add significantly to information, and even hindered it by delaying requirements. The primary effect of the securities acts was to raise the costs of securities issues and their trading.

As far as the securities acts are concerned, the answer to the question—What is the principal determinant of a law's influence on private economic decisions and markets: Congress, as revealed by the law as written; the law's interpretation and enforcement by the bureaucracy; or that which is acceptable to the market (private interests)?—is the last. Given the reports which had been required without benefit of law, the Securities Act of 1933 were redundant, the trading changes anticipated by the advocates of the Securities Exchange Act of 1934 were rejected by the industry, and the

1933 Glass-Steagall Act's separation of commercial and investment banking was meaningless.

Regarding the last, commercial banks had already dropped out of investment banking before Glass-Steagall because of the depression's decline in security issues, and they re-entered regardless of law when it became profitable in the 1960s. Congress (the House in particular) would not pass a law enabling the expansion of banks' activities, and agencies would not enforce the law as written, with the effect, the U.S. Court of Appeals pointed out, that different financial institutions were illegally performing each other's functions "without the benefit of Congressional consideration and statutory enactment." Under the pressure of the Court's finding, Congress passed the *Depository Institutions and Monetary Control Act of 1980*, which legalized existing activities. The formal replacement of Glass-Steagall by Gramm-Leach-Bliley in 1999 was superfluous.

There are more stories of relationships between laws and interests which show that the latter may anticipate, even initiate, as well as react to the former. The *Banking Acts* of 1933 and 1935 instituted federal deposit insurance and eliminated double liability for the stockholders of failed banks. The latter was thought unfair, especially after the large losses of the Great Depression, to small stockholders with little or no influence on bank decisions. Regulators talk of reducing bank risk, but history is replete with the opposite, for example, of bankers' shifts of the costs of risks onto government, that is, taxpayers. Double liability raised the costs of risk-taking and provided an incentive to close a declining bank before matters got worse. We saw in the 1980s that deposit insurance provided the opposite incentive, that is, to raise risk in the hope that an insolvent bank might recover. After all, with limited (zero) liability, what have the stockholders got to lose? Depositors' recovery rates from suspended banks fell with the end of double liability (Macey and Miller 1992; Kaufman 1992).

Banks have also taken advantage of Congress' and presidents' willingness to undertake bailouts, which Dodd-Frank has codified and encouraged in "too-big-to-fail." In summary, the New Deal had little effect on securities trading, Congress increased risk by means of deposit insurance, the elimination of double liability, and pressures on banks to expand lending on real estate, and moral hazard by means of actual and promised bailouts. Wall Street was not transformed, certainly not for the better, by the legislation of the 1930s.

A sufficient reason for the lack of effect of the securities acts was their aim at a nonexistent problem, although we cannot conclude that they would have been effective if they had been directed at real problems, for in that case they might have been stymied by the interests affected—such as practices that looked (to them) like the elements of a casino. In other words, they have lacked the expertise which bureaucracies have often been assumed to possess. That leads them into activities which allow the SEC to increase its size but have no or deleterious connections with investor well-being, including the operations running afoul of the courts because of inadequate cost analysis (Oesterle 2005; Zaring 2015).

White: SEC Role Bypassed by Court

WASHINGTON, Oct. 4, 2013 – SEC Chairman Mary Jo White Thursday criticized attempts to encroach on the agency's independence, saying recent moves by Congress and the courts inappropriately circumvent the SEC's expertise and judgment. In a dig at judges who have questioned the SEC's rules and its historic practice of allowing firms to settle cases without admitting wrongdoing, Ms. White suggested the courts were acting beyond the scope of their rules and should instead "defer to the agency's reasoned judgments." "We recognize that, under the law, a court can review a settlement," she said, in prepared remarks at Fordham Law School. "But a court that reviews a settlement [by] a law enforcement agency like ours ... has a more limited task."

Though she didn't refer to him by name, her remarks appeared to be criticism of U.S. District Judge Jed S. Rakoff for rejecting a proposed 2011 deal allowing Citicorp Inc. to pay $285 million to settle allegations the bank misled investors in a 2007 mortgage-bond deal. Mr. Rakoff said allowing companies to settle charges without admitting or denying wrongdoing is "hallowed by history, but not by reason."

Ms. White, who took over the SEC in April, has changed the agency's long-standing settlement policy and said it would insist on admissions of wrongdoing in certain cases of egregious offence, harm to investors or where public accountability is needed. But Ms. White suggested the shift was prompted by her background as a federal prosecutor and not by judicial criticism. *Wall Street Journal*, Oct. 4, 2013, p. C3.

Two more forces, or lack thereof, overlooked in general discussions of bureaucracies, are, first, that their purposes are sometimes founded on misconceptions. For example, the securities losses of the Great Depression were blamed by politicians and the press on frauds, secrecy, and speculations which called for more securities regulation, when they were more likely consequences of business losses that came with the depression's falling prices and. A more logical government response to these losses than that chosen would have been to try to develop a more responsible monetary system.

Second, the expertise granted to bureaucracies is frequently insubstantial or nonexistent. A complex economy in which individuals are dependent on their fellows may call for markets rather than bureaucratic committees. The railroad and truck routes of the ICC and the reporting requirements of the SEC have been based on no competent measure of the public good (except, in reverse, the encouragement of monopoly, the elimination of choice, and the discouragement of innovation), and are almost certainly inferior to those surviving the market test. The SEC had no economists at its beginning, and still takes inadequate account of the costs and benefits of information. It is only fair, the SEC seems to say, that everyone be given the same information, when in fact the competition for often costly information is at the heart of the financial (and other) markets.

All this, especially the changing political and economic conditions, brings into question the durability of bureaucracies. Useful or not, however, political agencies have defied termination, so that more or less regulation of an activity or industry has taken the form of changes in bureaucracies' budgets and membership. The rest of this chapter considers some of the developments of the SEC and Federal Reserve since the periods considered in Chaps. 4 and 6, respectively. They are renowned, and much has been expected of them, but have they mattered?

First consider some of the official and market responses to the substantial expansions of exchanges and other financial markets, after World War II. The SEC attempted to recover some of its original legislative initiative after its sleepy wartime and Republican years. Chairman William Cary called attention particularly to the SEC's recommendations arising out of its *Special Study of the Securities Markets*, begun soon after his appointment by President Kennedy (the *Report* of which was criticized by Professor Stigler; see Chap. 2 above).

President John Kennedy's administration raised the budgets of government agencies after several years of decline—allowing 250 new employees for the SEC alone—and appointed Columbia Law Professor Cary chairman. A student of William O. Douglas at Yale in 1934, and a member of the SEC's staff 1938–40, initially under Douglas, "Cary provided a link to the spirit and goals of the SEC." He had been a "determined reformer" and advocate of extended regulation as suggested by his article on "Pressure groups and the revenue code," which "echoed the tone and liberal convictions" of Douglas's paper on "Directors who do not direct," and "Federalism and corporate law." He revived several unfinished projects begun during the New Deal, including a statute extending the Securities Exchange Act's requirements to unlisted firms and "a highly publicized attempt to abolish floor trading." He renewed Douglas's accusation that the Exchange "still seems to have certain characteristics of a private club" (Seligman 2003, pp. 291–93).

On the other hand, Cary was not inclined to self-glorification or sensationalism in the manners of Douglas or Pecora. He wanted reform, but in a rational manner addressed to a problem, and "felt it important to behave like a lawyer." He began by obtaining funds from Congress for a Special Study of the Securities Markets stimulated by news of irregularities at the American Stock Exchange, increased speculation, and late deliveries to inventory. The SEC was authorized "to make a study and investigation of the adequacy, for the protection of investors, of the rules of national securities exchanges and national securities associations."

The commission produced a draft bill for Congress's consideration, although Cary was dismayed by the time and concessions required. It is not difficult to understand why. Two of the primary determinants of the rapid passage of the Securities Act (on May 27, 1933, twelve weeks after Roosevelt's inauguration) were vigorous Executive support and the securities and economic crises of the Great Depression. The Securities Act Amendments Act of 1964, on the other hand, took more than three years from the beginning of the *Special Study* and more than a year and a half from its completion and issue of its proposals—with little help from the administration.

FDR devoted much of his first inaugural address to the "unscrupulous money changers," whereas Kennedy's was entirely a "cold war" speech concerned with national security. They were speeches suited to their times, although further reasons have been given for the Kennedy administration's lack of support for the SEC beyond appointment of the liberal Cary.

"Kennedy's 1960 election had been accompanied by the loss of twenty liberal democrats from the House of Representatives, making the House far more conservative than the White House" and requiring the husbanding of "bargaining power for its most effective use," Arthur Schlesinger, Jr., wrote in his biography of Kennedy. No senior person in the administration was interested. Cary never saw President Kennedy on business, and the White House aide assigned to the SEC "literally had no free time to talk with us." Ralph Dungan had been a legislative aide to Senator Kennedy, on his presidential campaign team, and with Schlesinger was one of two White House Special Assistants to the President, and was interested primarily in foreign affairs (Seligman 2003, p. 292; Schlesinger 1965, pp. 707–713).

Finally, there was no crisis to be taken advantage of, least of all in the stock market. The bull market of the 1950s rivaled that of the 1920s, and peaked in 1966. So what was the problem, the public and Congress might have asked, if they had thought of it? Cary's answer to the unasked question was the standard SEC position regarding the existence of fraud, speculation, and other failures of investor protection which had attracted attention during the early years of the Wilson and Franklin Roosevelt administrations. Cary and the SEC, supported by their *Special Study*, still wanted to eliminate specialists and floor traders, and to segregate customers securities accounts. The SEC still could not understand why private speculators should be able to trade for their own accounts on a public exchange. But to secure a bill that was acceptable to a Congress not very much in favor of change, it was necessary to avoid potential opposition.

So the SEC settled for extending regulations to unlisted securities, raising standards for entry into the securities business, and barring fraudulent corporate publicity. One Congressman exclaimed: "Why, there isn't a single provision opposed by the industry." "Yet he failed to add," Cary wrote, "that if there had been strong objection the bill might not even have received a hearing – not to mention the fact that the bill would raise the cost of entry into the securities business." "Naturally the stock exchanges favored the legislation," Professor Lee Sclar (1965) observed.

Democratic Congressman Peter Mack, Jr., of downstate Illinois, Chairman of the Commerce and Finance Subcommittee of the House Interstate and Foreign Commerce Committee, helped the SEC get funds for its *Special Study*, but failed to be reelected in 1962 after the elimination of his congressional district following the 1960 census. Committee Chairman Oren Harris of Arkansas also sympathized with the SEC, but took "its oversight responsibility seriously. [I]t is not there simply to pass upon bills which an agency sponsors," Cary learned, "but even more to ensure that it is doing the job that Congress envisages, or not doing things to which it objects. [I]ts role as overseer extends beyond the Commission to the exchanges [as] evidenced by the critical and uncomfortable questioning of the" presidents of the NYSE and the National Association of Securities Dealers during the hearings held in connection with the bill.

The Senate accepted the bill expeditiously, but the House committee "proceeded in exactly the other direction, on the basis of letting the bill rest for an extended period of time in order that any opposition to it could be allowed to develop"—the opposite of Sam Rayburn's 1933 strategy of action before the opposition had time to form. "You have to let the dust settle" a committee member said. "Politically," Cary (1967, pp. 92–106) observed, "this is a technique for ascertaining public reaction to the bill and is well adapted to any committee chairmen who have sensitive antennae."

"[T]he Securities Acts Amendments are disappointing," wrote the reform-minded Professor Sclar, as indicated by the "provisions unduly favoring special interests," especially the reporting exemptions for banks and insurance companies on the grounds of alternative state and agency regulators. "These privileges did not result only from the power of lobbies such as those of the Comptroller of the Currency and the insurance industry. They also occurred because the SEC feared that by urging overly strenuous reforms, Congress would be driven to reject all of the Special Study's proposals. With the passage of time, however, the need to correct the deficiencies in the 1964 Amendments should become as clear as was the need to extend the Exchange Act to the OTC market," Professor Sclar (1965) concluded.

It would be difficult to ascribe long-term goals to the SEC's leadership, perhaps because of their political appointments. The same might be said of the staff since Cary had to go outside the organization, which had been in decline, to get the reform proposals he wanted. It may be said that there is a long-term upward bias in regulation, as suggested by Sclar, because of the difficulty of their legislative repeal. On the other hand, their enforcement depends on the interests and politics of the day.

A bonus to our discussions has been the appearance of Martin in both, first as one of the regulated, president of the NYSE, and second as a regulator at the Federal Reserve. The beliefs/ideologies of the participants also matter, although they may not dominate. Martin was skeptical of regulation and inclined toward free markets in both his capacities, and had some influence on practices, but he left both jobs under clouds, his efforts having eventually proved inadequate in the face of other forces.

The purposes of the Federal Reserve Act varied according to the interests concerned. The Act as written and publicly promoted was aimed at financial panics. The provision of an elastic currency intended to prevent currency shortages and the business declines and deflations that went with them.

The new and novel institution seemed an unlikely candidate for such a task when there already existed experienced agencies that had been developing along the necessary lines, such as the Treasury, clearing-houses, and the emergency powers of the Aldrich-Vreeland Act of 1908 (which worked well in 1914). An obvious structural improvement would have been the consolidation of banks. State anti-branching laws had led to thousands of small undiversified banks and frequent failures as well as destabilizing shifts of funds between money-center and rural banks.

These possibilities were rejected because of their lack of support by politically important groups, and branches were anathema in most of the country. European-style central banking was also unpopular. The Fed was finally adopted because its federal nature (rather than concentrated in New York after the models of London, Paris, Stockholm, etc.) made it politically acceptable and it contained several benefits for the big banks, who secured the support of Woodrow Wilson and Carter Glass. The Federal Reserve presented a ready source of funds for banks, bore the cost of the nation's gold reserve without competing with existing banks, and increased the access to international finance (Wood 2005, pp. 165–66).

A disadvantage, overlooked at the time of the Act's passage, was its retention of fixed reserve requirements for banks as well as the Fed, even though these had been criticized as contributors to financial crises in the United States, and the Bank of England had learned to suspend them in crises. Another disadvantage of the Fed was its self-supporting nature (its lending, or purchases of bank and government assets, was virtually costless while its revenue was the interest on those assets) which separated its fortunes from the economy's.

The Fed did well for its sponsors initially as it smoothed interest rates, assisted money-center banks' attempts to cartelize deposit rates (although unsuccessfully until they were fixed by the *Bank Act of 1933*), and financed federal deficits during World War I. The Treasury's demand for the Fed's support of its borrowing was excessive, however, and inflation continued almost two years after the end of the war. When the Fed got the freedom to raise interest rates—it became more insistent when its gold reserve requirement was approached—tight money was enforced almost to the end of one of the sharpest contractions (January 1920 to July 1921) in American history.

Monetary policy between 1923 and 1929, the "high tide" of the Federal Reserve, was principally managed by the Federal Reserve Bank of New York using the balance sheets of New York and Chicago banks as guides. This continued even after the '29 crash, when money, prices, and real GNP fell about a third between 1929 and 1932, and unemployment rose to 25 percent of the work-force. The Fed failed to respond, even when segments of Congress complained, because of concern for its gold reserve, money-center banks were stable, and perhaps most important, it did not feel the pain of the recession. In the past, most countries had suspended the gold constraint when it interfered with war spending, the Bank of England had been allowed to do so in the mid-nineteenth century, and the Independent Treasury took its time to resume after the Civil War, but the Federal Reserve was unmoved by the Great Depression.

The new administration effectively took control of the Fed in 1933, and dictated monetary policy during World War II and nearly six years afterwards. Even though its organization and powers were hardly changed, the Federal Reserve to which Martin came in March 1951 differed significantly from the original Fed because of the actions expected. The Employment Act of 1946 declared it to be the responsibility of federal agencies "to promote maximum employment, production, and purchasing power," which except for the last had not been considered primary objectives in 1913.

Traditionalists such as Martin still emphasized price and financial stability, but after the Great Depression and Keynes, many economists and politicians felt that more should, and could, be done by the Fed, if only to finance fiscal deficits. This conflict between traditional (classical) and interventionist (Keynesian) monetary policies has persisted in greater or lesser degrees.

Overall, it must be said that American monetary policy has been determined by (1) whether the gold constraint was active and (2) the federal government's fiscal policy. The first Bank of the United States at first financed Federalist deficits (1792–99), but behaved conservatively during the frugal administrations of Jefferson and Madison (1801–11). (Its charter expired before the War of 1812.) After its initial problems with the inconvertible state notes the second Bank of the United States had a solid record during the fiscal surplus years 1822–32, that is, until Jackson began to withdraw government deposits from the Bank.

The Independent Treasury System was operated by the U.S. Treasury Department under the oversight of a Congress that took its job seriously because of the electorate's concern for money, credit, and prices. The Independent Treasury (IT) had two contradictory jobs: (1) to maintain the gold value of the dollar, and (2) under the IT law of 1846, to keep its gold in its own vaults, rather than in banks, which subjected bank money and credit to the government's net receipts. That the Treasury undermined the law in order to maintain the gold value of the dollar, while at the same time responding to crises, seems to have been consistent with the popular will. The landslide losses in all three of Bryan's campaigns for the presidency suggest that the gold standard and price stability were favored by the electorate. Congress and the Treasury seemed to be in lockstep.

The effective end of the gold standard in 1933 (the devaluation of the dollar that year meant the end of the gold constraint, confirmed by the suspensions of the gold reserve ratios in the 1960s and the closing of the gold window in 1971), meant that money and prices would be determined by current political forces. The most important of those forces have been (1) finance and others favoring stability and (2) presidents and Congresses, unable or unwilling to raise the funds necessary to fund desired spending in other ways, thereby relying on monetization of the debt.

Some might regard Keynesian economists as a third force, but they have been nothing more than "intellectual" support of (2). Keynesian stability does not imply long-term inflation, but rather alternately easy and tight money during periods of low- and high-demand, with no implications for inflation in the long run. The notion that the 1951 Accord gave the Fed independence to pursue price stability is a fiction. The GDP deflator is almost eight times its value at that time; it rose more than 50 percent during Martin's 1951–70 tenure. In comparison, the price level was about the same in 1930 as in 1830.

Some Federal Reserve officials, such as Chairmen Martin and Paul Volcker (1979–87), have attempted to negotiate price stability, but theirs has been a losing battle. President Donald Trump's efforts to influence monetary policy are not new, as we have seen the big-spending administrations of Woodrow Wilson, Franklin Roosevelt, and Lyndon Johnson—most presidents, in fact. We must conclude that the Federal Reserve has had little or no effect on money, prices, or stability. Inflation has always, even before the Fed, occurred in the presence of fiat currencies (Selgin and White 1999). In fact, the two have been jointly determined. It could be said that the Fed's most significant effect was its destruction of the gold standard (which forced the adoption of fiat money) by its policies, especially during the Great Depression. On the other hand, it is likely that the expansive, fiscal deficit government policies of the last century would have forced the end of the gold standard with or without the Fed. Like the SEC, the Fed has grown in size and scope beyond the most vivid imaginations of its originators, but the institution probably has not significantly altered the courses of money and finance in the United States.

Wright Patman, Chairman of the House Banking Committee 1963–75, whom we saw in the last chapter was unhappy with the Fed, proposed a change in policy structure that struck at the heart of legislative-agency relations. "As far back as 1916," he opened a meeting of the Subcommittee on Domestic Finance holding hearings on *The Federal Reserve after Fifty Years*, "Elihu Root, in an address as president of the American Bar Association, with rare foresight, stated in referring to the growth of law by administration, that before these agencies the old doctrine prohibiting the delegation of legislative power has virtually retired from the field and given up the fight. If we are to continue a government of limited powers, these agencies must themselves be regulated."

What did he have in mind? "The law made by legislatures and by courts," he continued, "is readily accessible and relatively certain. But the essence of administrative power lies in determination of power. We must have a rule of law in America, not one of men. We would be remiss in our study of the Federal Reserve not to look carefully to insure that sufficient rules and guidelines are provided Federal Reserve decisionmakers to aid them in effectively and efficiently administering the Federal Reserve Act and contributing toward reaching the goals of the Employment Act of 1946. That discretionary power is preferable to fixed laws for the performance of some functions seems unquestionable, but definite norms must be present to guide progress toward clearly defined objectives."

He wanted responsibility along lines laid down by Congress, even a rule. "[T]he guidelines ... in the original 1913 act have for many years been inadequate for the severe demands of a more modern society. If Congress fails to implement its own will, not only will national goals be frustrated but there will continue the persistent erosion of the legislative power taking place in this country" (U.S. House 1964, pp. 1533–34).

This sounds a good deal like the legislated monetary policy of the pre-1914 Independent Treasury. No formal movements toward such a structure followed Patman, but monetary policies continued to be the outcomes of the usual conflicts between the usual parties: Congress, the president, and finance. We have seen that President Johnson's pressure on the Fed in the late 1960s brought an increase in inflation, which accelerated with President Nixon's pressures during the 1972 election year, and continued at least partly because of fears of the costs of disinflation. Finally, at the end of the 1970s, when double-digit inflation was damaging the political standing of President Jimmy Carter, he supported the new Fed Chairman Paul Volcker's sharp deflation.

The Great Moderation starting in the mid-1980s, during which the public and policymakers learned that low inflation was consistent with, and even conducive to, economic growth, allowed the Fed to increase its emphasis on low inflation (called "price stability"). It received significant support from Congress in the form of Stephen Neal's popular joint resolution in 1989 directing the Fed to target zero inflation, and even more from the fiscal surpluses after the Cold War (Wood 2009, pp. 173–174).

A strong signal that low inflation will not be with us long, however, is the enormous federal deficit. Adam Smith (1776, p. 882) observed that "When national debts have once been accumulated to a certain degree, there is scarce, I believe, a single instance of their having been fairly and completely paid. The liberation of the public revenue, if it has ever been brought about at all, has always been brought about by a bankruptcy; sometimes" repudiation "though frequently by a pretended payment" of currency devalued by inflation. That has been true of the United States so far, and it is unlikely that Americans will tax themselves to pay their debt.

Thomas Paine (1786) surprised many of his radical friends when he defended banks as means of enforcing government contracts. He distinguished between the powers of legislatures (1) to make laws that, depending on the perceived needs of the public, might override those of earlier legislatures, and (2) to act as agents or negotiators for the public. "A very strange confusion of ideas, dangerous to the credit, stability, and the good and honour of the commonwealth, has arisen, by confounding those two distinct powers."

"'Laws' as distinct from agency transactions ... may be altered, amended and repealed, or others substituted in their places" as the public interest directs. Agency transactions, however, are matters of business between the government and particular persons, and as sacred and enforceable as business contracts in general. Paine's first example is that "the state wants the loan of a sum of money; certain persons make an offer to government to lend that sum, ...the government accepts [their] proposals ... and an act is passed ... confirming this agreement. This act is final" and legally "binding on the state ... as much as if they had been made between two private individuals."

Paine was writing of the financial obligations of the Continental Congress and individual States during the American Revolution, and we know that Alexander Hamilton honored debts in the money (gold) that had been promised. Different attitudes prevailed in the twentieth century.

As part of the New Deal's inflationary measures, Congress abrogated gold clauses in American bond contracts. Since the silver scales of the late nineteenth century, when William Jennings Bryan threated the gold value of the dollar, most government and corporate bonds had been indexed to gold. For example, Norman C. Norman had bought a 30-year $1000 Baltimore and Ohio Railroad bond issued in 1930 with annual 4½ percent payable semiannually "in gold coin of the United States of or equal to the standard weight and fineness existing on February 1, 1930," that is, semi-annual coupons valued at $22.50 or 22.50/20.67 = 1.09 ounces of gold. After the government had devalued the dollar to $35 an ounce, Norman found that he had to sue for his contracted 1.09 × 35 = $38.15.

The case made its way to the Supreme Court, which by a 5–4 vote decided that Norman would have to settle for the old $22.50. Speaking for the majority, Chief Justice Charles Evans Hughes acknowledged that the legislation was part of a government policy of redistribution through inflation, but the Court was bound by "the constitutional power of the Congress over the monetary system," specifically the power "to coin money and regulate the value thereof" under Article I, section 8.

A dollar was whatever the United States said it was. "The contention," Hughes said, "that these gold clauses are valid contracts and cannot be struck down proceeds upon the [untenable] assumption that private parties ... may make and enforce contracts which may limit [Congress's] authority."

Oklahoma Senator Elmer Thomas had supported the policy in Congress at the beginning of the New Deal: The Thomas amendment to the Agricultural Adjustment Act, "in my judgment, is the most important proposition that has ever come before the American Congress.... It may transfer from one class to another class in these United States value to the extent of almost $200,000,000,000, ... from those who own bank deposits [and] bonds and [other] fixed investments, ... who did not buy it, who did not earn it, who do not deserve it [to] the debtor class of the Republic." (*CR*, April 24, 1933).

So, the value of money is policy—of uncertain effects, it might be added—and Martin and others who see it as a contract between the public and its government are fighting a losing battle. Martin was not a bad chairman. He presided over low inflation until the government wanted the Fed's finance—which it coughed up, just like central banks, and banks in general, before him. Neither he nor the Fed altered the course of monetary history. This study offers no general conclusions regarding the influences of bureaucracies, but has found that two of them have been primarily cosmetic. The SEC's requirements have added little more than the costs of doing business, and the Fed has not affected the monetary authority's primary purpose of monetizing government debt. Martin may have been useful to the Exchange in holding back regulation in the late 1930s; earning little thanks for his efforts and indeed it is unlikely that he substantively affected the market and bureaucratic forces at play.

References

Cary, William. 1967. *Politics and the Regulatory Agencies.* New York: McGraw-Hill.

Kaufman, George G. 1992. Capital in Banking: Past, Present and Future. *Journal of Financial Services Research* 5: 385–402.

Kiewiet, D. Roderick, and Matthew D. McCubbins. 1991. *The Logic of Delegation. Congressional Parties and the Appropriations Process.* Chicago: University of Chicago Press.

Lowi, Theodore, Benjamin Ginsberg, Kenneth A. Shepsle, and Stephen Ansolabehere. 2018. *American Government. Power and Purpose.* 15th ed. New York: W.W. Norton.

Macey, Jonathan, and Geoffrey Miller. 1992. Double Liability of Bank Shareholders: History and Implications. *Wake Forest Law Review* 1: 31–62.

Meier, Kenneth J. 1997. Bureaucracy and Democracy: The Case for More Bureaucracy and Less Democracy. *Public Administration Review* 57: 193–197.

Niskanen, William. 1971. *Bureaucracy and Representative Government.* Chicago: Aldine-Atherton.

Oesterle, Dale A. 2005. *Regulation NMS. Has the SEC Exceeded Its Congressional Mandate to Facilitate a 'National Market System' in Securities Trading.* Ohio State University Moritz College of Law Working Paper Series.

Paine, Thomas. 1786. *Dissertations on Government, the Affairs of the Bank, and Paper Money.* Philadelphia: C. Cist.

Poser, Norman S. 2009. Why the SEC Failed: Regulators against Regulation. *Brooklyn Journal of Corporate, Financial & Commercial Law* 3 (Spring): 289–324.

Schlesinger, Arthur M., Jr. 1965. *A Thousand Days.* Boston: Houghton-Mifflin.

Sclar, Lee J. 1965. The Securities Acts Amendments of 1964: Selected Provisions and Legislative Deficiencies. *California Law Review* 53 (5): 1494–1519.

Selgin, George, and Lawrence H. White. 1999. A Fiscal Theory of Government's Role in Money. *Economic Inquiry* 37: 154–165.

Seligman, Joel. 2003. *The Transformation of Wall Street. A History of the Securities and Exchange Commission and Modern Corporate Finance.* 3rd ed. Wolters: Kluwer.

Smith, Adam. 1776. *An Inquiry into the Nature and Causes of the Wealth of Nations.* London: Strahan and Cadell (Reprinted New York: Modern Library, 1937).

U.S. House. 1964. *The Federal Reserve After Fifty Years.* Hearings. Subcommittee on Domestic Finance of the Committee on Banking and Currency, 88th Cong., 2nd sess.

U.S. Senate. 1972. *Stock Exchange Commission Rates.* Hearings. Banking Subcommittee. 92nd Cong., 2nd sess.

Wood, John H. 2005. *A History of Central Banking in Great Britain and the United States.* Cambridge: Cambridge University Press.

———. 2009. *A History of Macroeconomic Policy in the United States.* New York: Routledge.

Zaring, David. 2015. The State of Cost-Benefit Analysis at the SEC. *New York Times*, July 13.

Index[1]

[1] Note: Page numbers followed by 'n' refer to notes.

J. H. Wood, *Who Governs?*, Palgrave Studies in American Economic History, https://doi.org/10.1007/978-3-030-33083-5

V

W

The manufacturer's authorised representative in the EU is Springer Nature Customer Service Centre GmbH, Europaplatz 3, 69115 Heidelberg, Germany. If you have any concerns regarding our products, please contact ProductSafety@springernature.com

Printed and bound by CPI Group (UK) Ltd, Croydon, CR0 4YY
30/09/2026
02225644-0005